To"
LaVerne

Blessings & Enjoy.

Jim Reed

www.MAgcloud.com

Tim&Tom

# Tim&Tom

## AN AMERICAN COMEDY IN BLACK AND WHITE

Tim Reid and Tom Dreesen
with Ron Rapoport

The University of Chicago Press | Chicago and London

The University of Chicago Press, Chicago 60637
The University of Chicago Press, Ltd., London
© 2008 by The University of Chicago
All rights reserved. Published 2008
Printed in the United States of America

17  16  15  14  13  12  11  10  09  08          2  3  4  5

ISBN-13: 978-0-226-70900-0 (cloth)
ISBN-10: 0-226-70900-0 (cloth)

Library of Congress Cataloging-in-Publication Data

Reid, Tim, 1944–
    Tim and Tom : an American comedy in black and white / Tim
Reid and Tom Dreesen, with Ron Rapoport.
        p. cm.
    ISBN-13: 978-0-226-70900-0 (cloth : alk. paper)
    ISBN-10: 0-226-70900-0 (cloth : alk. paper) 1. Reid, Tim,
1944– 2. Dreesen, Tom. 3. Tim and Tom. 4. Comedians—United
States—Biography. I. Dreesen, Tom. II. Rapoport, Ron. III. Title.
PN2287.R38A3 2008
792.702'80922—dc22
[B]

                                                        2008015674

To Rita, for the greatest blessings in my life:
Tim II and Tori

To Amy, Jennifer, and Tom Jr.,
who paid the dues right along with me

# Introduction

At the end of the quiet block in the San Fernando Valley, a street begins its rise over a hill that leads down into the land of dreams. Once Tim Reid and Tom Dreesen traveled that road in fear and trepidation. Today they make the journey in comfort and serenity. They have prospered in show business for more than three decades now—no mean feat, ask anyone who has tried—and they have done it on their own terms.

Reid has been an actor, producer, and director, on television and in the movies. If there is a living human being who has appeared in more television series than he has, Reid would like to meet him. Walking down the street, he will still hear the occasional shout of "Hey, Venus!" from someone who remembers him as Venus Flytrap, the preternaturally hip overnight disc jockey in *WKRP in Cincinnati,* one of the most beloved sit-coms from that genre's golden age.

Reid also has the satisfaction, bittersweet as it is, of knowing that as the star and executive producer of *Frank's Place,* he helped create a show whose hilarious and loving depiction of black life in New Orleans is as fondly remembered by its passionate fans as its untimely demise is regretted. Today, Reid makes films and documentaries at his own production studio in Virginia where he chooses the historical and cultural themes that mean the most to him. That is, he thinks, the only kind of show business success that really matters.

Dreesen does exactly what he likes, too, just as he did when he traveled the world with Frank Sinatra as the legendary singer's opening act during the last fourteen years of his career. He hones his stand-up routines at comedy clubs in Hollywood, then takes them on the road, often back home to Chicago. He appears regularly on David Letterman's late-night television show, although their warmest conversations, about the days when they were struggling young comedians, take place when the cameras have been turned off.

Dreesen performs in clubs, at corporate functions, and before so many charitable groups that Jim Murray, the late sports columnist for the *Los Angeles Times*, once wrote, "If you count the benefits he has performed without a fee, he has contributed more to charity than the Rockefellers." He is a low-handicap member of the celebrity golf tour, which features some of the top entertainers and athletes in the country. "I tell jokes and I play golf," Dreesen says. "Life is good."

Life is so good for both Dreesen and Reid that for years they resisted the idea of revisiting the time when it was not. They had an idea then—a sure-fire, can't-miss idea that was certain to make them rich and famous, to make them kings in the land of dreams. Now, however, as they sit in Dreesen's condominium near the road that leads over the hill to Hollywood, they have begun to look back, to try to come to terms with what went wrong, and to wonder. Were they ever that young? Were they ever that naïve? Did they really quit good jobs, abandon their families, throw away all they had accomplished in overcoming childhoods that would have strained the credulity of Charles Dickens to form an inter-racial *comedy* act?

"Do you remember what was going on in America then?" Dreesen asks. "Vietnam. Race riots. Cities burning. Protests in the streets. About the time we were getting our first gigs in Chicago, for instance, Fred Hampton was killed in an FBI raid on Black Panther headquarters and police were using tear gas to break up a race riot at my own high school. And here we were thinking we could make a difference by telling jokes. We must have been crazy."

"It wasn't going to happen," Reid agrees. "We took on the country's hatreds and fears in many ways. There was just so much pain in those days."

But there was laughter and adventure, too. And there were appreciative crowds, enough of them to keep Dreesen and Reid coming back for more, to keep them chasing the one big break they knew was just around the corner, to keep them from facing reality for almost five years. It all seems so distant now, so removed from who they are today. But as they remember the struggle and the danger of those days, and the fun and the excitement, they realize how much it has to say about where they are now, and perhaps where their country is as well.

Here, then, is the story of Tim and Tom, the first black and white comedy team in the history of show business. And the last.

Most of Atlantic City was still asleep when the party started at Club Harlem. It was six o'clock on Sunday morning, a sunrise service for the customers of nearby clubs that had closed at three or four a.m. The owners of those clubs were there too, and the entertainers, bartenders, waiters, and waitresses who worked in them. There was another client base, too, one that had come to town from brothels and back seats up and down the eastern seaboard.

The arrival of the pimps and their prostitutes, many from as far away as New York, Philadelphia, and Newark, was as carefully choreographed as any of the dance acts on the bill, and for the same reason. They were there to be observed, admired, and envied. Everyone knew that the pimps brought only the women who had done the most trade during the week. Those who did not measure up were not invited to Atlantic City, while those who did put on their most elegant gowns, those that fit the tightest and displayed the most skin, for a very late night on the town.

But the pimps were not only exhibiting their women, they were placing themselves on display as well. They would drive up in Rolls-Royces, Cadillacs, and Lincoln Town Cars and wear colorful three-piece suits with matching hats, gold chains and watches, and large jeweled rings. Stylin' at the Harlem, it was

1

called, and nowhere was it more evident than in the pimps' entrance to the club. What was the point of putting on a show, after all, if not to attract the widest possible audience?

They would arrive late, after most of the crowd had been seated, and walk the entire length of the room so everyone would see them and the women trailing behind. Since the Sunday breakfast show was invariably sold out, a lavish tip, as much as five hundred dollars, would have been delivered to the maitre d' hours earlier to reserve a table near the stage.

"Hey, you sure look good," a pimp would be told by friends and acquaintances as he passed by.

"Yeah, I do, don't I?" he would respond. And then, pointing to the women, he would say, "I'm doing good, too. This is my stable." Only then, would he and the women take their seats and wait for the show to begin.

Backstage, Tom Dreesen looked at Tim Reid and saw he was composed and calm. There had been little conversation between them since Reid had returned that afternoon from his sad journey to Virginia that had left Dreesen concerned for his friend and—he had to admit it—for their act on this big night they had been waiting for so long.

"Did you bury him?" Dreesen asked.

"Yes," Reid replied, offering no more details about his father's funeral.

"OK," Dreesen said. "Let's have fun out there."

They stood and watched the other acts on the bill, whose progression never changed. First, there was a twenty-minute dance act to rev up the crowd, get it applauding, laughing, having a good time. On this June morning in 1973, that role was filled by Mama Lu Parks, a large, energetic woman who danced by herself on the stage while half a dozen couples danced around her to songs from the 1920s through the '60s accompanied by a full orchestra. A male singing group, the Sons of Robin Stone, was next with some pop songs, and it was followed by the Quiet Elegance, three women whose songs ranged from laments about the men who treated them so mean to more uptempo numbers. After they had finished, the audience, energized now by all this music, knew there was one more act before the headliner of the evening, the young singing star Ronnie Dyson, came on. A comedy act.

Reid and Dreesen were ecstatic when, after years of trying, they were booked into Club Harlem. In its glory days in the 1950s, long before gambling came to Atlantic City, it was one of six thriving establishments in the resort city's Kentucky Avenue nightclub district, and at one time or another it had provided a stage for virtually every top black entertainer in show business. Sammy Davis Jr., Nat King Cole, Sarah Vaughan, and scores of other headliners had worked at Club Harlem and as the years went by they were followed by a new generation of top musical acts—the Temptations, Smokey Robinson and the Miracles, Gladys Knight and the Pips—and by young performers who had a hit record and were likely to draw a crowd. Like the other Kentucky Avenue clubs, some of which dated back to Prohibition, Club Harlem had seen better days and it had even been shut down for a time after a gangland shootout while Billy Paul was singing "Me and Mrs. Jones."

But the club still had its name and its reputation and during the summer it still drew large crowds of vacationers to the Jersey Shore. For Reid and Dreesen, who had worked in far less glamorous venues, it was a validation of the time they had spent polishing their act. And certainly no one could deny Club Harlem knew how to throw a party. Nowhere else on the Chitlin' Circuit, a loose confederation of black owned and operated nightclubs, was there anything like it. Not at the Apollo in Harlem, not at the 20 Grand in Detroit, not at the Sugar Shack in Boston, not at the High Chaparral or the Burning Spear in Chicago. Club Harlem, which put on shows at 10 p.m., 2 a.m., and 6 a.m., stood alone.

"And now," they could hear the emcee say, "are you ready for some comedy?"

A few cries of "Yeah!" were heard, accompanied by more clapping, but the emcee wasn't satisfied.

"I *said*, are you ready for some *comedy?*"

A larger cheer went up this time as the audience, having fun now, filled the room with sound.

"Well, we got us a comedy act. They came all the way from Chicago and . . ."

A voice in the audience interrupted. "They better be good."

"They're good, brother," the emcee said.

"They *better* be good."

"Now, man, don't hold me to it. To tell you the truth, I ain't seen these turkeys myself. Don't blame me if they ain't good. And now here they are, the comedy *team* of Tim and Tom."

A polite round of applause greeted Reid as he walked out on stage alone. A few women whooped in appreciation of the tall handsome young black man as he approached the microphone.

"Thank you very much," Reid said. "*We* are so happy to be here. *We* just came in from Chicago and *we've* never been here before."

As Reid kept repeating "*we*," the audience rose to the bait.

"*We?*" a loud voice called out. "Who this motherfucker calling *we?* I don't see no *we*. I see *he*."

Reid held up his hand, as if he were about to continue, when a spotlight fell on a lone figure standing at stage left. The audience began to react, slowly at first, and then with gales of laughter, at the sight of the only white man in the club, on stage or in the audience. Shading his eyes with his palm and peering out into the crowd pretending to be searching for someone, Dreesen took a few tentative steps onto the stage and a female voice rang out.

"*Look* out! What we got here?"

Reid, oblivious, continued talking.

"*We* drove here from Chicago and *we* had a hard time finding a room," a line that drew laughter from the crowd as it considered the implications while Dreesen tiptoed toward the microphone.

Finally, Reid noticed Dreesen, stopped in midsentence and waited impatiently for his partner, eyes still shaded by his hand, to take the last few steps to the center of the stage.

"Where the hell have you been, man?" Reid said. "And what *are* you looking for?"

"I don't see any of my people out there," Dreesen said nervously, still looking around.

Big laugh.

Reid walked to the edge of the stage, ducked his head under the stage lights, brought the edge of his hand to his forehead, and looked left to right around the room.

"No, I don't think any of your people *are* here," he said.

Bigger laugh.

"Well, then we better be funny."

Still bigger laugh.

"What do you mean *we*, white man?"

Biggest laugh yet.

They felt comfortable now, relaxed, sure they had the room on their side. Confidently, they swung into a set routine.

"Let's get on with the show," Reid said. "These people came here to see something funny."

"Wait a minute," Dreesen interrupted. "Every time we perform somewhere, you get to be the black guy."

Laugh.

"Just once, *I* want to be the black guy."

Big laugh interspersed with calls from the audience of, "Ain't gonna happen tonight, brother." And, "You got a long way to go." And, simply, "Sheeee-it."

"Tom," Reid said, "black isn't just a skin color. It's an attitude. It's spirit. It's soul. You understand what I'm talking about. Soul, Tom, soul."

"Well, I think I can do it. I want to try."

"All right, man, I'm going to give you a test. I'm standing here waiting for a bus. You're a brother and you're going to come up and start a conversation with me."

Dreesen walked a few steps away, then abruptly turned around and returned.

"What corner are we on waiting for this bus?" he asked.

"What difference does it make?"

"It's important. I've got to get into the spirit of the thing, right? What neighborhood are we in?"

"Oh, all right. We're in Harlem, 125th and Amsterdam."

"125th and Amsterdam? Come *onnnn*, bus."

Huge laugh.

"Stop that now," Reid said. "Just come up and start a conversation with me, all right?"

Dreesen walked off, then returned and said, "Look here, man, do the bus stop here?"

Boos and catcalls came up from the audience as Reid buried his head in his hands.

"Look," he said. "*You* wait for the bus and *I'll* be the black guy—wait a minute, of course I'm the black guy, now you're getting me confused—and I'll come up and start a conversation with you."

Reid walked off, muttering "Do the bus stop here?" then turned and returned to center stage with a confident strut.

"Look here, brother," he said rapidly. "Is this where I catch Big Mac? I've got to ease up town, get me some new rags, a couple of fronts and a pair of gators so I can check out them traps, do a little night crawling through the hood."

Reid smiled as the crowd reacted with approving laughs and shouts of "Talk that talk, brother," and "Tell him about it now."

"Damn," Dreesen said. "I didn't know you spoke a foreign language, Tim."

Laugh.

"That's not a foreign language, Tom. That's soul talk. Now, you come up and repeat what I just said."

Dreesen walked away frowning, mumbling to himself as if trying to remember what Reid had said. When he reached the edge of the stage, he turned around and, in an uncoordinated version of Reid's walk, approached.

"Look here, man," Dreesen said, "is this where I catch big rag? I want to ease up town and buy me a bus, get in front of a couple of gators and trap them so I can go through the neighborhood at night with a hood on."

Big laugh and catcalls. "Look out now!"

"I don't think you better be crawling through any black neighborhoods with a hood on," Reid said as the audience, applauding now and cheering, shouted, "I hope you heard that, white boy!"

They paused for a moment, smiling at the audience and at each other. Things could hardly be going any better, and now it was time to address the audience directly.

"I'm Tim Reid . . ."

"And I'm Tom Dreesen . . ."

"And in case you can't remember who's who, just remember," Reid said, "I'm the taller of the two."

"And I'm the Italian," Dreesen said.

"Oh yeah, and one more thing," Reid said. "You never call a black man Tom."

People were laughing now, laughing hard, but then, as they prepared to move on, a man stood up in the back of the room and began shouting.

"Hey, white boy!" the man yelled. "Hey, white boy! I'm talking to you, goddammit! Listen to me now! I'm talking to you, honkie!"

Reid and Dreesen were used to hecklers, and had devised ways to handle them, but this one was different from any they had faced before. He was not interrupting them out of anger, or bitterness, he was responding to the *act*, to Reid saying, "You never call a black man Tom."

"Are you listening to me, white boy?" the man called. "Why don't you call him a nigger? That's what you'd call him in Mississippi."

For the first time since the customers had entered Club

Harlem, the room fell silent—Reid and Dreesen could hear them breathing—until with no hesitation, without so much as a thought, Dreesen said, "Hell, I've called him a nigga in Chicago."

To Dreesen, it seemed as if all the air had been sucked out of the room, and he could feel his heart beating in his chest. He'd screwed up, he thought. His past had betrayed him. All the hanging out with black guys back home in Harvey, Illinois, all the scuffling around they'd done together, the trouble they'd gotten into, the sports they'd played, it had all come back to haunt him.

Nigga—that's the way it was pronounced, not nigger—was a sign of affection, of respect, of a friendship so tight it could be symbolized by the most loaded of epithets. And it was true. He *had* called Tim nigga in Chicago. He had said it to every one of his black friends at one time or another just as they had said it to each other. He wouldn't think of saying it to anyone *except* a friend, in fact. But now he had gone too far. He was sure of it.

Suddenly, the room was rocked by an explosion of laughter. The sound started out loud and grew louder, then louder still. In a moment, it was echoing off the walls and people were pounding the tables, a few even standing and applauding, including the man who had asked the question. He pointed a finger at the stage, nodded his head, and Dreesen could see him mouthing the words, "That's real, brother."

Thinking about it later, Reid and Dreesen realized why the line had worked. It was honest. Nothing else would have been acceptable—no fumbling, no apologizing, no "Oh, I don't use words like that." Only the hard-core truth. At another place, another time, it might have been a disaster. But for this audience on this night, Dreesen's instinctive reaction was the right one. It brought the biggest laugh of the night—one of the biggest he would receive in his life—and it allowed them to regain their rhythm and take back control of the stage.

"Damn, Tom," Reid said later. "That was gutsy, but I have to admit it was right on."

They finished the act with their *Dating Game* spoof, in which Reid, really cooking now, played all the men. Bachelor Number Three is gay and more interested in Bachelor Number One than in the woman trying to choose among them, played by Dreesen wearing a wig. The audience was howling when they were through and they walked off the stage to a standing ovation while the emcee called out their names in tribute.

Outside on Kentucky Avenue, they blinked in the early-morning sunshine, physically exhausted, desperately in need of sleep, but on an adrenaline high they did not want to end. They had left a stage so many nights feeling not just the emotional pain of rejection, but physical pain as well. But as low as those moments were, that is how high they felt now.

"This must be what it feels like to be on heroin or cocaine," said Reid, who had never used hard drugs, as they stood outside the nightclub.

"Or what women mean when they say they don't remember the pain of childbirth once that beautiful baby is in their arms," Dreesen replied.

They had finally made it. Four years of struggle, of so many ups and downs, and now they had an act that was not only funny, but was relevant, too, that spoke to the times, to the American condition. They were on their way now—they were sure of it—on their way to becoming the biggest comedy team that ever hit show business. They felt bonded, believing they had stood up to a test no other comedy team had ever faced. They were not only friends and partners, they also felt a strong sense of brotherhood. No matter what happened now, personally or professionally, they would always be there for each other. Nothing would ever drive them apart.

**2**

On a Sunday afternoon in October 1944, a young woman named
Tina Wilkins got into a car parked at the curb outside the New
Calvary Baptist Church in Norfolk, Virginia, and lay down on
the back seat. Hearing parishioners emerge from the church
a few minutes later, Wilkins raised her head and spotted William
Lee Reid and his wife chatting amiably with the minister
on the front steps. She got out of the car and shouted profanities
at Reid while pointing at her bulging stomach. Certain that
she now had the attention of the entire congregation, Wilkins
picked up a broken piece of brick from the ground and began
to break every window in the car, which belonged to Reid. Her
actions would be a popular topic of conversation in Norfolk's
black community for years to come.

Two months later, the birth of Wilkins's baby was just as
chaotic: Shouts of "Boil water!" as people rushed in and out of
the room. Fears the infant would die because he was coming
into the world feet first and his exhausted mother's legs had
collapsed around his neck. A midwife extracting him from the
womb with great difficulty, then worriedly turning her attention
to the mother, terrified that two people might be lost that
morning. "To say I had a turbulent birth is putting it mildly,"
Tim Reid says.

"I was a bastard child," Reid says. "Many war babies are, you know. Daddy's off fighting and mama's working at the factory. A lot of women in that era were on their own and very independent. My mother was certainly fiery, which explains what happened when she found out my father was married. Even though she was engaged to another man at that time, too."

Wilkins's fiancé, Timothy Isabel, was in the army overseas but she used his name on her infant son's birth certificate, calling him Timothy Isabel Jr. "I hated that name," Reid says. "In school, they used to call me Queen Isabella and every time they did there was a fist fight." Reid never met his namesake, and his mother never saw him again, though Isabel sent checks for child support until he was sixteen years old. As for Reid's biological father, that information was kept from him until he was nine.

"I'd see him when I went to visit my grandmother," Reid says. "I was told to call him Uncle William Lee and I never questioned it. Sometimes, I'd go to church with my father and one woman or another would come over and give me a nickel or a quarter. Then, we'd go have dinner at one of their homes and maybe visit another one later. I was still little, but I understood what was going on. There were a lot of women in my father's life."

A baby was the last thing Tina Wilkins needed. How could she be starting a family when she never had one of her own? "It was rumored that her father was white—I'm not sure her mother really knew—and she could pass for white except for the coarseness of her hair," Reid says. "So when she appeared in a family where everyone had a darker complexion, they just gave her away. Basically she grew up in somebody else's house. She was a gorgeous woman—tall and slender, what they called high-yella—and she was a hot commodity. Men chased her constantly. But then I came into her life and all that ended. I was a real burden for her."

Wilkins was industrious, though. After quitting school in the ninth grade, she worked as a barmaid and as a domestic in the homes of white people, constantly moving from one job to another and one city to another. Nashville, Baltimore, New York, wherever there was somebody she knew or the promise of work. Occasionally, she would accompany the families who employed her to their summer homes, sometimes traveling as far as Long Island or Lake Placid, New York, and taking her young son with her. "I was always on the move," Reid says, "always being shuffled about. I had a fear of abandonment and I never let myself get attached to something, or someone. It took me a long time to come to grips with that."

Reid's sense of isolation increased after an operation on veins that had grown together under his arm. "A doctor told my mother if I fell and hit that spot I'd bleed to death before she could get me to a hospital," Reid says. "So every time I went out to play, she would come out and yell, 'Stop!' She didn't want me to do anything physical." His mother's compulsion extended to cleanliness, too; two baths a day and constant changes of clothes were the norm. "Her whole life centered around trying to keep me clean and safe," he says. "I never understood the reason."

Wilkins's life, and that of her son, took a menacing turn when she married George Bright, a Baltimore street hustler and heroin addict. Reid's stepfather gave him a new name, George Bright Jr., and, when he was not strung out or going through withdrawal, some of the affection he craved as well. "He gave me an electric train when I was eight," Reid says. "I still have it today, and it still runs."

Bright's periods of sobriety never lasted long, however, and his new family paid a heavy price. It was constantly on the move—"We used to joke that whenever the rent was due was moving day," Reid says—and constantly subjected to Bright's drug-fueled fits of violence. "He would shoot up and beat my mother," Reid says, "once so severely she ran out into the street naked. I was very young, but I knew my mother's life, and mine, were in danger. And of course Baltimore itself was one of the most dangerous cities in America. The places we lived were just frightful. I would cry myself to sleep every night."

With Bright spending almost everything he earned on drugs,

Reid and his mother survived on the few jobs she could find and the occasional kindness of strangers. She would send her son to a neighborhood grocery store with a quarter and instructions to buy a few cigarettes ("you could get two for a nickel"), a couple of slices of bread, some baloney, and BC headache powder. "A Jewish man owned the store and lived with his family on the second floor," Reid says. "They and a few other shop owners were the only white people in the neighborhood, except for the insurance men who came around to collect on the policies of the people who could afford them, and sometimes men looking for a black girl. That man was like an angel to me. Sometimes the twenty-five cents wouldn't be enough and he'd let me sign my name on a bag. It got to the point where my mother just stopped going—I guess she was ashamed—and would say, 'You go. He likes you.' He was very important to our survival."

Reid also took a part-time job brushing the clothes of customers at a nearby shoeshine stand. For this, he would receive several pennies or a nickel, though one day, after a customer dropped a twenty-dollar bill, he received a larger reward.

"Sir, sir, you dropped this!" Reid said, running after him with the money.

"Why, thank you, young man," he said, and gave Reid a quarter.

"I was so proud of that quarter. I'd never gotten that much," Reid says. But his mother had a different reaction.

"You had *twenty dollars?!*" she yelled. "We could have lived on that for a *month!*"

"I will never forget that beating," Reid says. "She beat me within an inch of my life."

Reid's mother did insist her son receive one advantage, a Catholic school education, though Lord knows where she found the money. She enrolled him in St. Mary's elementary school where he performed well enough to skip a grade, learned that corporal punishment was not confined to the home, and witnessed one more example of his mother's fierce protectiveness. After committing a playground infraction one day, Reid was summoned by the tough-looking nun in charge of the yard to crawl through her legs. Frightened, he complied, only to have the nun lock her legs together, trapping him inside the folds of her habit, and beat him with a strap.

Suspecting what his mother's response might be, Reid tried to keep the incident from her by asking to forego his afternoon bath. But she insisted and, upon seeing the welts, demanded to know what had happened. When Reid woke up the next morning, he found his mother fully dressed to take him to school.

"Is that the one?" she asked Reid as one nun appeared.

"No, ma'am," he said fearfully.

"That one?"

"No, ma'am."

When the playground supervisor did arrive, Reid pointed her out and the next thing he knew he was being dragged across the yard where his mother dropped him in the dust, grabbed the nun by the back of her habit and began to swing her around. "If you ever lay your hands on my son again, I will kill you!" she shouted, as children arriving at school began to cry while their parents and other nuns tried to intervene. Wilkins continued to swing the unfortunate nun wildly by her habit until a monsignor intervened and calmed her down. A conference in the rectory followed with some soothing words from the monsignor and an apology from the nun.

"For the next year, it was as if I was in a country club," Reid says, laughing at the memory. "The nun was always giving me gifts, bringing me lunch. She was scared to death of my mother and I don't blame her. So was I. It seems that most of the women in my life were hell-raisers. Maybe that's one reason I've always adored strong women."

Occasionally, life in Baltimore would become too much for George Bright—if the police weren't looking for him, his drug suppliers were—and he would pack up his small family and their few possessions and drive to Norfolk. There they would hide out in a small room on the third floor above a store on

Church Street owned by his sister Belle until he felt it was safe to return home. To Reid, these trips were an adventure because of all the people entering and leaving the second floor of Belle's home, which, despite its location across the street from a whites-only YWCA, was the largest whorehouse in the city.

Aunt Belle was the most exotic creature imaginable. Her beautiful dark skin, the unusual cast to her features that made her look like an Indian woman in a cowboy movie, the fact she dressed only in filmy lingerie, and that she was always in bed, all combined to make her an endless source of fascination to an eight-year-old boy. As did the stories he was told about her. "Aunt Belle had been jilted by her lover—he just walked out one day with one of her girls—and she swore she'd never get out of bed," Reid says. "It was one of those big beds you see in the movies, with huge pillows, and she did all her business right there. She was so good with money she didn't have to work any more herself so she just ran the place from her bed. There were only three things ever allowed on that bed—her cat, her money, and me."

For hours at a time, Reid would sit on Belle's bed in the spacious room on the second floor as the light streamed in through large Victorian windows and his aunt conducted business. A customer would ring a bell on the sidewalk below and, once he had been identified, someone would pull a rope operating a pulley that opened a door to the stairs leading to the second floor. From her bed, Belle could look into an adjoining room where the women chatted with their customers and danced to the latest hits on a jukebox before taking them to bedrooms down the hall.

"Come on in here, George," one of the women would call into Belle's room.

"Go on, honey. It's all right," Belle would say, and soon Reid would be dancing to the music as the women and their johns threw coins his way.

"If I ever got a dollar my mother would take it," Reid says, "but I didn't care because I was so happy dancing and being around all those women. I loved it when they'd pick me up and smother me in their breasts. And they would all laugh because I let them *know* I loved it. They would laugh and say, 'Look at this little pervert,' and they'd hug me some more. Sometimes I think I can still smell the scent of the gardenias they wore in their hair."

One day, a white Norfolk police sergeant with a young boy in tow entered Belle's second-floor bedroom in the building on Church Street. Not long afterwards, Reid got his first glimpse of the road to his future.

"Here you are, sergeant," Belle said as she handed him an envelope filled with cash. "How are you and your family these days?"

"Thank you, Belle," he said, placing the envelope in his uniform pocket. "We're all just fine. This is my nephew. I'm taking him around with me today."

"Would you do me a favor?" Belle asked. "My nephew here has been cooped up in this house for days. Would you take him on your rounds with you?"

Soon Reid was sitting in the back seat of a police car next to a boy about his age and eating an ice cream cone as the policeman drove around Norfolk making his weekly collections. "Black people weren't allowed in some of the areas we went," Reid says, "but we'd get out of the car and the cop would knock on the door and we'd all just walk right in. As long as I was with a policeman, everything was fine."

Their final stop was at a door that ushered Reid into the largest room he had ever seen, a cavernous space that extended as far as he could see and had no apparent ceiling. Off in the distance, there were lights, and men and women wearing costumes and talking animatedly to each other, which prompted laughter and applause from people he could not see. "I'd never been in a theater before and here I was backstage," Reid says. "I was just fascinated by the ropes and the curtains and the stagehands. They took us over to the side curtain and let us watch the play and I thought, 'Wow!' I couldn't have been there for more than fifteen minutes, but the whole time I was thinking, 'I want to be out there.'"

Back in Baltimore a few years later, George Bright was giving Wilkins a particularly savage beating one night when her son tried to intervene. "I jumped on him and he hit me and knocked me across the room," Reid says. "That was it. My mother knew I wasn't going to make it so she called Norfolk and told my father he had to come get me. I know she hated doing it, but it was the only thing she could think of to save me."

William Lee Reid, who was a brakeman on a coal car for the Norfolk and Western Railroad, acknowledged his son in a number of ways. There were walks around town that always included ice cream, and there was the occasional train trip, including one to the 1956 World Series in New York. A good pitcher once himself—good enough to spend the war years playing baseball at the Pensacola Naval Air Station in Florida—he wanted Reid to see Jackie Robinson and Roy Campanella play against the Yankees. And their few trips to church were a clear signal to Norfolk's black community of their relationship. But as a married man with a family of his own, there was a limit to what Reid could give his son, a limit that included a home. So Reid moved in with his grandmother and her common-law husband, Clyde, at the boarding house she ran at 719 Chapel Street, which served the black community in a number of ways.

"Selling whiskey by the drink was still illegal in Virginia then," Reid says, "but at boarding houses you could buy one for fifty cents a shot. And for a dollar and a quarter, you could get a meal with your whiskey. There wasn't really a bar as such. People would just sit at the kitchen table and eat and drink. Navy beans, pig tails, pig feet, collard greens, thick cornbread fried in a skillet—something was always on the stove. Part of my job was serving the food and pouring whiskey for people. Another part was taking slips of paper around town to the guys running numbers, which was our version of the lottery. I looked

at my grandmother like somebody out of the Old West, like An-
nie Oakley. She was another tough woman in my life."

To a nine-year-old boy, Beulah Reid's wood-frame three-story
boarding house seemed as large as an aircraft carrier and, like
his Aunt Belle's whorehouse, it was an enthralling place to live.
"Something was always going on," Reid says. "Eating, drinking,
dancing, and singing, either to a record player or along with
somebody playing a guitar." And since the clientele ranged from
couples renting a second-floor room for a day or two to entire
families, he never lacked for playmates. "The adults would be
drinking and talking and we'd be outside playing," he says. "My
grandmother would say, 'Here, take a dollar.' I went from being
a kid where a dollar would feed us for three days to one who
always had a dollar in his pocket. It seemed like all the money
in the world to me."

Reid was also fascinated by his uncle Joe, Beulah Reid's
younger brother. A handsome man in his forties who wore zoot
suits and chains and lived on the streets by his wits, he would
show up before church on Sundays to tie the boy's tie and give
him an allowance that included fifty cents for the collection
plate. "Put in 10 cents for yourself and the rest for me," he would
say with a laugh. "Tell God I ain't as bad as he thinks."

God's judgment was rendered a few years later when, during
a trip to North Carolina, Reid saw his uncle beat a man who had
been flirting with his wife outside an establishment in Elizabeth
City. "We just sat there watching, not saying a word," said Reid.
"I was too scared to cry, scared of my grandmother and scared
of my aunt Lucille, who was the meanest woman I've ever seen
in my life. She and Uncle Joe were always fighting. They loved
each other, but they loved fighting more."

The tide of the battle turned when Joe's victim returned with
a tire iron and knocked him down with one terrifying blow to
the head. "They wouldn't let me see him in the hospital until
finally a nurse snuck me in," Reid says. "He was paralyzed and
he stayed that way for the rest of his life. But when I see him in
my dreams today I see him whole. I saw so much violence and

pain in those days, but what I remember most is the joy and love they all gave me."

Late nights in the boarding house, after the regulars went home and the kitchen was quiet, were spent watching old movies on television with his grandmother. Joel McCrea, Randoph Scott, George Raft, and Brian Donlevy were Beulah Reid's favorites. "We watched everything," Reid says. "Westerns, crime movies, comedies, horror movies, whatever was on. I think I know more about what was on the late show than just about anybody else alive."

If his grandmother's lifestyle and occupation were unconventional, so were her notions about raising a child. "She spoiled me rotten," Reid says. "She knew what it had been like living with George Bright and she wanted me to have as much fun as possible. She'd say, 'Go downtown and look in the windows. Buy yourself a spinning top or some marbles.' Or if it was hot, she'd say, 'Go ride the bus and cool off,' and I'd ride to the end of the line. I came and went when I wanted. I roamed the streets. My grandmother gave me my wings. For the first time in my life, I was free."

But this freedom came at a price, beatings that became more frequent as he grew older, and as his father's carefree life began to seem more appealing. "He was such a cool dude, driving this nice car, doing these interesting things and I wanted to live with him," Reid says.

"Things go on in this house, dad," Reid told his father. "You know what I mean."

"I'm trying," William Reid said. "Stay here a little longer and I'll work it out."

Standing unseen on the boarding house porch and listening to this conversation, his grandmother put an end to Reid's thoughts of leaving. "I'm going to teach you a lesson you'll never forget," she said, taking out an electric cord. "Don't you ever disrespect this family. What happens in this house stays in this house."

"She whipped me with that cord until she got tired," Reid

says. "Finally, Clyde said, 'Beulah, stop before you kill that boy.'"

After the city condemned the boarding house to build a highway, Reid's grandmother purchased a more modern building not far away. "It was right across the street from an elementary school," Reid says, "but I was staying up so late at night that I was late every morning. I had the worst attendance record in the school."

As for the education Reid received on Norfolk's streets, it lacked one thing even a perfect attendance record would not have provided: a meaningful association with white people. "I never had a white friend when I was growing up," he says. "I never spoke to a white person socially. We lived in a completely isolated, functioning black environment. The first white person I ever talked to on a social level for more than twenty minutes in my life was Tom. Tom Dreesen was the first white friend I ever had."

This lack of contact led to beliefs about, and experiences with, white people that ranged from the comic to the ominous. "The women who worked in white folks' homes would tell stories in the boarding house and in church about how white people lived and they were aghast," he says. "They'd come in when they were done cleaning up after them and say, 'These people are nuts. They live like heathens.' Learning through the eyes of a domestic is not the way to grow up with a healthy respect for white America."

What Reid found most fascinating were the stories he heard about how white parents treated their children. "They said they didn't discipline them and the kids talked back to them all the time. The idea that a child would tell his parents to go to hell was amazing to me. I said, 'You mean they don't hit them? I want to live with white folks.'"

But the first time Reid ventured out on his own, he saw another side of America's racial divide. Though Tina Wilkins knew Reid was safer now, she felt guilty about sending him away and stayed in touch as best she could. Occasionally, a package would arrive at his grandmother's boarding house containing a gift she had bought or, more often, a used item she had been given by one of her employers. And during the summers, as she traveled with a vacationing employer or looked for work, she would send for Reid to join her for a week or two. Which meant stepping into a different world.

"The first time I left the cocoon of my community to be with my mother," he says, "my grandmother got out my Boy Scout uniform and said, 'I want you to wear this. White people are nice to military men.' That's the way she thought, that wearing a Boy Scout uniform would protect me on a bus filled with white people."

The bus stopped for lunch at a restaurant outside Richmond, Virginia, and Reid followed the crowd inside, took a tray, and stood in the buffet line. Suddenly, all movement and conversation in the restaurant stopped. "I could hear every sound: trays being put down, people shuffling their feet," Reid says. "I could even hear them breathing. I looked around and everybody was looking at me—the customers, the cashier, the people behind the counter serving food. I thought 'What?' and then I saw a black woman in the kitchen staring at me with the most evil look on her face. She walked over to a table where the food was laid out and just *slapped* it with her hand and said, 'Come over here! Come over here right now!'"

Confused and frightened, Reid walked over to the woman who snatched his tray away, said, "Get out of here! Go around the back!" and shoved him out the door. "What a mean woman," Reid thought as he went outside with every eye in the silent restaurant still on him.

"Come here! Come here!" a man behind the restaurant, who had seen what had taken place, shouted as he ran up to Reid. "See that window over there? Go over there. Just go over there and be quiet." Reid did as he was told, but when he saw the woman who had shouted at him, he was ready to run. Then he saw she was close to tears. "Come here, baby," she said. "Don't you know you're not supposed to be in there?" She then wrapped her arms around him and stacked a tray with more food than he could eat.

"She was so afraid for me," Reid said. "And I didn't know any better. I'd always been in the black community and when I went downtown we were taught what to do. When you get on a bus, you go to the back and sit. You shut up and put on a face. Every kid my age got that lesson. But here I was all alone for the first time in the middle of white people and I didn't know how to behave."

By the time he was twelve, Reid was running with the Corner Boys, a Norfolk street gang whose major activity was rolling sailors as they stumbled out of the bars in the black part of town. "If you lived in my neighborhood, either you were a Corner Boy or you didn't come out much," he says. "So we started early, running errands for the bigger guys. They called us the Junior Corner Boys."

Reid's best friend among the Corner Boys was Raymond, who was a few years older, brilliant, and violent. "Raymond never seemed to go to school, but he did all my homework for me," Reid says. "And he was a great organizer. He could get anybody to do anything, and tell them how to do it. He was another bastard child living with his grandmother so I guess he thought we had something in common. I was lucky that he was there to look out for me."

The Junior Corner Boys confined their activities to staying out late and the occasional petty theft in neighborhood stores until one Saturday some older gang members convinced them to break into the elementary school across the street from Reid's grandmother's house. "We trashed the place, threw paint on the walls, and hauled some stuff out," Reid says. "But the older guys knew the principal kept forty or fifty dollars in a box in his office so while we were vandalizing the school they stole the money."

Any notion they had committed the perfect crime ended Monday morning when they were called into the principal's office and told a neighbor had identified them. A threat of reform school and fifteen licks on each hand with a ruler ("He beat me till I peed in my pants") quickly produced the names of the older boys, and then the principal handed down the sternest punishment of all. "Go home and tell your grandmother what you did," he said. "Tell her we're going to have to decide what to do with you."

Terrified of the beating that awaited him, Reid tried to stay away from his grandmother, but she got the news through the neighborhood grapevine soon enough. So did his father, who took the step he had been trying to avoid. "You have two options," he told Reid as they went for a ride. "Either you come to live with me and go to school, or I kill you. What's it going to be?"

"I think he would have, too," Reid says, laughing at the memory. "I didn't really want to go by then. He was living out in the country, which I hated because it was away from all my friends, but I didn't have a choice."

But if convincing his son a change was needed was a simple matter for William Reid, selling the idea to his grandmother was something else again.

"You're not taking him from me!" she shouted. "I won't have it!"

"You're ruining the boy, Beulah!" Reid's father said. "He's running wild. He has no discipline. This is the only way to save him."

Reid's grandmother tried everything—begging their pastor to intervene, even threatening to have her own son arrested—but she had no recourse. At the age of twelve, Reid moved in with his father, who took out adoption papers and gave him yet another name. Once Timothy Isabel Jr., then George Bright Jr., he was now Timothy Lee Reid. "You can see where they scratched out Isabel on my birth certificate and wrote in Lee Reid," he says. "That was when my father officially acknowledged me."

Reid was also accepted, if not embraced, by Novella, his father's wife, who had witnessed Tina Wilkins's tantrum outside the New Calvary Baptist Church a dozen years earlier. "There was no real warmth, but she was decent to me," he says. "She said, 'Here's your room. What's in there is yours. What's out here is mine. Understand?' And I did. I understood that for a man to bring a son he fathered by another woman into their home was not easy for her. Especially since she couldn't have any children of her own. I stayed there for five years, until I graduated from high school. I'm convinced that's what kept me out of prison, or from dying violently like so many of the guys I ran with. I owe that woman a lot."

Whenever life in the country grew too oppressive ("Sometimes I thought it was just me and the mosquitoes"), Reid would go back into Norfolk, and soon he was spending most weekends back at his grandmother's boarding house. This allowed him to continue running with the Junior Corner Boys and, when he was sixteen, led to the confrontation with another gang that changed his life.

"We went into a store where the Princess Anne Road Gang hung out," he says, "but apparently they heard we were coming and they didn't show up. You could see the owner of the place figuring there might be trouble and looking relieved when nobody else came. Raymond and I were sitting in a booth with some of the older guys, including one who had just escaped from jail. He drank a cup of coffee and then got up and said, 'Nothing's going to happen tonight. Let's get out of here.' As he was walking out the door, he threw the cup through a big display case and shattered glass flew all over the room.

"I was the last guy in the store and I knew I had to be cool, not show any fear, just walk out, not run. But just as I got to the door I felt something hard pressed against the back of my head. I turned and saw it was a German Luger. The owner looked me straight in the eye and said, 'Run.' I was two steps from the door and I remembered something my father had told me: If you kill somebody inside your store, you'll get off because you're defending your property. If he falls on the other side of the door, out on the sidewalk, you're probably going to have to pull some time. All I could think was if I could just go through the door, I'd live.

"The guy said it again, 'You hear me, boy? Run,' but I took those last two steps as slowly and deliberately as I could with the gun pressed to my head. As I got to the door, I felt the gun come up off my head and I walked outside. Then I took off. I would have run over Jesse Owens that day. I caught up with Raymond and the other guys and I said, 'That's it. I'm through. I'm not doing this any more.'"

William Reid was active in community affairs and president of the Civic League in Crestwood, a small black town on the outskirts of Norfolk. This enhanced his status in the neighborhood, and worked to his son's advantage as well. "I was a horrible student," Reid says of his high school days. "I was arrogant in class and used to terrorize the teachers. One poor woman sent me to the principal and the first thing he said to me was, 'Would you take this note to your father for me?' My father's stature gave me that leeway."

But the protection William Reid could offer his son did not extend to his own dealings with the world outside Norfolk's black community. His good job on the Norfolk and Western, where he had worked for ten years, disappeared in an instant after an argument with a white supervisor. And his efforts to rebuild his fortunes by opening a nightclub came to an equally unhappy end. "He built it with his bare hands," Reid says of the Combo Terrace, the club his father erected in Chesapeake, a few miles outside of Norfolk. "He had painters put an amazing scene of the Harlem Renaissance on the back wall. It was iridescent and when he shined blue lights on it, it looked three-dimensional. There was a bar and restaurant in one section and a stage in the back where you would pay a cover charge and see a show. There was nothing like it in the black community, and since we couldn't go to white night clubs back then it was the place to be. I never would have thought my father could have created such a wonderful setting."

William Reid hired well-known performers, such as Ruth Brown, Gary U.S. Bonds, and the Showmen, and soon customers' cars were parked up and down the road. To his son, a senior in high school with no particular plans, it seemed like salvation. "I was popular." Reid says. "I was vice-president of the student council, I had lots of girlfriends, I was on the track team, I had a little money in my pocket. It was the best my life had ever been. But when I looked ahead, I was scared. It seemed as if everything was coming to an end, that it would be all downhill. I certainly didn't have the grades to go to college. I didn't see a future. But when my father opened the club and it was so successful, I figured I'd work with him. I thought we were going to be rich."

The end of William Reid's dream came in stages. First, the owner of the Swing Inn, a juke joint across the street from the Combo Terrace, set up a bust. He sent a minor into the club to buy a drink and then paid off a policeman to walk in after him. The policeman locked the front door, arrested William Reid, and picked up the phone. "They pulled the paddy wagons up to the back door and arrested everybody in the place, 128 people," Reid says. "To this day, it's one of the largest raids in the history of the state of Virginia."

But while the lurid case was dismissed because the setup had been so transparent, the Combo Terrace finally succumbed to a charge that was far more mundane. "The way the show worked was you had a hoochie coochie dancer, a comedian, and then a singing act," Reid says. "The dancer was not a stripper—all she did was dance—but what my father didn't know was that if you had a dancer in your club, you needed a license. And that's what they got him for. He didn't have a five-dollar dance license. So they took his beverage license away and closed his business down. It ruined him and he never recovered, spiritually, emotionally, or financially. It took him another ten years to die, but that's what killed him."

As invested in the dream as his father had been, Reid was stunned. "All because he didn't have a piece of paper? How could a thing like that happen?" He had to learn something about the world of business, he thought. Somehow, some way, he had to go to college. Even if he didn't have the money, or the grades.

Money was the easy part. Reid was walking down the street to the air force recruiting office one day when a car pulled up and a man leaned out to ask for directions to Virginia Beach. "The *air* force?!" he said as they struck up a conversation after Reid offered to show him the way out of town and climbed in the car. "Don't you know what's going on in the world? There's a war coming."

"I figured that's how I'd get the money for college," Reid said, but the driver, who taught at Florida A&M and supplemented his salary by working as a waiter in the summer, had another idea. "I'll tell you what," he said. "Help me find this place I'm looking for and I'll give you ten dollars. You can join the air force tomorrow."

Two days later, Reid found himself wearing a shirt that was too big, a jacket that was too small, and a bow tie the likes of which he had never worn before. He was now a waiter at Steinhilber's, an exclusive white Virginia Beach restaurant that employed a more discreet method of subverting the state's liquor laws than the one his grandmother had used. "The governor ate there, so you could bring a bottle and they'd give you a setup," Reid says. "And if you didn't have a bottle, they could work it out."

The pay wasn't much, ten dollars a day, but an industrious waiter who had a sunny personality and a ready smile, and who didn't mind coming and going by the back door, could earn as much as eighty dollars more in tips. "It was a gold mine," Reid says. "No wonder faculty members at black colleges were waiters at resorts in the summer. They could make more there than they could teaching school. By the end of the summer, I had fifteen hundred dollars, enough for tuition, clothes, everything I needed. I'd never had so much money in my life. Then my mother called and said she wanted to come home so we got an apartment. It was the first time in nine years we'd spent more than a couple of weeks together."

Getting into college was not as difficult as he had expected, either, though it was humbling. Today, Norfolk State University places Reid high on its list of most prominent alumni. But at a time when the school was known as the Norfolk Division of Virginia State College, he was granted only probationary status because of his high-school grades. Nor was Reid's first year in college especially promising. His job at Steinhilber's, which remained open through Thanksgiving, and his growing fondness for liquor houses, and the women he found there and on campus, all took precedence. "I'm drinking heavily, I'm chasing girls, I'm working at night," Reid says. "By the time I get in, it's two or three in the morning. Then I get up at eight and go to class. If I go to class."

At one point, he disappeared altogether and moved in with a woman he met at a bar, leaving her place only when it was time to go to work or out drinking. "Everybody was looking for me," he says. "Even my mother didn't know where I was." In desperation, Tina Wilkins did what she'd done the last time she had feared Reid's life might be in jeopardy. "I went home after being away for a week to pick up some clothes and my dad was there," Reid says.

By then, William Reid was a man of broken dreams. The strong and powerful figure who had once held a prestigious job, run a popular nightclub, and been a figure to reckon with in the black community had been reduced to driving a cab at night, and nursing his grievances with whatever liquor and women came to hand. Where once he could threaten his son with physical violence if he didn't mend his ways, his only weapons now were a few quiet words—and his own example.

"All he said was, 'I am so disappointed in you,'" Reid says. "He had tears in his eyes. It just tore my heart out. I respected my dad and everything he had done for me. I knew what he had gone through and I could see I was giving him more pain. I said, 'That's it. Things have got to change.' And they did. I went back to school, I started making my grades—I even made the dean's list—I did the first acting I'd ever done in a play, and I met Rita."

Reid's theatrical baptism came about by purest chance. There was no theater department on campus and there would have been no theater either but for Stanley Wilson, an English professor who loved Shakespeare and whose class Reid inadvertently disturbed one day. "I was chatting up this young lady out in the hall and I guess I was talking pretty loud when Stanley came out of the room to tell me I was interrupting his class," Reid says. "He sized up the situation right away and he told the girl, 'This man means you no good,' and she took off. Then he turned to me and said, 'I think we can put that voice of yours to better use. Who are you?'" Soon, Reid was answering Wilson's casting calls and taking the elective drama classes the professor had convinced the college administration to offer.

As Wilson was presenting Reid with one important new experience, Rita Ann Sykes was offering another. A quiet and studious young woman from Berkley, just across the Elizabeth River from Norfolk, she had been raised in the sort of close-knit middle-class family Reid never knew. She had three sisters and a father who worked in a navy yard, came home to his wife and family every night, and took them to church on Sunday. She had one other attribute that helped Reid pull himself together as well.

"She is a saint," Reid says. "I could not have made it at that time in my life without her because she always made me believe I could do anything I wanted to do. And she did it in a way that was so matter-of-fact it was almost as if I had already done it. If I had come home one day and said, 'I think I'm going to be an astronaut,' she would have said, 'OK, I'll pack your lunch.' The Bible says, 'Let he who is without sin cast the first stone.' Rita could throw that stone. If I even bent down to pick it up, I'd get hit by lightning. I married above myself, way above."

Reid immediately hit it off with Rita's family, particularly her father, who had been a drummer as a young man but gave up a chance to go to New York rather than risk his job at the navy yard. By October of his junior year, Reid was a married man and a father, living with his wife and mother, working at Stein-hilber's, keeping up his grades, helping supervise a campus job internship program, and getting caught up in the civil rights movement that was sweeping through America's black colleges like a prairie fire.

Reid's racial consciousness was forged while he was in high school at the Goody Goody Barbershop on Church Street, a few blocks from the site of his Aunt Belle's whorehouse, which had long since been torn down, and his grandmother's house across the street from the elementary school. It was where he hung out after quitting the Corner Boys and where he joined many black men in discussing the news of the day. And more and more, the news of the day had to do with civil rights.

The Goody Goody was run by the four Thompson brothers and the heated arguments over the best way to improve the sta-tus of blacks would continue long after their barber tools were put away and the doors were closed. "Willie Thompson was go-ing to college and he was a real radical," Reid says. "The sum-mer before I went to college, he got me involved in SCAD, the Student Committee Against Discrimination, which was very militant. Most of us lined up on the side of Stokely Carmichael and the Black Panther Party. I was on my way to becoming more radical than Malcolm X, and I stayed that way until the March on Washington."

Reid had not planned to be in Washington on August 28, 1963. It was not until after midnight that he set off on the spur of the moment with Willie and Bones Thompson. Lying down inside the back window of their two-seat Austin-Healey 3000 during the three-hour journey, he arrived at the Washington Monument before dawn. "There were just a few people there and it was so warm we fell asleep at the base of the monument," Reid says. "The screech of the PA system woke us up a few hours later and there was a massive crowd. I thought, 'This is amazing' and we all began moving, the force of the crowd just pulling us along. About an hour later, Peter, Paul, and Mary started singing 'If I Had a Hammer,' and the crowd kept growing. I lost sight of the Thompson brothers and the crowd kept swirling around, hundreds of thousands of people just moving, moving. One minute I was standing next to Wilt Chamberlain and the next minute I was a few steps right behind Martin Luther King. There was no structure to anything. There was a sense that everybody could go wherever they wanted."

Hours later, as King was about to give his historic speech, Reid climbed a tree near the platform to listen. The effect was profound. "Sometimes, you hear something and you say, 'That's true,'" Reid says. "A bell rang for me that day and it said, 'This is the truth.' Dr. King changed my whole attitude about militancy and violence. I knew we had to focus on living together. I went home and resigned from SCAD." When he arrived at college a few weeks later, Reid joined the campus chapter of the NAACP and two years later became its president.

"We helped integrate the YMCA, we helped integrate the lunch counter at Woolworths, we helped integrate White Castle," Reid says of his journeys with other students into Norfolk's business district. "White Castle was the toughest. They were one of the last chains to integrate. To this day, I can't bring myself to eat a White Castle hamburger. It's the only hangover I have from the civil rights movement. Woolworths was tough, too. They would take the seats off the stools and there would be no place to sit. So we would sit on our schoolbooks, which really pissed them off. They spit on us, and once the police brought in dogs and made us leave."

But as tumultuous and dangerous as those times were, Reid discovered a sense of purpose in the civil rights movement he had never known before. And something else, too, something that would inform the movies he produced about the era decades later. "I get a little upset when Hollywood or documentaries on public television show young blacks in that era so persecuted and oppressed and worried," he says. "It's always, 'Oh,

God, they're going to bomb that house!' Let me tell you some-thing that those of us who were there still talk about. We had a *ball*. We partied, we had meetings, we debated. You should have seen us reading from Robert's Rules of Order. We saw our pic-tures on the front page of the papers and on the local news. We took over a building in town and the mayor and the city council had to meet with us. Sargent Shriver gave us some money to buy a building that is a Boys' Club to this day. Yes, there was the Klan, which always seemed to know when we would be marching. The police would line up in the middle of the street between us, supposedly for our protection, but the dogs would be facing toward us, not the Klan. But we knew the cause was important and we were excited to be a part of it. Those were wonderful times, the best times of our lives."

The civil rights movement offered something else to young men like Reid as well, a chance to channel their aggressions in a healthy way. "It gave me an opportunity to express myself, to exercise my warrior nature, which has nothing to do with race and has been built into us since we were cavemen. White boys from middle-class families had it easier, I think, because of all the socially acceptable ways they had to vent. I talk to black students about this today, that they shouldn't deny their warrior nature but use it constructively. I know it gave me confidence later on."

In the spring of Reid's junior year, a frightened young white man just out of college arrived on campus from Wilmington, Delaware. A representative of DuPont, he was making the firm's first recruiting trip to a historically black college. "The poor guy was scared to death, just trembling," says Reid, who was helping to coordinate his student interviews. "I said, 'Hey, man, relax,' and went out into the hall to try to find some people for him to talk to. But by the end of the day, he'd only had four or five interviews because nobody thought a white company was going to hire a black person. They all said, 'DuPont? Yeah, right.'"

Finally, almost out of desperation, the recruiter said, "Look, how about you? Come up to Delaware. We'll put you up in a nice hotel, you'll eat at this great restaurant, you'll meet the people who run our management training program. What else do you have to do on a weekend?"

A few nights later, after playing the priest in *Oedipus Rex*, Reid removed his costume and, realizing he had not brought a shirt suitable for a job interview, borrowed one from Stanley Wilson. Then he hurried to catch a train that would take him to Wilmington, and a new life.

"I still have that shirt," Reid says. "It and the train George Bright gave me are the only things I have left from my youth."

Tom Dreesen's earliest memories of growing up in Harvey, Illinois, are of the noise. The noise of the Grand Trunk Railroad trains rolling through on the tracks that separated the city's residential section from its industrial base. The noise of the pounding from the Wyman-Gordon factory just beyond the tracks where parts for airplane engines, crankshafts, propellers, and landing gear were manufactured during the three shifts that filled every hour of the day. The noise of the jukebox in Polizzi's Tavern below the second-floor apartment where Walter and Glenore Dreesen lived with their ever-growing family.

"How can you stand all this noise?" Dreesen's grandmother once asked when she paid a visit.

"We didn't know what she was talking about," Dreesen says. "It was part of us."

Dreesen's mother was a bartender in the tavern downstairs, which was owned by her sister's husband, Frank Polizzi. It was one of three dozen bars in Harvey, a town of some 30,000 souls nineteen miles south of Chicago's Loop. Founded in 1889 as a temperance community, Harvey soon abandoned that social experiment and years later a factory worker finishing his shift could meander from bar to bar on his way home. "On the corner was Sparrow's Tavern," Dreesen remembers. "Down the street was Johnny's Gay Club—gay meant happy in those days—around the corner was Al's Corner Club and down the street from Al's was Fuzzy's. And that was just on our block."

But the bars were not only places to drink. They also served as Harvey's social centers, places where the word was spread about births and deaths, marriages and divorces, and how the children were doing in school. Work in scores of manufacturing plants in and around Harvey was such a popular topic of conversation that at times the taverns seemed to be the site of unofficial union meetings. But so were world events. The Korean War, which many draftees from Harvey fought in, was much on the minds of the city's families then.

Most fascinating to Dreesen as he hung around his uncle's bar was how highly regarded tavern owners were. They were the town's celebrities and their presence on the street was as notable as that of any politician or entertainer. "See that guy over there, Tommy," Walter Dreesen would say to his son. "That's Bill from Bill and Lottie's." Bill was a pot-bellied, bleary-eyed, red-faced boozer, but the fact that he owned a tavern meant he was important.

The taverns' influence also extended beyond their doors. They sponsored bowling leagues, basketball teams, and teams in the Chicago area's native sport: sixteen-inch softball. Every summer, they joined together to put on a picnic in Thornton Woods where they set up tents, served food and drink, and organized games as Harvey's families took their ease. A particular measure of an owner's stature in the community was seen when he appeared in a competitor's tavern. "People would say, 'Joe from Joe and Mary's is in Bill and Lottie's buying a round for everybody. What a good guy,'" Dreesen remembers. "And later, Bill would visit Joe and Mary's and he would buy a round."

But a tavern owner's popularity was most evident when he stood behind his own bar. Just as his name was on the sign above the sidewalk, he was the star attraction inside. An owner had to be ready with the latest jokes and stories, with the most up-to-date news of the neighborhood and, most important, with a personality that kept the customers coming back. "If a guy was a jerk, he wouldn't have much business, would he?" Dreesen says. "So there would have to be something likeable about him."

By the time he was seven years old, Dreesen was attending Ascension Catholic grade school and moving from bar to bar afterwards, shining shoes and drinking in the atmosphere along with the Pepsis the owners gave him. His last stop, usually about the time the shifts at the plants were changing and the traffic was heaviest, was at his Uncle Frank's place where he would observe the purest expression of the tavern owner's art. "I would watch him behind the bar and hear him tell these wonderful stories," Dreesen says. "The whole bar would listen and laugh as if he was onstage. He would tell jokes and I was fascinated that he could cause this sound to come out of another human being's body. His vocabulary and his inflection, just the way he said a word, would make everybody erupt in laughter. It was the warmest sound to me and I was always gravitating toward it, trying to figure out what made people laugh."

Polizzi had a band that played in clubs around town in the evenings, Frank Polizzi and the Venetianaires, in which he played guitar and saxophone and sang. Dreesen's father played the trumpet and sometimes his mother would sing harmony. "Being a tavern owner was the epitome of success to me," Dreesen says. "They always had money in their pocket. They were always buying drinks for people. I grew up thinking one day I would be a tavern owner. I could see it: Tom's Bar and Grill."

But there was another side to owning a tavern, one that introduced Dreesen to old-fashioned codes of honor and made his admiration for his uncle even stronger. "You never went into Frank's bar and gave him any shit," Dreesen says. "If you did, you were out on the sidewalk. He threw teamsters out of the bar two at a time. I must have seen him in fifty fights and I never saw him lose. My dad told me that Frank was on stage singing one night and he saw a guy fooling around with his sister, my aunt Ann, while the guy she was engaged to was playing saxophone in the band. Frank stopped singing, walked off the stage, decked the guy, then came back up and finished the song."

The single most memorable display of Polizzi's toughness, one that secured his place in Harvey lore, occurred one afternoon when two men drove up in a truck and wheeled a shiny new jukebox into the bar. Polizzi's Tavern was the only one of Harvey's bars with a jukebox that wasn't supplied by the local syndicate, which was run by Babe Tuffenelli out of the south Chicago suburb of Blue Island. Polizzi confronted the men and, when they refused to remove the jukebox, he wheeled it outside himself and dumped it on the sidewalk, where it fell with a crash and broke apart. As the delivery men fled, Dreesen watched his mother and Polizzi's wife, his Aunt Marge, all too aware of the possible consequences of Polizzi's act, fall to their knees and begin saying the Rosary. Half an hour later, Babe Tuffenelli himself, accompanied by one of his larger associates, drove up in a big car and entered the bar.

"You broke my fucking jukebox," the mob boss told Polizzi.

"I told your goons to get it out of here," Polizzi said. "I told them like a gentleman, twice."

"You broke my fucking jukebox," Tuffenelli repeated.

"I didn't order your jukebox," Polizzi said and he pointed across the room. "See that jukebox over there? I broke my back working in a factory to buy that jukebox. Why are you fucking with me? I'm from the old country, too. Go fuck with the *medigans.*"

The bar was perfectly still, the neighborhood drinkers rooted to their stools waiting to see what would happen next. Finally, Tuffenelli broke the silence.

"I tell you what I'm going to do," he said. "I'm going to walk out of here and I ain't saying nothing. But if you ever leave this place and go to work anywhere, you've got to promise me you'll come to work for me."

"I'd never work for you," Polizzi said and the confrontation was over. Tuffenelli never returned.

"It was amazing he didn't get killed," Dreesen says. "My uncle had steel balls. Most people who saw him in action lived in pure fear of him. My father was one of them."

Walter Dreesen was the sort of man who would tip his cap to women as he passed them on the sidewalk. Soft-spoken and well-dressed, Dreesen played the trumpet well enough to claim first chair in the Thornton High School band as a freshman and later to play in bands in New York. On one of his trips home, he ran into Polizzi who told him his band needed a trumpet player. An introduction to his wife's sixteen-year-old sister, Glenore, followed. Not long afterwards, Glenore became pregnant and, very quickly, Mrs. Walter Dreesen.

Walter Dreesen had an aptitude for numbers that qualified him for jobs in the time and motion study departments of Harvey's factories and he was seldom out of work. But his drinking and his gambling affected every aspect of his life, and the lives of everyone close to him. "Here's what an alcoholic's mentality is like," Dreesen says. "Whenever my father saw somebody he respected, he would tell me, 'See that guy, Tommy? He can go in any bar in town and get credit.' That was success to him—being able to drink without reaching into his pocket."

Dreesen was the third of eight children and with each new arrival their father's drinking increased while their living conditions declined. Before long, they had left the apartment above Polizzi's Tavern and were living in a shack behind the Wyman-Gordon plant near the railroad tracks. It had no bathtub, no shower or hot water, and five of the children slept in one bed. "We were raggedy-ass poor," Dreesen says. "To this day, some of my brothers and sisters can't talk about it. It's hard for us to go deep into it because it seems surreal."

To ward off the rats that burrowed beneath the shack the family employed a method that was as simple as it was ineffective. "We took bottles from behind gas stations and taverns, broke them, and put them in the rat holes so they couldn't get out," Dreesen says. "Of course, the rats would just dig another hole. I came home one night after setting pins in a bowling alley and there was a rat under my sister Alice's crib. Both my parents were out drinking and I was afraid it was going to hurt the baby so I got a broom and tried to chase it outside. But it ran past me into a little pantry and I couldn't find it. I lay there all night long, dreaming about that rat."

What little heat there was in the shack came from a coal stove in the kitchen. "If you stood up real close to it, your front side would get warm, but your back would be cold," Dreesen says. "Then you would turn around and warm your back and you would be cold in front."

Dreesen and his older brother, Glenn, furious at the thought of their parents sitting in a warm bar while they and their brothers and sisters froze, helped solve the problem by obtaining fuel from a source nearby: the coal cars attached to the trains rolling through just behind the house. "There was a certain spot where the trains would stop for a moment while they unhooked them," Dreesen says. "I would climb up on top and throw the coal down to Glenn who put it in a gunnysack. Then I'd jump down before the train started lurching forward and we'd run away. We always had to watch out for this one railroad dick in particular because we knew if he saw us we'd be in trouble."

Years later, Dreesen was tending bar in Harvey when a man he recognized walked in.

"You don't know who I am, but I want to buy you a drink," Dreesen said.

"I know who you are," the man replied. "You're that little shit who lived in the shack near the tracks. You and your goddammed brother used to steal coal off the train cars."

"You knew we were there?"

"Of course, I knew. One of the other cops knew where you lived and what you were using the coal for. He said I should turn my back and pray to God you didn't fall off the goddammed train and get yourself killed or I'd have it on my conscience. No, you can't buy me a goddammed drink."

The one place Dreesen could get away from the cold was in church. He became an altar boy when he was in the third grade, learning the Latin of the mass during his lunch hour, and he discovered a peace he could not find at home or on the streets. Dreesen found comfort in the warmth of the building, the singing of the choir, and the chanting of the congregation. There was something else about being an altar boy that appealed to him, too.

"That was the first time I was in front of a crowd," he says, and in the years to come, his stories about priests and nuns and Catholic school became such a staple of his act that letters would arrive at NBC's studios after his appearances on *The Tonight Show* addressed simply "to the Catholic comedian." Being an altar boy was not without its temptations, though, particularly the coins lying on top of the collection plate. "I took a dime once and long after I forgot what I bought it haunted me," he says. "I've put thousands of dollars in collection baskets since then because of that dime."

Glenore Dreesen left Walter once, but with only an eighth-grade education and no place to go, she returned. That was the turning point. "Everybody liked my mother," Dreesen says. "She was very compassionate and would sit and listen to your problems for hours. But when she realized she could never leave my father she threw in the towel. She started going out with him every night and matching him drink for drink. That's when the neglect really started."

On payday, Glenore would take a cab to the train station—the family never owned a car—where Walter arrived from the Acme Steel plant in Riverdale. They would cash his check at a currency exchange and she would bring a few groceries home. Then she would get back in the cab and join Walter in a bar near the train station, leaving the children alone while they drank up the rest of his paycheck.

The clothes the Dreesen children wore to school grew more threadbare, which made them stand out, particularly by the time they would arrive at Thornton High School, the one place where every element of Harvey's population—black and white, rich and poor—mixed on a daily basis. Maryellen Sebock, the

Harvey girl Dreesen later married, said there were three classes of girls at Thornton: the cashmeres, the fur blends, and the orlons. "She left one out," Dreesen would tell his audiences one day. "The gunnysacks. That was my group."

Their meals became more meager, too: cornmeal pancakes for dinner or gravy made of flour and water over day-old bread. On the days when a hearty thirty-cent lunch was served at Ascension—a barbecue sandwich, potato chips, and a soft drink—Dreesen would sit in the classroom eating his dried Karo syrup sandwich as the delicious smells wafted up from the lunchroom on the floor below.

"On the days they didn't serve lunch, we ate in the classroom and we would all spread our lunches out on our desk," he remembers. "There was one girl, Mary Jo Feldes, whose mother made her roast beef sandwiches with sliced tomatoes and gave her an apple or a banana. She was a thin girl and didn't eat much—a little bite of the sandwich, a little bite of the apple—and then she'd throw the rest in the wastebasket. I would wolf down my food as fast as I could and bolt out of there because I knew if I waited until everybody left I would go in the wastebasket and eat what she threw out. I didn't want to be tempted to do that."

Dreesen's mother had her pride, too—no holiday baskets of food from the Elks or Kiwanis or Rotary Clubs were allowed in the shack along the railroad tracks. "My husband has a job," she would say. "We're doing fine." It was all her children could do not to run after their would-be benefactors and grab an orange or an apple, food they rarely saw at home. "I think that's why I do so much charity work to this day," Dreesen says. "I know what it's like to be on the other side."

Somehow, the Dreesen children found in themselves the strength their parents lacked. They spent the better part of their childhoods looking out for each other as best they could, and they all grew into responsible adults with good jobs and children who lacked for nothing. Dreesen was particularly cared for by his two older siblings, his brother Glenn and his sister Darlene.

"Glenn was like a father figure to me even though he was only three years older," Dreesen says. "He's the one who showed me what a work ethic is all about—paper routes and shining shoes and setting pins in the bowling alley and caddying. He was a hard-working guy. He still is. He went in the navy when he was seventeen and when he got out he opened a photography studio and took in my sister Judy and my sister Darlene. And when I got out of the navy, he took me in, too."

If Glenn was Dreesen's de-facto father, then Darlene, though just eighteen months older, was his mother. "As far back as I can remember, she was always there," he says. "When I was little, she held my hand and told me when to cross the street. When I sold newspapers, Darlene sold newspapers. When I was an altar boy, Darlene went to church with me every day. When my mom and dad were out drinking, Darlene would watch over all of us. She had no childhood of her own."

Dreesen speaks slowly and emotionally as he tells the rest of Darlene's story. The bad marriage she made when she finally got out of the house. The diagnosis of multiple sclerosis not long after her second marriage to Walter Bethman, the good man she deserved. The steady deterioration from cane to walker to wheelchair to bed, and finally to the grave while she was still in her forties. "I'm not a religious person," Dreesen says. "But if there is a heaven, there is no justice if Darlene isn't there. She never did one wrong thing, not one. I think about her every day."

Once, when he was fifteen years old, Dreesen and a couple of friends hitchhiked to Biloxi, Mississippi. Feeling guilty after several days and certain his mother must be worried sick, he called her at the home of the closest neighbor with a telephone. She hadn't realized he was gone. But though he was living essentially without adult supervision, he did not lack for examples of the choices life offered. One was represented by the Bowl Center where he organized the other pin boys to ask for a few more cents a line, which led the owner to call him "Brains." The other was the golf courses where he caddied.

The bowling alley was connected to a pool hall where the pin boys were free to play when they were off duty, and free to get into trouble. They formed gangs, hand-painted their leather jackets, and hit the streets late at night. By the standards of a later era, their transgressions were innocent enough—petty theft, fighting, carousing after curfew—but they led to arrest records and nights in jail. "I set pins with some pretty tough guys," Dreesen says. "It was not a sissy job and you learned to fight. If a guy called you out for no reason, which happened all the time, you had a choice. Either you defended yourself or you were nobody. If you were a tough guy, you got respect. I wasn't getting much respect anywhere else in the world so I learned how to handle myself. At least there were no drugs then, only liquor and beer. Marijuana was just coming onto the scene— people were talking about it like it was heroin—but we never saw any."

By the time he was sixteen, Dreesen had quit school ("There was no one at home to tell me I couldn't") and was running the streets full time, hoping to stay one step ahead of his probation officer. "He was a mean son of a bitch," Dreesen says. "I still remember his name: John T. Lane. We had a little reprieve from curfew so we could set pins, but we were supposed to be home at ten o'clock. Once he told me, 'I've got 350 kids and I can't handle them all. If you fuck up just once, I'll put your ass in jail because it will make my life easier.' He would have, too."

But while the bowling alley and pool hall pointed Dreesen in one direction, Ravisloe Country Club, located a few miles south of Harvey in Homewood, offered a glimpse of something else. Designed by the legendary golf course architect Donald Ross and considered a hidden gem in golf-mad Chicago, Ravisloe was something of an anomaly: a Jewish country club that hired gentile caddies from all over the city. "We were Irish, Italian, Polish, you name it," Dreesen says. "And for a lot of us, it was the first time we had ever met doctors and lawyers and business-men. I caddied for Mr. Florsheim of Florsheim Shoes and for Mr. Balaban, who owned the Balaban and Katz chain of movie

theaters. I had never been around people like that before and
I began to see there was something beyond owning a tavern. I
saw a world on that golf course that changed my life."

The Ravisloe members doted on their caddies, tipping well,
making sure they ate lunch, and allowing them to play for free
on Mondays. "How ironic is that?" Dreesen says. "We were some
of the poorest kids in the whole Chicago area, but we learned
to play golf on one of the best courses anywhere." At the end of
each season, all 150 caddies at the club were invited to a ban-
quet where they received gifts and the mothers of the top dozen
were given a watch. Two were awarded Evans Scholarships that
allowed them to go to college. "I had never seen benevolence of
this magnitude," Dreesen says. "All those stereotypes you hear
as kids about different ethnic backgrounds, how Jewish people
are cheap and so on, Ravisloe took that right out of me. They
didn't treat us like servants. They treated us like young men."

Dreesen discovered something else at Ravisloe, something
that not only found its way into his stand-up routines but helped
him understand where comedy came from, and why so many
comedians were Jews. "They encouraged comedy in their children," he says. "I'd see them sitting at the table and telling their
friends, 'This is my nephew, Sidney. Sidney, tell Joe that funny
thing you told me this morning.' Sidney might be eight or nine
years old but they'd sit there and listen and tell him how funny
he was. 'Tummeling' was the word they used—I heard a lot of
Yiddish at Ravisloe—and it was part of the Jewish tradition. In
Irish and Italian and Polish families, children are to be seen and
not heard and they didn't encourage that kind of behavior. You
start telling jokes in Catholic school and they'd take a ruler to
your ass. That was the difference."

During one of his appearances on *The Tonight Show* in the
mid-1970s, Dreesen decided to push the envelope a bit as he
talked about his hometown. "I grew up in Harvey, Illinois," he
said, "and there are 40,000 people living there, 20,000 white
and 20,000 black, and they haven't had a racial incident since

1969. They are expecting a little trouble next July, though, when the 20,000 black people get out of jail."

For months afterwards, black people would approach Dreesen and say, "That was right on, brother. They're always putting us in jail." Whites, on the other hand, would say, "You're right. Those people are always committing crimes and going to jail." Johnny Carson had another response. "That's the ballsiest joke anybody ever told on this show," he said.

Between 1960 and 1980, Harvey's racial makeup changed dramatically as the town's black population rose from 7 to 66 percent. Racial incidents became common at Thornton High School and in 1969 the city was struck by a full-blown riot, which resulted in many arrests. "There was no riot control in those days and nobody knew what to do," Dreesen says. "Police cars came rushing into Harvey from cities all around—Hazelcrest, Markham, Homewood—and they started putting every black person they saw in jail. They picked up a guy on his way to church and a nurse going to work. So the irony of that joke is how politically correct it was, and how misinterpreted. I didn't care. I was comfortable telling jokes like that. Maybe that's one reason I was so comfortable working with Tim."

As far back as Dreesen could remember, he was surrounded by, and friends with, black people. Playing basketball and football on otherwise all-black teams. Shagging golf balls that flew over the fence of a local course and returning them to their owners for a dime apiece. Playing Mumble the Peg, a game with a knife whose object was not so much to win as not to lose. ("The last guy had to crawl through everybody else's legs and they'd take their belts off and whip the crap out of you.") "It made me very competitive as a child," Dreesen says. "Maybe it was inherent, but it was also being raised among all these black guys who were very competitive, too."

Dreesen's path was eased a bit by the intimidating presence of a large black youngster several years his senior named Everett Nicholson, known throughout Harvey as Goochie. "Goochie was very quiet but very tough," Dreesen says. "Everybody feared him." After watching several black youngsters gang up on Dreesen and steal the money he had made shining shoes or wrestle away the golf balls he had recovered, Goochie put a stop to it. "From now on, when you fight that white boy you've got to do it one at a time," Goochie told them. "So the word got out that I was Goochie's boy," Dreesen says. "I would follow him around. To this day, I don't know why he liked me, only that he was a decent guy."

The fact that Harvey was strictly segregated was not a barrier to his friendships with Goochie, Tutu Brackens, and other black kids because the poor white neighborhood where the Dreesens lived abutted the black one, and because they all had one thing in common: poverty. "I was different from so many of the white guys they knew," Dreesen says, "Maybe they associated with me because we were so poor, because of the holes in our shoes and the raggedy clothes. And maybe that made me more sensitive to being looked down on. At some point I realized I was having thoughts other white kids didn't have."

The easy nature of these childhood relationships led to a growing familiarity with a world that many of his white friends didn't know. Playing on black basketball and football teams, for instance, introduced him to "the dozens," or trash talking. "We'd do it for the same reason they do today," Dreesen says, "to get into your opponent's head, to get him pissed off at you and get him out of his game. I'm embarrassed when I think about it now, but this is the kind of things we'd say when we were kids:

"If you want to play the dozens and you want to play the game, well the way I fuck your mama is a goddamn shame."

"I saw your mama with a mattress on her back, yelling, 'Curb service!'"

"I don't play the dozens, I play the eleven and a halfs—I fuck your 11 sisters and your half-assed mama."

In later years, Dreesen would see that these juvenile games of one-upsmanship had introduced him to a mindset that, though foreign to white America in the 1950s, would serve him well in show business. "One of the things that fascinated me about growing up around black people was they had their own language," he says. "White men were Charlie and white women were Miss Ann. They'd say, 'Charlie's there, it's not going to happen,' as a warning. Or 'Miss Ann's behind the counter' if a white woman was waiting on them. Little Richard had a song that went, 'Oh, oh, oh, Miss Ann, you're doin' something no one can.' Black people knew what he was talking about, and I learned."

Dreesen also learned the sort of black response that stemmed from slavery and later it became a part of his act. "I called it the mumbles," he says. "When the slaves were being berated by the white master they learned how to look him in the eye and just mutter something under their breath. I could see how that carried over to today—I was fascinated by how black people talked among themselves—so sometimes when I was working in black clubs I'd do a boss yelling, 'Get back to work, you lazy so-and-so.' Then I'd say, 'Yeah, boss, right away,' and then whisper into the mike, 'Kiss my black ass,' and they'd all start laughing. Their culture was just so different and I grasped that as a kid."

Another place Dreesen could see this difference was in Harvey's black churches, or rather outside them. "Catholic kids were not allowed to visit any other churches in those days," he says, "but I'd go by Goochie's old Baptist Church—it was nothing more than a tar-paper shack—and sit on the sidewalk and wait for him. I heard more joy coming out of that church, the singing and the praying, than I'd ever heard in my life. In Catholic churches, the praying was quieter and this was so different. Whatever the preacher said, the congregation would say, 'Uh, huh! That's right! Tell him about it!' They seemed so overjoyed with their faith, not always suffering the way we did."

Later, Dreesen would see how the response of black church-goers had prepared him for performing in front of black audiences. "Whether they were heckling or not, they would react to what you're saying," he says. And the exuberance he was exposed to became another feature of his act. One routine he developed had to do with the difference between white and black cheerleaders at football games, which Dreesen performed in front of an all-black audience for an album called *That White Boy's Crazy*. The white cheer was "Big apple, little apple, Susie Q. Come on, team. We're rootin' for you." The black cheer, by contrast, was "Ooom gowa! Soul power! You'll all be dead in just an hour!"

Goochie also became a regular part of Dreesen's routines, the neighborhood character who represented the rough and tumble of life in Harvey. "Goochie was tough," Dreesen would say. "Young kids today brag about they know how to use Kung Fu. Goochie knew how to use Car Tool. I went to an all-white Catholic school in an all-black neighborhood called Our Lady of the Courageous Caucasians. The first day I got in trouble and they sent me down to Mother Superior. They said, 'Thomas, this is Mother Superior.' Well, I'd been hanging around with Goochie so I said, 'Yo, mama, what's happening?' She went in the drawer to get a ruler and I got scared. But I remembered something Goochie taught me. He said, 'If you're ever afraid, you've gotta woof.' Woofing is acting like you're not afraid. So when she got the ruler, I said, 'Hey, you better be pulling out a gun. That's right, I'm talking to you, Batman's wife.' She went, bam, bam across my knuckles with the ruler. I said, 'Damn, baby. I was only fooling.'"

Goochie went on to work for Wyman-Gordon and saved enough money to open a bar in one of Harvey's toughest neighborhoods where Dreesen would visit him when he was in town. "Hey, white boy, come over here," Tutu Brackens would say, playing to Goochie's crowd of regulars. "Let me tell you about this white boy. I knew him when he wasn't shit, sitting around telling his goddam silly-ass jokes. Buy me a drink. You got all kinds of money."

"Go easy on my friend," Goochie would say. "He's just here for a short time."

Laughing and putting some bills on the bar, Dreesen couldn't help thinking how good it was to be home.

Dreesen can't remember when he first heard the word "nigger," whether it was from the white residents of Harvey, whose racism was so deep-seated in the community, or from black friends and their parents whose use of the word turned its hateful origins on its head. All he remembers is that he was very young and that he came to understand how the word could be used in a number of ways. "Black folks used it affectionately as well as to be mean," he says. "I heard black mothers say, 'You little nigga, get in here. I'll whoop you upside your nappy head.' Or a black guy would tell his girlfriend, 'You're my pretty little nigga.' Remember now, they weren't called black in those days, they were colored. They called *themselves* colored. To call somebody a black this or a black that was calling him a bad name. Black didn't become beautiful until about the time I met Tim."

There was no nuance in the way "nigger" was used in the pool rooms, of course. "A lot of the white guys there were from the South—they'd come north because of all the factories in Harvey—and there was nothing friendly about the way they used the word, just anger and rage," Dreesen says. And soon enough this hatred would be directed at him.

While the white and black populations of Harvey came into contact every day, there were lines that neither crossed. They lived in their own neighborhoods, went to their own bars and, though Thornton was Harvey's only public high school and fully integrated, the white and black students separated themselves in class and the lunch room and patronized their own after-school hangouts. "The races were so divided," Dreesen says. "Somebody was always starting fights, and blaming the other side. The only time we'd get together was to root for the football team or the basketball team." This gulf explained the reaction of his white friends to his relationship with blacks. "What's that all about?" they would say, eyebrows raised, and before long he was hearing himself called nigger lover. "I was wounded by it," Dreesen says, "but then I would be with my black friends and I didn't care. Later, I heard it when I was touring with Tim and I realized not much had changed."

Almost intuitively, Dreesen understood one key require-
ment of his relationship with blacks: don't try to act like them.
"I'd see white boys who wanted to be black—the blacks called
them 'wiggers'—go around saying, 'Man, what's happening, you
jive-ass mother?' I never did that. Even in my night club act,
I approached it from a white boy's perspective. I was on the
outside, observing. I never tried to be a brother. Now, if I was
alone with one of my black friends and he was brother-talking
me, I could brother-talk back, but only if it fit that particular
circumstance."

Occasionally, though, Dreesen found himself in uncomfortable situations. Among Harvey's top celebrities as he was growing up was the singing group the Dells, whose 1954 recording of
"Oh What a Night" propelled them to national stardom, which
they continue to enjoy to this day. Dreesen became friendly
with Marvin Junior, the group's lead baritone, and their relationship was so free and easy that they developed something of
a routine when they were together. "You know what, Tommy?"
Junior would say. "You're my nigger even if you never get any
bigger. And if you do get bigger, you'll just be a bigger nigger."

Dreesen was delighted when, in the early 1970s, Tim and
Tom were signed to be the Dells' opening act at the 20 Grand, a
popular black club in Detroit. One night, he was part of a large
group backstage and, as was often the case, the only white person around. "Marvin was niggering everybody," Dreesen says.
"'Man, we told these niggers this . . . and those niggers said
to us'—things like that. Well, pretty soon, a guy from Detroit
grabbed Marvin and pointed at me and said, 'Hey, man,' and
whispered something. Marvin looked over and said, 'What the
hell is *wrong* with you? That's just Tommy. He's our home boy.'
And he went on with his conversation. But that didn't mean
I could start using the N-word all over the place. It was their
language, their culture. Even as a child I knew that, and I knew
my place."

As Dreesen made his way in show business, his relationships
with his black friends were a constant source of surprise to

other performers. Paul Mooney, the black comedian who created Homey the Clown for the television series *In Living Color*
and whose deconstruction of the word "nigger" was an integral
part of his act, used to doubt Dreesen's stories of his childhood.
"You don't know no brothers, man," Mooney told him. "You
make up that bullshit."

Once, when Goochie and his wife were visiting Dreesen in
Los Angeles, they ran into Mooney at a comedy club. "This isn't
Goochie," Mooney said after the introductions had been made.
"You went to Rent-a-Nigger."

"Paul was lucky because Goochie smiled and took it in good
spirits," Dreesen says. "He could have taken his head off."

But if the Goochie who appeared in the act surprised
Mooney, he once astonished Dreesen himself. The night before
playing in the Jackie Gleason Inverrary Classic in Florida in the
mid-1970s, Dreesen was introduced to President Gerald Ford.

"Oh, yes," Ford said as they shook hands. "Betty and I have
watched you on television at the White House."

"Thank you very much, Mr. President," Dreesen said, not
believing for a minute the Fords had ever seen him perform.
"What a politician," he thought. "No wonder he's president."

The next day, Dreesen hit a long drive off the seventeenth
tee and, as he walked down the fairway, he ran into Ford coming up the eighteenth in the company of Jackie Gleason and Tip
O'Neal. Noticing where Dreesen's ball had landed, Ford looked
back toward the tee and said admiringly, "Who hit that one,
Goochie?"

Dreesen was speechless. "He was telling the truth," he
thought, and for the rest of the day he pondered the power of
television and the fact that Goochie was known to the president
of the United States.

But for all that Dreesen's career and Goochie's bar meant
they had overcome the days when they scrambled after golf
balls, fought in alleys, and evaded the police, there would always be a part of Harvey in them they could not escape. When
Goochie's first wife was killed by a shotgun blast to her head,

Goochie called to tell him the news. Shocked, he returned to the dinner table and told Maryellen, "You won't believe this. Gerri had her head blown off by a shotgun."

"*No!*" Maryellen said. "I don't believe it."

"Yeah, wow . . . pass the potatoes, will you? Wait a minute. Do you realize what I just said to you? I said somebody I've known since I was a kid had her head blown off, pass the potatoes. That's how desensitized I've become to the gangland killings in Harvey. The violence creeps in and before you know it, it becomes a way of life."

Goochie also died before his time, the victim of another of his home town's vices. "He got to drinking more than he should have sitting in that bar of his," Dreesen says.

As he entered his teens, Dreesen began to realize something was not right. His brothers and sisters were blond and had blue eyes and freckles, whereas he was darker and had coal black hair. "Look at this," a boyhood friend told him as they looked at a photograph of the eight Dreesen children. "It's a bunch of Cocker Spaniels and one Airedale."

Frank Polizzi had always treated him differently, too. There was the cowboy outfit, complete with two six-shooters, Polizzi gave him for his sixth birthday, a far more elaborate gift than any of his brothers and sisters ever received. There were all those afternoons watching his uncle behind the bar that somehow made him feel as if the tavern, and not the shack along the railroad tracks, was where he belonged. There were his own feelings, too, feelings he did not understand, for the man who had such respect in the community, who could entertain his customers with a joke or a song, who was so different from his father. Finally, when he was fifteen years old, Dreesen summoned up the courage to approach Polizzi.

"I need to talk to you," he said.

"Why?" Polizzi said.

"I don't know how to say this," Dreesen blurted out before he lost his nerve, "but I think you're my father."

"Why do you think that?"

"Because I don't look like my brothers and sisters and I don't look like my dad. I look like my cousins, and like you."

Part of Dreesen wanted his uncle to laugh at him, to tell him he was imagining things, to say his suspicions were absurd. But Polizzi told him the truth.

"I *am* your father," he said quietly. "Your mother and I had an affection for each other and you were the result. It was one of those things that happen. I want you to know this because I don't want you to think we were a one-night stand or something in the back seat of a car. And now you have a decision to make. You can tell the world if you want to. It will ruin your parents' marriage, and it will ruin mine, and you know how close your mother and your Aunt Marge are. But you're entitled. It's up to you."

Though he was confused and hurt, and desperate to talk to somebody, Dreesen realized that he was not angry, either at his mother or Polizzi. He kept his distance from Polizzi for a time, and he kept his silence on the subject for years, not even mentioning it to his mother until after his father died many years later.

"I don't want to talk about this, Tommy," she said when he finally confronted her. "Your Aunt Marge and I love each other. It would kill her. It would kill *me.*"

"I'm not talking about it, Mom," Dreesen said. "I just want you to know that I know. Do you think I care who put the seed in there? You're my mother and you've always told me you loved me. Dad never did that, so I didn't lose anything." In time, his mother finally accepted the fact that he knew who his father was.

His last conversation with Frank Polizzi was also one he would never forget.

"I don't have long now, Tommy," Polizzi said from his hospital bed in 1992. "You've got to tell me. Do you have any regrets, any anger or rage you want to get off your chest?"

"No," Dreesen said. "Everything I have, everything I am,

is because of you. What about you? Is there anything you regret?"

The old man, who had once thrown troublemakers out of his bar two at a time, who had introduced Dreesen to the art of making a room full of people laugh, began to cry. "The only regret I have is that every time I was in the bar and you came on TV, I could never say, 'Hey, that's my son up there. Put down those drinks and take a look. That's my son.'"

It was years later, sitting in a bar after a performance late one night, when Dreesen told the story to someone outside his family for the first time. "Tommy, that kind of thing happens in more families than you can imagine," Frank Sinatra said. "The only difference is you learned the truth."

When Dreesen was seventeen, Glenn came home on leave from the navy. Admiring his brother's neatly pressed uniform, and fascinated by his stories of sailing the Mediterranean on the *USS Ticonderoga*, Dreesen did what he had done so often in the past. He followed Glenn's example. First, though, he had to convince John T. Lane.

"Will your probation officer release you?" the recruiting officer asked Dreesen when he learned of his scrapes with the law.

"He'll be glad to," Dreesen said. "He told me he's got too many guys to handle."

But Lane had other ideas. "Hell, no, I'm not letting him go in the navy," Lane told the recruiter.

"I couldn't believe it," Dreesen said. "I thought he wanted to get rid of me. That recruiter had to do a heavy sales job." In the end, Lane relented and Dreesen's life changed overnight.

He had a uniform and a head shaved bald that made him equal to everyone else around him for the first time in his life. He had his own bed, another first. He had enough hot water to take three or four showers a day if he wanted to, which he did. ("Everybody thought I was nuts. I didn't care.") He had all the clothes he needed, including *two* pairs of shoes. Amazing. And he had a regular paycheck. Not a lot of money, but something to put in his pocket. How much did he really need, anyway? The navy took care of everything.

Then there was the food. Three hot meals a day, every day, for the first time in his life. And if a couple of navy staples always seemed to be on the menu, he would never complain. "We called ground beef on toast shit on a shingle and chipped beef foreskins on toast," Dreesen says. "Guys were always bitching about them, but not me. I thought they were delicious."

After navy boot camp, Dreesen was transferred to Quonset Point, Rhode Island, where he was placed in a marine unit requiring advanced training that was almost a cliché—relentless physical activity that brought him near the breaking point, marine sergeants yelling awful things about his mother in his face, constant insults to his manhood that would have demanded immediate retaliation back in Harvey, but here had to be endured. But once he figured out what the object was, to separate those who could stand up to the abuse from those who couldn't, he knew he would be all right. "One day they just brutalized us and I went to bed ready to go AWOL," Dreesen says, "but then I made up my mind I was going to die before I let them know they got to me. After that, it got better. I started walking a little taller. I felt like I was starting to become a man."

Before long, the navy had been transformed from an ordeal into an adventure. Dreesen joined a navy boxing team, was assigned to a Naval Air Torpedo Unit and sailed on the *USS Tarawa* to the Antarctic. Crossing the equator for the first time, he and the other young sailors were transformed from "pollywogs" into "shellbacks," a ritual dating back to Marco Polo that included having their heads shaved and crawling through a gauntlet of veterans who beat their behinds with paddles soaked in seawater to make them harder.

But there was another part of shipboard life that might have been the greatest revelation of all—the conversation. "You would sit around and have these really heated debates with the kind of people you had never met before," Dreesen says. "There would be a Jewish guy from New York, a black guy from Detroit, a white guy from North Carolina, a kid from a farm in Arkansas and they'd be talking about Jews and blacks and Italians, about all the stereotypes they'd grown up with. It would really get heated with one guy saying what his grandfather told him about Italians and black guys arguing with somebody from the South about what *his* grandfather thought about blacks.

"When you talked to people like that in my neighborhood, it was ass-whipping time: 'What did you call me?'" Dreesen says. "Your teeth might come flying out of your mouth. So I'd sit there thinking there was going to be a fight. But it was *intellectual* combat. Guys would be in each others' faces, but then someone would say, 'You know, I never heard that before. I'll have to think about it.' I'd never seen debates where two people would sit there and yell at each other and then shake hands when they were done. It fascinated me."

After sixty-six days in the Antarctic ("the only land we saw in all that time was an iceberg; I can't tell you how lonely that was"), the crew was given liberty in Brazil where Dreesen walked into a bar one day and met Rosa Maria Carlos, who was twenty years his senior and amused by the young sailor with the ready wit. Soon, they were a couple. "I thought I knew how to make love—every eighteen-year-old boy thinks he knows how to make love—but I didn't know a thing," Dreesen says. "Sigmund Freud said the basic motive for human drive is sex and who am I to argue with the father of psychoanalysis? I should have been learning that in school, not algebra."

"Slowly, Tommy," Rosa Maria said. "We'll do everything you want to do, but patience. Start when you wake up in the morning. If you plan on making love to a woman that night, you say, 'Do you know what it's like for me to open my eyes and the first thing I see is your beauty?' When you get in bed that night, you will get the total woman."

(Years later, Dreesen could not resist turning this lesson into material for an audience of one. "I came in off the road late one night and slipped in bed next to Maryellen and fell asleep.

When I woke up she had her back to me and I said, 'Do you know what it's like to lay here beside you and know that soon I'll see your beautiful face?' She said, 'Gee, Tommy, that's so sweet' and rolled over. I said, 'Oh, my God, I'm *home*.' She said 'Jokes! Fucking jokes at seven in the morning!'")

Rosa Maria taught him one more lesson before the *Tarawa* left for home. Certain he was in love as only an eighteen-year-old boy can be, he began to talk about jumping ship and staying behind with her.

"What's wrong with you?" she demanded. "You've got to go back. You belong in America and I belong here."

"I'm just afraid that one day you'll forget me," Dreesen said.

"Yes, I will, Tom," she said. "But you'll never forget me."

Perhaps the most lasting lesson Dreesen took away from the navy came on his first trip home after boot camp. The anticipation had been so exciting—walking down the streets of Harvey in his sharp new uniform, hanging with all his old friends at all the old places. But almost from the moment he arrived, he realized that everything had changed. His friends, many still in high school, were doing what they had always done together—attending football and basketball games, going steady, shooting pool, trying to get into trouble, or stay out of it. For the first time in his life, he didn't feel he belonged.

"All the places I used to go—the pool room, Tony's Pizza Parlor, the barbershop—I didn't feel comfortable there anymore," Dreesen says. "And I didn't feel comfortable around my buddies, either. Everybody was talking about the same old stuff we had always talked about. It just seemed so mundane. I felt empty. It was a lonely time for me." His mother and father were still drinking steadily; his clean surroundings back on the base made life in the shack by the railroad impossible. Dreesen realized how different his life had become after just a few months.

"I knew I didn't want to make a career of the service," Dreesen says, "I didn't know what I wanted to do. All I knew is that I couldn't do it in Harvey."

They met, of all places, at a meeting of the Junior Chamber of Commerce at Smith's Lounge in Harvey. Nothing in their pasts could have predicted such a prosaic setting, but in the spring of 1968 they were nothing more remarkable than two young businessmen seeking to advance their careers.

At loose ends after leaving the navy, Dreesen returned home and resumed the life that seemed to be laid out for him. Nothing really took, though. "I worked in the factories, I poured concrete, I cleaned sewers, I got my Teamsters card, I loaded trucks," he says. "I was a bartender, I was a photographer, I was even a private detective for a while. I just went from one job to another."

He was also a family man. Walking into Tony's with some of his buddies one night while home on leave from the navy, Dreesen spied a pretty girl named Maryellen Sebock and the attraction was immediate and mutual. "Later she told me that as soon as she saw me she went into the ladies' room and redid her hair," Dreesen says, smiling at the memory. "And when I saw her walk out the door, I left too and got my car and offered her a ride." Not long afterwards, Maryellen became pregnant and they were married.

Only later did Dreesen realize that, like Reid, he had married a girl whose upbringing was worlds apart from his own. Mike

Sebock, Maryellen's father, had started working at Allied Steel when he was seventeen years old and worked his way up from the factory's lowest rung to plant manager. And while Dreesen had a restless streak that might never be satisfied, Maryellen wanted a husband like her father—one who went to work every morning, came home to dinner every evening, supported his family, and bowled on Tuesday nights. It was a conflict that would never be truly resolved.

One day, Dreesen ran into an old friend in a bar who, in the course of trying to sell him life insurance, said, "You know what, Tommy. You could do this. You'd be good at it." And he was. Very good. Two weeks of training in Columbus, Ohio, and he was on his way. You mean all he had to do was hit the streets, talk to people, make them like him, convince them he was doing them a favor? Piece of cake. In his first year working for Columbus Mutual, Dreesen sold enough disability, hospitalization, and life insurance to join the firm's Million Dollar Round Table. As for joining the Jaycees, well, what better way to make his name known in the local business community, and to meet young men who needed, and could afford, exactly what he was selling?

Reid arrived by a different path after DuPont made him the first graduate of a historically black college to be hired for its marketing management trainee program. "They sent us to Rochester, New York, for training and on the first day they asked everybody to stand up and give their name and their school," he says. "Everybody was from MIT, Stanford, Michigan, Georgia Tech, these famous universities. I was the last guy to stand—I was the only black person there—and I said, 'Timothy Reid, Norfolk Division of Virginia State College.' It wasn't even a college; it was a *division* of a college. Everybody looked at me as if to say, 'He'll be gone in twenty minutes.'"

But he passed DuPont's tests and was sent to Chicago, where he arrived the day after Martin Luther King was assassinated. His first images of the city were of smoke rising from burning buildings off in the distance and armed soldiers patrolling the streets. Some months later, his father arrived as part of the Virginia delegation to the 1968 Democratic National Convention and Reid drove him downtown to the Chicago Amphitheater. "We were next in line to drive into the underground parking garage when protesters rushed the barriers and the police waded into them," Reid says. "The next thing I knew they were beating a guy on the hood of my car. I felt like we were watching a movie in a drive-in. We couldn't go forward, we couldn't go back, and we certainly weren't going to get out of the car. Finally, the police beat a path through the crowd and we drove into the garage. So my first few months in Chicago were pretty dramatic. But in a strange way I liked it because it reminded me of the civil rights struggles I'd been involved in back home."

DuPont gave him a three-state territory in which to sell the company's photographic products and he and Rita moved into a three-bedroom house in Markham, a town just west of Harvey. "In school, we used to say, 'Some day, I want to make $10,000 a year,'" Reid says. "Well, it happened like that. One day, I was living in the projects in Norfolk and the next day I was a businessman in a three-piece suit, smoking a pipe, and driving a Plymouth Fury with blackwall tires. I was sitting at home watching football on television. My wife was in the kitchen cooking dinner. My son was playing with his toys on the floor. In just a few months, I had realized the American dream. And I was bored to tears.

"I'd always been active, on the go—school, two jobs, campus plays, the civil rights movement. And then, suddenly, nothing. I thought, 'This is it?' So I started to drink. I had a $600-a-month expense account and if I spent it all on liquor that was fine, as long as I was drinking with a client. Sometimes, I drank myself into blackouts. I'd wake up not knowing where I was."

Somehow, he was able to conceal his breakdown from Rita. Wrapped up in her teaching job and their young son, she didn't see how much trouble he was having adapting to his new life. *She* certainly wasn't bored, nor did she have to adjust to a middle-class existence. "I grew up with a mom and a dad in a three-bedroom house in a great neighborhood," she says. "We were like *Leave It to Beaver*. My father died in the house he was born in when he was seventy-seven years old. I had a completely different upbringing from Tim's."

The moment when Reid could no longer hide his problems from her arrived one night in the fall of 1968 when he returned home after a long evening with a sales manager during which he drank a dozen Brandy Manhattans. When he woke up the following morning, he had thrown up all over himself and while Rita had tried to clean him up, his clothes reeked. When he walked outside, the door to his car was open and it had run out of gas because he had not turned off the ignition. This has to stop, he told himself as he reached for the paper.

WANTED! YOUNG MEN OF ACTION! JOIN THE JAYCEES! The display ad in the *Harvey Tribune* might have been written just for him. "If there's anything I need now, it's action," Reid told himself, and he made a note of the date and time of the group's next meeting at Smith's Lounge.

Dreesen moved quickly upon joining the Jaycees, attaching himself to a program he believed he knew something about, one aimed at helping teenagers in trouble with the law. "I wanted to work with kids who were like me, who came from the other side of the tracks," he says. Remembering his own experiences with John T. Lane, he approached a local judge, Ron Crane, and suggested an alternative to the juvenile probation system that hadn't done him any good. Instead of giving misdemeanor offenders fines that their parents would pay, or sending them to a juvenile detention home, why not put them to work? Have them perform community service on weekends. Get them involved in something positive. Encourage them to think about something beyond themselves.

Crane approved the idea and soon Dreesen was spending many of his Saturdays leading cleanup crews as they cut weeds in the summer, shoveled sidewalks in the winter, cleaned trash from alleys and senior citizens' basements, and did other odd jobs. On their lunch breaks, he talked to the youngsters in language they understood about his own days on Harvey's streets. One day, his brother Glenn followed them around with a camera and the pictures ran in the *Harvey Tribune*, raising the profile of the program, and Dreesen's stock in the Jaycees.

But as he continued to work with the city's juvenile offenders, he realized they were different from the members of the gangs he had run with in one fundamental way. He and his friends had drunk their fair share of beer, but they had seldom gotten as loaded as the boys in his work crews did. And while marijuana was around in his era, hard drugs had now entered the scene. Heroin, LSD, amphetamines, and other drugs were at the root of juvenile criminal activity. Until this was dealt with, he realized, all the work crews in the world would not help.

What the Jaycees really needed, Dreesen thought, was a drug-prevention program in the city's grade schools, before the children were introduced to drugs. Open the sessions with music, he thought. Tell a few jokes to get everybody relaxed. Talk to them on their own level. Get them thinking about the choices they had to make. The members of the Jaycee board were skeptical at first—"If you talk to kids about drugs, you're going to get them interested in drugs," was the refrain—but drawing on his own background Dreesen was able to convince them that the temptations were already there and had to be addressed.

Sitting in the back of the room at his first Jaycee meeting, Reid had one reaction as Dreesen proposed his plan to the general membership: He should be a part of it. "All of my memories about drugs, especially about George Bright and heroin, were about violence," Reid says. "That was my personal reason for wanting to get involved." But there was something else, too, something Reid knew instinctively. The program needed a black voice.

"If it was going to be based in reality, it would have to say that drugs were a black and white problem," Reid says. "White America didn't want to accept the fact that their kids were sniffing glue and their housewives were popping pills. It said, 'Oh, that's just a black thing.' What the program needed was a way of showing we are all in this together."

"I'm Tim Reid," he told Dreesen after his presentation. "I'd like to work with you on this."

"Gee, I'm sorry," Dreesen said. "I've already got a partner."

The rejection lasted one day, which is how long it took John DeBoer, the Jaycee member Dreesen had enlisted in his program, to say he had taken a job in another town. Dreesen called Reid and asked if he was still interested. After two short conversations, they were a team.

"Tim was absolutely right, of course," Dreesen says. "John and I would have failed. Two white guys were going to go into integrated schools and talk about drugs? It never would have worked. But a young black guy and a young white guy—now that got their attention."

"Oh the games people play now / Every night and every day now . . ." The Joe South lyric rang out through the classroom as Reid and Dreesen entered. "How many of you have heard that song?" one of them would ask and every hand in the room would go up. "Well, that's what we're here to talk to you about today, about the games people play and some things that are going down in the community." There was no set routine, just casual, light-hearted banter back and forth as they presented some basic facts about the hazards of drug use and tried to get their message across. And soon they saw that their very presence was as important as any of the statistics they were quoting.

A black man and a white man—hip, up from the streets, at ease with each other—had come not to lecture or frighten the students, but to make them laugh, to get them to think about what they were doing rather than simply going along with the crowd. Reid and Dreesen would ask them what they already knew about marijuana, heroin, and other drugs. The hands would shoot up—as Dreesen had suspected, the kids knew plenty—and soon he and Reid were directing a spirited conversation, answering questions, and dropping in more information while joking back and forth with each other. "Here was a black guy and a white guy who lived in their community and were concerned about them," Dreesen says. "We made a connection."

"Now that you've heard us, what do you think? Do you want to help us spread the word?" they would ask as the sessions wound down, and they would pass out surveys asking the students what they thought about what they had learned. Invariably, they would find themselves in the middle of a scrum of youngsters asking questions, asking what they could do to help, while a recording of the Isley Brothers singing "It's your thing / Do what you wanna do" filled the room.

As word of the program spread, Reid and Dreesen found themselves in ever greater demand. Schools all over the city brought them in, sometimes in the company of their friend Paul Hollingsworth, a Harvey police officer, and within months they were building on their success. "Every school we went to, we asked them to vote for somebody to represent them," Dreesen says. "We put together a float for the Fourth of July parade that had a boy and a girl riding on it holding up signs saying, 'Keep Off the Grass' and 'Acid Can Burn Holes in Your Life.'"

Soon, the interest spread beyond Harvey. The program was written up in the Jaycees' national publications and copied by other chapters. "The Jaycees were good at designing kits that showed how to put programs together," Reid says. "So they basically copied our ideas and sent them around the country. It became a model program and I was damn proud of it."

"I can't tell you how many times in the last thirty years people have come up to me and said, 'You don't remember me, but you came to my school years ago and talked about drugs,'" Dreesen says. "'You were so concerned about our well-being and that really impressed me.' That just means so much to me." For their efforts, Reid and Dreesen were named National Jaycees of the Year.

Dreesen still remembers her name, Joanne Cerufka, and the exact words she spoke: "You guys are so funny. You ought to be a comedy team." He wishes he could say her words registered immediately, but he was too busy talking to other eighth-graders, asking them what they thought of the program. Nor was he sure that Reid had heard her until several days later when they were chatting at the bar in Smith's Lounge before a Jaycee meeting. Then they grew quiet.

"Are you thinking about what that girl said?" Reid asked.

"Yeah," Dreesen replied. "I guess I am."

"Would you do that?"

"Hell, I'd do it if you'd do it."

"Let's do it then."

Though Maryellen Dreesen was less than thrilled about the plan—"Her exact words were, 'That's the dumbest thing I've ever heard,'" Dreesen says—Rita Reid could not have been more supportive. So they began working on material in her kitchen, and occasionally in the office above Smith's Lounge, which belonged to Larry Dirksen, a lawyer and fellow Jaycee member. The first thing they realized was they were starting from scratch. Presenting their message in schools had given them a small taste of performing in front of a crowd, but this was entirely different. What would they say? How would they present themselves? They had no idea. They did have one common experience they could draw on, however.

"We approached it as salesmen, as if we were selling a product," Reid says. "We did what salesmen do: gather information, decide who your audience is, try to figure out the best way to give your customers what they want. When we realized we needed material, for instance, we knew exactly what to do: analyze other comics."

Reid bought all the comedy albums he could find—as many comedians and as many styles as possible. "Jonathan Winters, Moms Mabley, Bob Newhart, Pigmeat Markham, Jackie Vernon, Nipsy Russell, Lord Buckley, Dick Gregory, Lenny Bruce, Godfrey Cambridge, I bought them all," Reid says. "To this day, I have one of the largest comedy collections anywhere." They started watching comedians on television and taking notes. They began looking for whatever humor they could find in their own lives. Was this funny? Did that have the makings of a routine? It was almost as if they were outsiders, looking in on a pair of strangers.

"The act developed through us sitting down and saying, 'What if I did this? What if you said that?'" Dreesen says. "Neither of us had a clue about what would work or how to write a routine. We listened to the comedy albums and watched people on television. We didn't know what else to do."

One day Dreesen bumped into Dick Owings, a boyhood friend who had always made him laugh. Now a junior high school English teacher in Markham, Owings had never considered writing jokes, but when he accepted Dreesen's plea for help he brought an important sensibility to the creation of the act. Owings had been born without the lower portion of his right leg, but had always pretended there was nothing wrong with him physically. He had played baseball and basketball and participated in gymnastics, and he had reacted to the natural curiosity of his peers with scorn.

"Kids would say, 'I hear you've got a wooden leg,' and I'd say, 'No, I don't, do you have a wooden head?'" Owings says. "But it was not a joking matter with me, even as an adult. I was in an advanced state of denial, in constant fear that people would find out about it. And a lot of people actually didn't know. You couldn't tell anything was wrong with me by watching me walk."

Owings's experience made him particularly sensitive to Reid's position in the act. "Tim's blackness was like my leg," he says. "It could be an object of the humor—everything else was material, why not that?—but it couldn't be personal. Tim had to be above the stereotype. He could be laughed with, but not at." All three men soon came to see that while Dreesen would generally be the act's manic free spirit, its Jerry Lewis, Reid would be its cool and collected observer of his partner's antics, its Dean Martin. Occasionally, the two men would switch roles, but the intelligent, well-spoken image Reid projected on stage made it clear he would never be subservient to Dreesen because of race.

"Tim was really the most sophisticated and articulate of the three of us," Owings says. "He projected the image of the successful black guy, not one who is the butt of jokes. What we started to do was consciously poke fun at white America's attitudes about blacks. We'd exaggerate redneck stereotypes. It was so broad that even the racists in the audience could laugh and say, 'Oh, that's not me.' So we blundered along trying different things and luckily Tim was open to looking at stereotypes without getting offended or being defensive. It created a very free-wheeling atmosphere where everything was fair game."

After working with Reid and Dreesen for only a short time, Owings realized that he was learning something that went beyond the creation of a comedy act. He was learning something about himself as well. "Compared to the issues we were discussing, my situation was small potatoes," he says. "If we could try to find the humor in them without Tim getting insulted, then why not my leg? Why wasn't it OK to make comments about that, too? I told myself, 'You've got to get over this.' I went from denying anything was wrong with me to wearing shorts. Whenever people asked me why I wasn't sensitive any more, I said it was working with Tim and Tom."

Early on, Owings sensed that the increasingly contentious nature of race relations in America might have an effect on how the act was accepted. Chicago in particular was going through an especially difficult transformation. "There was a huge white exodus out of the south suburbs," Owings says. "The school district I taught in was infamous for block-busting tactics by realtors. The area in Markham where Tim lived, which is where I went to junior high school, went from 100 percent white to all black in just a couple of years. I had always been a wide-eyed liberal—my parents taught us to be racially tolerant and my brother, Trent, was a minister at a church in Oak Park and marched for civil rights. It was very painful to see this kind of racism so close to home."

One hot summer evening, Reid and Dreesen came to visit Owings. It was just before dusk and a number of people were outdoors taking the air and watering their lawns when Dreesen began to pretend he was a salesman showing Reid around. "I'm sure you'll enjoy this house," Dreesen said in a loud voice. "These are all fine people who live around here."

"My neighbors started looking at me very strangely," Owings says, laughing at the memory.

Watching television one night, Reid and Dreesen nearly fell out of their chairs when the Committee, an improvisational comedy group from San Francisco, appeared on *The Tonight Show* and one cast member started teaching another how to be black. "It was manna from heaven," Reid says. "We didn't steal it word for word, but we knew we could adapt it so it would work for us. That got us thinking about racial stereotypes in general and how we could use them." And slowly, several routines that became staples of their act began to take shape.

"Are you sure he's not with the bossa nova?" Tim asks as they meet Tom's Italian father.

"Now that's a stereotype," Tom says. "And it's Cosa Nostra, and no he's not."

"Well, tell him to put away his gun."

"Hi, Pop, this is my friend Tim . . . What do you mean where is his basketball?"

They invented Super Spade, who traveled about town disguised as Clark Dark, a mild-mannered reporter for *Muhammad Speaks*, and his trusty sidekick, Courageous Caucasian.

"I just got a call from Mayor Daley," says Courageous Caucasian. "There's a race riot down on 54th Street. He wants us to get down there right away. He says two old white ladies, school teachers, were on their way to school when ten big nig . . . uh, colored guys, attacked them without provocation."

"Let's see if I have the details correctly," Super Spade says.

"Ten despicable hardhats attacked a black five-year-old choir-boy on his way to church."

They did a bit where Tim expresses frustration at the nervousness of white people when they are around blacks.

"I don't know why they get uptight when the brothers wear big hats and drive Cadillacs," he says. "They say, 'Look at that pimp,' when the guy could be a banker. Now I don't believe in militancy at all. I'm a pacifist at heart. I feel a black man can get anything he wants with a gracious smile . . . and a .357 magnum."

Though race was not at the center of all their routines, popular culture was never far away. The drug scene was a natural. Told he is being interviewed on television, Harry Hash, America's No. 1 dope addict, says, "Hi, Mom. Don't go in my room." Their spoof of *The Dating Game,* in which Tom wears a wig and affects a woman's voice, allowed them to send up not only the television show on which it was based, but also the relationships of gays—with each other and with the straight community.

"My friends call me the Gayfather," one contestant says. "Everybody up against the wall . . . facing me."

The news of the day was fertile territory, too.

"The Senate by a wide majority turned down the president's proposal for budget reform. Reached at the San Clemente White House, Mr. Nixon commented he viewed the actions with misgivings. Miss Givings said she had no comment . . .

"In a report issued today, the government stated that despite total unemployment, phase 33 appears to be working. And that the American yen is strong . . .

"Thunderstorms and high winds ripped through three major cities in Alabama today. Officials there estimated the damages may run as high as eight dollars . . .

"Last night at a political dinner, two of the most outspoken women in American politics met for the first time. The beautiful and controversial Jane Fonda was presented to Martha Mitchell wearing a skin-tight, topless leather jumpsuit with cutaway buttocks and transparent crotch panels. Miss Fonda wore a simple blue evening gown with gold trim."

Later, as they became more self-assured, this commentary grew more elaborate, and more pointed, as when Tim interrupts Tom as he is trying to start the act.

"This Watergate thing has got me upset . . ."

"Yeah, well, we don't want to talk about that. We're here to make these people laugh . . ."

"Do you know what it's like after all these years to find out white folks steal?"

"Look, Tim, that's not what . . ."

"You don't understand. White folks taught us religion. They taught us about God. Some white missionaries came over to Africa and saw these natives and said, 'I want you all to start reading the Bible.' Ever since then, I've been reading and they've been finding diamonds. I'm going into the diamond mine and look for Jesus."

As they continued compiling material, their sessions in Dirksen's office and Reid's home became more intense. After several months, they realized they had gone over the same material so many times they could no longer tell what was working and what wasn't. So they turned to a captive audience for help.

"Rita, do you think this is funny?" one of them would ask. "What if we did it like this?"

"One day, we must have asked her every five minutes if something was funny," Dreesen says, "and finally she said, 'You can't come over here any more. I can't help you. Go do it somewhere else. Get up on a stage somewhere and find out if it's funny.'"

She was right. It was time to find a larger audience. But not before Rita told Dreesen something else as he was leaving.

"You know, I pray for you, Tom."

"You pray for me?"

"I pray for my husband. I pray that all his dreams come true. And you're his partner so I pray for you, too."

Speechless, Dreesen began to understand the pressure he

and Reid were putting on their families with their precarious undertaking. And he began to wish he had the same support at home.

The place they had their eye on was the Party Mart Supper Club in South Chicago. It served dinner, had live music and drew a hip young crowd that looked like their kind of audience. So what if they had never set foot in the place or met the owner?

"We knew how to get in doors, how to meet people," Dreesen says. "We were far better salesmen than we were comedians. We sold the sizzle, not the steak."

"Comedians, eh?" the owner said as he looked over the two young men dressed neatly in suits and ties as they made their pitch. "We've never had comedy here before, but if you guys are crazy enough to try it, I'll give it a shot. Come in Thursday night. I've got a jazz trio performing. You can be on the bill, too." And as easy as that, they had their first job as comedians. Not that the owner offered to pay them, or that Dreesen or Reid dared to ask. It was understood they would be working for free.

On a September night in 1969, Reid and Dreesen stood in the kitchen before the show—the Party Mart had nothing as elaborate as a dressing room—nervously awaiting the moment of truth when the leader of the jazz trio walked in after finishing his set. "You guys are on," he said. "I'll introduce you. What do you want to be called?"

What did they want to be called? Good grief! The act needed a name, didn't it? It had never occurred to them. What a time to be reminded how green they were.

"Um, Reid and Dreesen," Dreesen said.

"No, Dreesen and Reid," Reid said.

"Oh, hell. He's Tim and I'm Tom. Just call us Tim and Tom," Dreesen said

"OK, just for now," Reid said, and they followed the leader of the trio out of the kitchen.

They were a disaster. Looking as nervous as they felt, they bolted through their act as if they were double parked.

"*Hi,we'rethecomedyteamofTimandTom.He'sTimandI'mTom*,"
Dreesen said, and they raced through their routines one after
the other. "We remembered every line but we didn't wait for
anybody to laugh. We just kept going and going."

"Hey, slow down," somebody in the back of the room
shouted.

"Oh, please, sir, don't heckle us," Dreesen said. "This is our
first time doing this," and they continued the act at 100 miles
an hour.

"How'd we do? What do you think?" they asked the owner,
their adrenaline still racing, after they left the stage.

"Whoa, slow down, will you?" he said. "I couldn't even tell if
you guys were funny or not. You never gave me a chance. Come
back tomorrow night and try it again. But you've got to slow it
down."

Feeling a little more comfortable now—at least their show-
business careers would last more than one night—Dreesen
and Reid brought their wives, Larry Dirksen, and several other
friends with them to the Party Mart the next night. Take it slow,
they told each other as they stood in the kitchen. Wait for the
laughs. Give ourselves a chance. The piano player called their
names and they walked out into the large room.

Reid said something funny. People laughed. Dreesen said
something funny back to him. People laughed. The act went
just as they had envisioned it—state the premise, proceed to
the set-up lines, wait for the audience response, drive home
the punch line. The racial material, casually delivered between
two men who were obviously friends, got the knowing appreciative response they were after from the all-white audience.
The laughs continued one after another and when they were
finished the crowd applauded and shouted out words of praise.
It was all they could do to wait until they left the room before
they started hugging each other.

"It was like a scene out of a B movie where the dark clouds
open and the sun bursts through," Dreesen says. "I kept thinking, 'People are laughing at something we wrote.' And our

friends and spouses were laughing, too, and maybe beginning to think we weren't so crazy after all. At that moment, I realized I'd never had a dream. I never really knew what I wanted to do with my life. I was just wandering aimlessly. The idea that we could make a living by making people laugh just overwhelmed me. I thought, 'I want to do this. I have to do this.' I was so hyper I couldn't sleep all night. The next day I went to Ascension Church where I'd been an altar boy and sung in the choir—it was Saturday and there was no service so I was there alone—and I lit a candle and prayed. I said, 'Please, God, let me make my living as a comedian.'"

Reid's reaction was less emotional but just as delighted. "When all those people were sitting there laughing at us," he says, "all I could think was, 'We're on our way.'"

The Golden Horseshoe in Chicago Heights seemed like the perfect place for their first paying gig. The first actual nightclub Dreesen and Reid had ever performed in, it had a stage, tables and chairs facing it, and a progression of acts that made for a full evening of entertainment. The Golden Horseshoe featured singers, musicians, and the rocking up-tempo organ playing of Eddie Warner, the club's owner, who dressed, acted, and played his instrument like Liberace. "Eddie's big thing was to end his act playing 'Night Train' as unbearably loud as he could," Reid says. "The glass walls inside the room would actually shake. You could get a nosebleed listening to him play 'Night Train.'"

The fact that the Golden Horseshoe catered to a working-class white clientele made Reid feel anything but comfortable—"I felt like I was walking into Alabama in 1932"—but he realized it was something he was going to have to get used to.

"All right," Warner told Reid and Dreesen after they had talked their way onto a weekend bill, "you'll do four shows on Friday, four shows on Saturday, and two on Sunday. I'll pay you thirty dollars."

"Only thirty bucks apiece for ten shows?" Dreesen asked.

"Thirty to *split*," Warner said. "It's not my fault there are two of you."

"We didn't care," Dreesen says. "It was the first time anybody paid us and it was a legitimate room where people sat down and paid attention to the entertainers. It was a real boost for us to play a place like that."

They were confident now, at ease with each other, sure of their material. Even a lackluster response to their first show didn't bother them. And sure enough, the second show received a more enthusiastic reception, and the third one went better yet. By the time they left the stage after their final performance, the applause was ringing in their ears and, not wanting the night to end, they took seats at a table so they could continue to bask in the glow.

"That's something we got pretty good at," Dreesen says with a laugh. "When we had a good show, we always just happened to be out by the front door where the audience could see us as they were leaving. We'd be talking to the doorman . . . 'Do you know where our car is?' . . . and people would come by and say, 'Nice show,' . . . 'Oh, thank you very much.' But when we bombed, we were hiding."

"You couldn't find us," Reid says.

"Well, this night," says Dreesen, "we should have gotten the hell out of Dodge."

Sitting among some appreciative customers, they were approached by a woman singer who had been on the bill carrying a champagne bottle. The audience had enjoyed her performance, too, and she was happy for another reason as well.

"Look," she said, pointing to her ring finger. "I'm engaged."

"Wonderful," Dreesen said, and he kissed her on the cheek.

"That's great. Good luck," Reid said and he did likewise. The woman poured them some champagne and returned to the party at her table.

Chatting happily with each other, neither man saw it coming. All they knew was that suddenly somebody had pushed a lit cigarette into Reid's face. Howling in pain, Reid grabbed the man's arm and thought, "Oh, shit." It was the biggest arm he had ever seen. Dreesen jumped up, reached across the table, and grabbed the shirt of the assailant and threw the hardest right hand he could. He had been in more than his share of barroom brawls, and boxed when he was in the navy, but he'd never given away so much weight before. With Reid still hanging on, the man pulled Dreesen across the table and began to squeeze with both arms. Unable to breathe, Dreesen could feel his rib cage starting to give way. Reid grabbed a full bottle of ketchup off the table and hit the man on the head as hard as he could from behind.

"Not only did the bottle not break," Reid says, "the man didn't recognize he had been hit. He didn't even flinch. That scared me even more." Customers screamed and overturned tables and chairs as they scrambled to get out of the way until finally two bartenders interceded and managed to pull the man off Dreesen. Eddie Warner joined the fray, too, scratching the attacker, sticking a finger in his nose, and falling to the floor as if he'd been shot when one of Dreesen's off-balance punches inadvertently hit him in the face.

Staggering out of the club, they assessed the damage. Reid had an angry red scar on his face where the cigarette had landed while Dreesen had bloody knuckles and was wheezing from some rib muscles that would keep him breathing in pain for a week. "Welcome to show business," Reid said, and they both laughed as hard as their physical conditions would allow.

"I went in the next day to get our money and there was Eddie Warner with a black eye," Dreesen says. "I started telling him how sorry I was, but he just looked in the mirror and said, 'I've never had a shiner before.' He was proud of it."

Dreesen took precautions against a repeat occurrence during the remainder of their run at the Golden Horseshoe, and at later gigs as well. "I brought some of my boys from the neighborhood," he says. "We had the place packed the next two nights and there were some guns in the room, too. Tommy Johnson, Mike Crowder, Sammy Eubanks, a lot of the guys I'd set pins and played pool with. They had gone into the service, too, and then come home and sort of picked up where they left off. But we were all still buddies and when I told them we needed help they were right there."

While Dreesen was the first white person Reid had ever really known, his "boys" were a revelation, too. "Here I was in a town where I had no friends, and Tom had a cadre of white guys I never would have associated with," Reid says. "But I was comfortable with them because their street sense was the same as the rogues I used to hang out with. And they saved us so many times. I was certainly glad they were in the Golden Horseshoe the next night when I went out there with a scar on my face."

Dreesen's boys provided Tim and Tom protection from unruly crowds through one simple method, intimidation. "Oh, you think you're funny," one would say to someone who interrupted them. "How about this line?" And he would punch the heckler in the face.

"It could get kind of hard to do the act sometimes," Reid says with a laugh, "but we appreciated the gesture. And they helped us in other ways, too, sitting and talking with us, mellowing us out when we didn't have a good night. The fact that Tom's friends, who were not all liberal people—some of them were downright racist—felt protective toward us and believed in what we were doing was one of the things that made me think we would succeed."

Years after the brawl in the Golden Horseshoe, Dreesen was in a Chicago restaurant when a waitress approached and said, "Tom Dreesen?"

"Yeah," he said, preoccupied. "What's the soup of the day?"

Suddenly, she started to cry. "You don't remember me, but that was my boyfriend who picked that fight in the Golden Horseshoe. The son of a bitch, I broke up with him. He was trying out for the Bears. He didn't make the team but he played on their taxi squad. He could have killed one of you. Every time I see one of you guys on television, it reminds me of that night."

"What was his problem?" Dreesen said. "Was he mad at Tim for kissing you on the cheek like that?"

"No, that wasn't it. He was just a miserable bastard."

It all seemed so easy now. Their ability to sell themselves, and Dreesen's lack of inhibition about approaching perfect strangers, got them in door after door.

"You're comedians?" said Vince Sanders, who hosted a show on WBEE, a black radio station in Harvey, when they appeared in his studio one day. "Go ahead, make me laugh." As Sanders played a record, Reid and Dreesen did a few routines and Sanders said, "I like you guys." The next thing they knew they were on the air and had a manager, one with local show-business connections and a professional sensibility of what was good about their act, what was not, and, most important, how much harder they had to work at it.

"Vince had been an actor and he would call rehearsals as if we were doing a play," Dreesen says. "He was tough on us. He talked about our dress, our material, our timing. He became the third eye we needed."

Sanders seemed to know everybody in the black community and he began taking them around to Chicago-area jazz clubs, record parties, charity functions, and other black radio stations, including WVON, where they hit it off with a young announcer named Don Cornelius. "Would you mind if my boys got up and did a few minutes?" Sanders would ask and they would do one or two bits from the act. Though they were not being paid, they realized they were spreading the word about who they were and what they did. Soon, they found themselves performing at South Side jazz clubs between sets played by well-known local and touring musicians—Sonny Stitt, Gene Ammons, Eddie Harris, Les McCann, and others. Sanders also introduced them to Merri Dee, the host of a local television show that was popular with black audiences, who had them on several times and booked them at live shows she produced in the Chicago area.

"Vince flaunted us around the black entertainment

community and that was very important," Reid says. "We had to find our niche audience first, establish ourselves as being 'hip.' If we didn't have that, we'd be dead."

They also started going to clubs to see other comedians, watching them work with a professional eye and approaching them afterwards to ask for advice. Sometimes their recommendations were more amusing than helpful—"Go out there with a drink and a cigarette," Slappy White told them, "it will help your timing"—but often the advice was valuable.

"How long have you been together?" Dick Gregory asked them when they met after the famed black comedian had appeared on Sanders's radio show.

"Eight months," Dreesen said.

"You're not ready," Gregory said.

"We're not?" Dreesen said.

"No, you're not," Gregory said. "You've got a long way to go."

"We were offended," Dreesen says. "He had never seen us. How would he know? But he was absolutely right. We still had so much to learn. So we started looking at how different comedians built their routines, their rhythm, how they spaced out the jokes. It helped us improve the structure of the act and bring things together."

The more they worked at it, the easier it got. With their newly purchased powder-blue tuxedos—"All the acts in show business had uniforms then," Reid says—and their publicity photos taken by Dreesen's brother, Glenn, they began to feel like the professional entertainers they had set out to be.

The stage manager of the cavernous arena inside Chicago's famed Union Stock Yards looked incredulously at the two young men standing before him. "You're who?" he asked.

"We're Tim and Tom," Dreesen replied. "We're a comedy team."

"You're kidding me," the stage manager said as he took in their blue dinner jackets, black tuxedo pants, cummerbunds, and black patent leather shoes. "Really. Who are you?"

"We're Tim and Tom. We're on the bill," Dreesen insisted.

This isn't going very well, Reid thought. First, they'd had to talk their way past a security guard into the arena and now they were having to fight their way onto the stage. And nobody seemed to know who they were. Making the situation even more disconcerting was their surroundings. Vince Sanders had told them this first Black Expo, which was organized by Jesse Jackson, was going to be a big deal, but nobody had expected anything like this. "It was huge," Reid says, "the first gathering of black artists, businessmen, politicians, and leaders in other fields ever held. It's gone on to become a very important national event since then—a lot of cities hold local Black Expos, too—but in 1969 it was all brand new and very exciting."

Especially when 10,000 people filled the room, including many celebrities. The mood was festive and everybody seemed to be dressed in the height of fashion, particularly the entertainers who represented a Who's Who of popular black culture. "And here we are dressed in our little tuxes like we were performing at a supper club," Reid says. "We looked ridiculous."

"OK," said the stage manager, who had finally found their name on his list. "You'll go on right after Stevie Wonder."

*Stevie Wonder!* Who'd want to listen to them after he performed? They'd be eaten alive.

"Stevie sang, Stevie danced, Stevie played the drums," Reid says. "He brought the house down. Ten thousand people were standing and cheering so loud you could feel the building vibrating. Then they took him off the stage and the announcer said, 'And now we bring you the comedy team of Tim and Tom.' All of a sudden, you could hear the echo of the microphone in this huge room. We walked out and you could hear a pin drop. People had just heard Stevie Wonder—and were waiting for Howlin' Wolf, the great blues man, who was coming on after us—and you could just see them thinking, 'Who are these guys?'"

They killed. "47th and Drexel? Come *onnnn*, bus." Pandemonium. It was their first good reception at the Party Mart a thousand times over and it left them euphoric. "We were used to working in rooms with twenty people in them," Reid says. "You know those science fiction movies where the force of the surrounding field enters your body and you're possessed by it? That's the way it felt, like we were taking the energy from the stage off with us. We went home thinking we'd have our own television show within a year. Remembering that kind of reception is one of the things that kept us going during some of the hard times."

In the early 1970s, Chicago was night-club heaven. On a given evening, someone looking for live entertainment could choose between Bette Midler at Mr. Kelly's, Erroll Garner at the London House, the Smothers Brothers in the city's bustling Old Town section, and, scattered throughout the city at clubs and hotels, Steve Lawrence and Eydie Gorme, Shecky Greene, and Jack Jones, not to mention some of the top jazz and blues musicians in the country. So Reid and Dreesen were thrilled when, less than a year after they began performing, Dave Silver brought them downtown.

Silver owned Punchinello's, a small Rush Street nightclub that not only had entertainment, but also served as a gathering place for entertainers in other clubs when they were through performing for the night. You never knew who you might see there so Reid and Dreesen were more than a little wide-eyed when they walked in one day to audition. Sitting with Silver as they did their routines was his friend Rip Taylor, a zany comedian with a long career in nightclubs and on television, who thought they were a riot. Watching Taylor's reaction, Silver was intrigued. Soon, Tim and Tom were performing at Punchinello's and Silver was taking them under his wing.

"He sent us to his publicist, Aaron Gold, who called Irv Kupcinet at the *Chicago Sun-Times*," Dreesen says. "The next thing we knew we were in Kup's column, which was really a big deal, and performing on his Purple Heart Cruise for wounded veterans with Bette Midler, who had just been on *The Tonight*

*Show,* and Barry Manilow, who was her piano player. Kup put us on his TV show, too. He was so important to us, and his assistant, Stella Foster, always made sure he knew when and where we were performing and that we got in the column regularly. I gave Stella a rose once and told her she'd get the other eleven when we made it big. Every time I see her, she says she's still waiting for them. Stella was one of the few black women who played a major role in the mainstream press in Chicago back then and we were both so happy for her when she took over Kup's column after he died."

"Dave opened the door for us downtown," Reid says. "All of a sudden, we're on television, meeting marketing people, getting introduced to Chicago night life. Hugh Hefner invited us to the Playboy Mansion, which had a pool upstairs where people would dive in naked and wave at the folks downstairs. It was a pretty heady trip for guys like us and it made us feel like we were getting into the mainstream. We began to carry ourselves like we were in show business. I never really felt like an entertainer until we met Dave. As long as we were on the South Side, we were just hustlers trying to make things happen. But Dave gave us the idea we could do something bigger. He accelerated the dream for both of us."

Silver had his own dreams and ambitions, too, which extended far beyond Punchinello's. Though barely in his thirties, he had show business connections around the country and, more important, an innate feel for how the industry would develop. "Dave could see further ahead than other people," Reid says. "And he saw things in us we couldn't see ourselves." So while Vince Sanders had been invaluable in instilling the work ethic they needed and helping them find work, it was clear that Silver represented the next step. "Dave didn't want to be in show business the way Vince did," Reid says. "He wanted to *own* show business. Sometimes meeting just one person can be a catalyst for your career taking off. That's what Dave was going to be for us."

As they were going over some material for the act one day,

Reid asked Dreesen if he had called Silver about the cable television deal he had mentioned to them. "I've been meaning to do that," Dreesen said. "I don't even know what cable television is. Do you?" And he picked up the phone.

"*What!?*" he said. "*Dead!?* He can't be. I just talked to him a couple of days ago."

"I'm sorry, Tom," Silver's wife said. "It happened very suddenly."

"My God! Where is he being laid out? I want to pay my respects."

"He was buried yesterday."

"We didn't even get a chance to say goodbye," Dreesen says. "He was only thirty-two years old. I found out later his father had died at thirty-four and his brother at twenty-nine. They all had defective hearts."

"We were devastated," Reid says. "It took all the wind out of our sails. All of a sudden, we were back to having a part-time dream. I've always believed that had Dave lived things would have been very different for us."

When Reid and Dreesen began performing, it never occurred to them that their success on any given night might depend on the racial makeup of the audience. Funny was funny, wasn't it? What else mattered? "We thought that if we could show race wasn't an issue with us, it didn't have to be one with them," Dreesen says. "We were so naïve."

As they began working before integrated crowds on college campuses and as the opening act in some of Chicago's more elegant supper clubs, they noticed a disconcerting phenomenon. At times, it seemed that people were wondering whether they needed permission to laugh, whether their jokes, and their relationship, were a fit subject for humor. "Every time there was a black person in the audience, not a single white person would laugh until they looked at him," Reid says. "If the black guy laughed, it was OK. It was as if they were on a three-second delay. If there were two or three black folks in the audience, I felt sorry for them because people were always turning around and looking at them as if to say, 'Is this funny, Negro? You're the specialist.'"

But a black audience did not guarantee they were home free, either. "You could see them sitting there trying to figure out why is this black man up there with this white guy? Is it some kind of Uncle Tom situation?" Reid says. "It would take two or three minutes before they became receptive to what we were doing, let alone laugh. It seemed as if the crowds were always on edge when we first came out. For every audience, black or white, there was that initial moment of shock."

"It was almost as if we were an interracial marriage," Dreesen says. "I was performing at the Laugh Factory in Hollywood last year and there was a young blonde girl sitting with a black guy on one side of the room, a black girl with a white guy on the other side, and an Asian guy with a white girl in the back. All I could think while I was performing was nobody was staring at them. They damn sure would have stared when Tim and I were performing and I'm talking about blacks *and* whites. But today, nobody thinks about it. This was important because one of the things I learned in sales is true in comedy, too: when people don't know you, you only have a minute or two to make a favorable impression. So if people have negative feelings about you going in, you don't have much time to turn them around."

Reid and Dreesen were also surprised by what seemed to be the different expectations of black and white audiences. "When we worked the black clubs, they didn't expect anything out of us except to be funny," Dreesen says. "They didn't expect us to be political or say profound things about race. But with white audiences, it was as if they were saying, 'Where is the message?'"

"I think black audiences pulled for us in a different way," Reid says. "A lot of them, particularly those who moved up from the South, were like me—they had not been around white people in a social situation. But now they're seeing a black guy and a white guy who are relaxed with each other so once we worked through the initial resistance they began to pull for us. I think they understood what we were trying to do even before we saw it. You have to remember the context of the times. We were only five years removed from the passage of the Civil Rights Act, five years from my having the right to vote. And it was just one year since the assassinations of Martin Luther King and Bobby Kennedy and the riots at the Democratic convention. There wasn't a day that what was happening in Chicago, and what was happening in America, didn't affect how audiences saw us."

"Because things were so polarized it affected what people thought about us as much as the jokes we were telling." Dreesen says. "What I realized was those who wanted us to succeed didn't see color while those who didn't want us to succeed saw nothing *but* color."

Reid and Dreesen felt this ambivalence wherever they performed. "Some people wanted to like us," Reid says. "They'd tell us, 'When you came out I thought, please, God, let them be funny.' But others said their first reaction was, 'Here we go with this racial bullshit.'"

Integrated audiences also paid close attention to the relationship between the two men. Was Dreesen the top banana with Reid playing his foil? Was Reid subservient to Dreesen, even in a sharp-witted way, as Rochester had been to Jack Benny? It was almost with a sigh of relief that they saw the two men deal with each other on even terms, taking turns playing straight man and delivering punch lines. "Black audiences had never seen that," Reid says, "and liberal white audiences didn't want to see a black man playing the buffoon."

Dreesen experienced the ambivalence of white audiences some years later when he made his comedy album *That White Boy's Crazy* in front of a black crowd. Program directors at black radio stations immediately put it on the air, knowing their audiences would relate to his stories about growing up among blacks. But white radio stations balked. A white man talking about black people? What would their listeners think? Better not take any chances.

But there was one quality Tim and Tom projected that played

a key role in their acceptance: the two men obviously liked each other. "People would tell us that it was apparent it wasn't just an act," Dreesen says. "That came across on stage and it made all the difference." Years later, Dreesen spoke with Jerry Lewis, who said he and Dean Martin had experienced the same phenomenon. Even when they used some of the oldest, most hackneyed material imaginable ("Jerry, did you take a bath today?" "Why, Dean? Is one missing?") the audience would laugh because of the chemistry they created. "They knew we loved one another," Lewis said. "And it lasted until it was clear that we didn't love one another any more. That's when the act fell apart."

"You couldn't always convince everybody, though," says Reid. "I remember a black guy coming up after a show and saying, 'Do you guys really get along? Come on, tell me the truth. He probably calls you nigger.' Tom might have been thinking about that when he said that crazy thing at Club Harlem."

After a while, Dreesen and Reid came to see that it was not just audiences that were approaching them with mixed feelings. More surprising, and more frustrating, was the fact that people in show business did not know what to make of them, either. Many of the agents, promoters, business managers, club owners, and television producers they met—even those who dealt extensively with black performers—were uncomfortable with the idea of an integrated comedy act. Here, the country was going through a racial upheaval that had created great suspicions on both sides of the divide and Reid and Dreesen were *laughing* with each other about it?

"We could see that they weren't just judging the act for what it was, they were analyzing the business part of it," Reid says. "And I think the bookers were worried that we might bring a black clientele to their clubs. So despite all the places we worked, and all the great performers we worked with, we were not absorbed into the industry. I thought for sure somebody would see the potential in what we were doing, would see that race is something we're going to be talking about in this country for a long time and would want to develop us. But even when the audiences showed they were willing to accept us, the industry wasn't. That was very hard to get used to."

Steve Sperry, a Chicago-based manager who lined up some of their college dates, was also surprised by this resistance. While handling the comedy team of Edmonds & Curley, Sperry had booked them on *The Tonight Show* half a dozen times and on a number of other national television shows, too. Sperry was so successful getting jobs for Edmonds & Curley, in fact, that the William Morris Agency paid him the ultimate compliment of stealing them away from him. But now he believed he had a much better act to sell.

"The first time I saw Tim and Tom perform, I thought they were brilliant," Sperry says. "They were so different from anything I had ever seen before. The way they pushed the envelope on racial stereotypes was much funnier and more interesting than Edmonds & Curley and I thought selling them was going to be a piece of cake. But there was nothing I could do for them outside of the college circuit. The TV talent coordinators and the people who booked live shows just weren't comfortable with it. I thought, 'What's the matter with you people?' It puzzles me to this day."

There was something else they had never considered, too, something that shocked them when Marvin Junior explained it to them one night in the Junction Lounge in Harvey, a bar run by a church-going woman named Doll Franks, whose insistence on proper behavior included donations to a "swear jar" from anyone whose language she objected to.

"You know people are going to try to break you up, don't you?" said Junior, whose many years of success singing with the Dells had prompted Dreesen and Reid to ask for his advice.

Break them up?

"It's a game they play called Divide and Conquer," Junior said in his gruff, streetwise voice of experience. "They going to come up to Tim and say, 'You don't need that white boy in your act.

You're funny without him.' And they're going to tell Tom, 'What are you working with that nigger for? He's holding you back.' I'm telling you it's going to happen. Be ready for it."

"We left the Junction Lounge that night saying that would never happen to us," Dreesen says. "We were shoulder to shoulder, two soldiers in a foxhole. Nobody was going to break us up. No, sir. We had so much to learn."

**5**

It was time to take the act on the road. Chicago was home, comfortable and welcoming, and it was a thrill to be hired to open for some of the great black entertainers who came to town: Count Basie, Lionel Hampton, Sarah Vaughan, Stevie Wonder, Diahann Carroll, Dionne Warwick, Leslie Uggams, and more. So what if the headliner was making $10,000 a night while they were lucky to split $300? They were in the big time, weren't they? Even if only on the fringes. And look at the people they were meeting, people whose managers were becoming familiar with them. This had to lead to something down the road, didn't it? But in the meantime, they had to go where the work was. And that meant venturing out beyond the city limits.

They worked in big towns and small towns, hotels and motels, college campuses, and prisons. They worked Playboy Clubs and the Chitlin' Circuit. They worked in restaurants, night clubs, supper clubs, jazz clubs—any place that would book them, often on a moment's notice.

"Whenever another act fell out, missed a plane or something, boom, we were there," says Reid. "We were the National Guard of comedy teams."

They worked Michael's of Mankato in Minnesota, where Reid told the audience. "I hear they've got a bad black problem here."

"Really?" Dreesen said.

"Yeah, the guy died." Laugh. "They don't have many brothers in Mankato. I knew I was in trouble when I saw a white man delivering the mail." Bigger laugh.

They played a large arena at the University of Illinois, where someone in the crowd threw a ball of ice that hit Dreesen in the face and drew blood. "Turn on the lights!" he shouted, while Reid, unaware of what had happened, was startled at his partner's outburst. "I want to see your face, you chicken-shit son of a bitch!"

"Look, Tom, that's terrible, but you have to suck it up," Reid said when Dreesen told him how he had been hit after the show. "You have to be professional."

"Tim, the ice ball was thrown toward your side of the stage. I think it was aimed at you and I just got in the way."

"That dirty son of a bitch! I'd have gone down there and killed him!"

They played before an audience of eight at a Holiday Inn in Springfield, Missouri, where Reid told Dreesen, "Why don't you entertain me?" and took a seat at a table. The next evening, before a gathering that was only slightly larger, it was Dreesen's turn to sit while Reid worked solo.

They worked prisons where their Dating Game routine was always a big hit, particularly when they introduced Bachelor No. 3 as Percival Prudence from the laundry. "In almost every prison, the gay guys worked in the laundry," Dreesen says. "All we had to do was say the word laundry and there would be howls of laughter."

They worked in a club in New York before an audience that was almost entirely Japanese. "They didn't understand a word we were saying," Dreesen says. "They had a translator and we'd say, 'Hi, we're the comedy team of Tim and Tom,' and then we'd have to stop while the guy said it in Japanese. We died like dogs."

As soon as they were done, they bolted down the stairs, out

the door and, accompanied by Vince Sanders, who had made the trip with them, walked four blocks without saying a word.

"Why are we walking so fast?" Reid asked.

"I think they're gaining on us," Dreesen answered.

When they arrived at their hotel, they stood outside to catch their breath and observe New York's late-night street life.

"Would you ever go with a hooker, Tim?" Dreesen asked innocently, nodding his head toward Sanders as they watched some ladies of the evening stroll by.

"Never," replied Reid, picking up on where Dreesen was headed.

"Now Vince, you've got to buy pussy," Dreesen said, "but look at us. We're two young good-looking guys, we don't have to buy it."

"Damn you, Tom," Sanders protested. "I would never . . ." and at that moment a provocatively dressed black woman walked past, smiled at Dreesen, said "Hi, Tom," and continued walking.

"Wait a minute, no," Dreesen said to Reid and Sanders, who were cracking up not only at the woman's greeting, but at her perfect timing. "I swear to God I didn't," and he chased her down the street.

"How did you know my name?" he asked when he finally caught up.

"I saw your act last week," she said with a smile. "'You never call a black man Tom,' remember?"

"Yeah, sure," Sanders said when Dreesen reported the conversation. "Club Harlem. Right."

"I couldn't convince them I hadn't been with a hooker," Dreesen says. "I was really pissed."


Reid and Dreesen performed at dozens of colleges in the Midwest, but they were never quite as successful as they had thought they might be. "We'd hoped that colleges would be our bread and butter because there were so many of them," Reid says. "But we didn't always go over very well, even with the racial material, because we were more of a nightclub act. We didn't get into the Vietnam protests or talk about politics much, which was what they were looking for. So we never really took off."

Working the college circuit did give them a new kind of hope, though, as they found themselves opening for singers like Neil Diamond, Brook Benton, and the popular soft rock group Bread. "We thought maybe we'd be blessed with that show business miracle that sometimes happens," Reid says, "that one of them would book us to go on the road with them. We'd tell each other, 'Do you know how many gigs Neil Diamond does?' What we didn't know was that the headliner hardly ever *saw* the opening act. He'd be backstage getting ready. The only act that ever took us around to open for it was the Dells, who took us to five or six places. They were really good to us."

So as much as they traveled, and as much as they hustled work in Chicago, there were times when they wouldn't have a paying gig from one month to the next. But late in 1971, after two years of scrambling, they got a big break: an offer of regular work at Playboy Clubs around the country. There were so many Playboy Clubs, and comedians were a staple of their entertainment lineup, that it was almost like having steady jobs. Before long, they were performing at clubs in New York, Boston, Baltimore, Cincinnati, New Orleans, St. Louis, and Kansas City as well as Chicago. They had to split the $750 fee so there was no way to get ahead financially, but it was worth it to be able to perform in a sophisticated environment where customers were receptive to, or at least tolerated, their brand of social commentary.

"Playboy Clubs were like an island within the city," Reid says. "They had their own entertainment philosophy and if it didn't appeal to you, you didn't go. And they were the first clubs to give black comedians a chance to work before multiracial audiences. Dick Gregory, Godfrey Cambridge, Nipsey Russell, they all worked there. Playboy Clubs were the closest thing there was to a comedy circuit at that time."

The setup at Playboy Clubs provided a learning experience, too. Each club had two showrooms, the Play Room and the Penthouse, where entertainment took place simultaneously, and the performers would move from one to the other during the evening. "We'd follow a girl singer, who would work in one room and then go upstairs," Reid says. "When we were halfway through our act, she'd start singing in the second room. Then when we were done, they'd bring another act into the room we'd just left. And if the rooms were full, they'd open a third one to catch the overflow. The idea was to have things happening all at once so the customers would want to stay and see what they had missed. It was like a factory. Playboy Clubs wouldn't let a nickel walk out the door if they could help it."

Their down time at Playboy Clubs gave them a chance to study other comedy teams, which made them understand just how important timing was to an act like theirs. "We'd never seen a team work except for maybe three or four minutes on *The Ed Sullivan Show*," Dreesen says. "We walked into the Chicago Playboy Club one night and saw Tracy & Veder and we were fascinated. Their rhythm, the way they worked off one another, their patter, how they set up the punch line—it was amazing. Everything they did was bing, bing, bing. It was eye-opening for both of us."

With this inspiration, and with the Playboy Clubs' regimen of five or six shows a night, their act began to improve. "Doing one show after another made us really sharp." Reid says. "The Playboy Clubs gave us what we needed—a chance to work at it. It was on-the-job training for us, almost like getting paid to rehearse."

Wherever they went, they tried to drum up business by appearing on local radio and television, chatting with disc jockeys and talk-show hosts, who often had their own agendas. "There was a guy named Bob Braun who had an afternoon talk show in Cincinnati where he sold his own line of products," Dreesen says. "He was talking to us about the act once and suddenly he said, 'But sometimes comedy's painful, isn't it, Tom? . . . like the pain a lot of our viewers have from hemorrhoids.' And he started selling Bob Braun's salve."

There were also interviewers who didn't know who Reid and Dreesen were and didn't care. While talking to the host of one radio show, they realized he wasn't listening to them. He would ask a question, look at some paperwork on his desk, then motion to the engineer in the control room to queue up a tape. "How did you two meet?" he asked at one point, and again began fiddling with some papers.

"We knew each other when we were very young, working on my father's farm," Dreesen said, winking at Reid, who looked at him quizzically. "We were best friends all the time we were growing up. And then, one day . . . my father sold him."

"Hey, that's great," the host said, still oblivious, as Reid and Dreesen laughed so hard they all but fell on the floor. "I've often wondered what his listeners were thinking," Dreesen says.

The contrast between their appearance on stage—two hip, good-looking, well-dressed young men—and the reality of their lives on the road could not have been more stark. No one who saw them working in the fanciest club in town would have believed how little money they were making—often no more than $100 a night apiece—or that they could not afford the luxury of separate hotel rooms. But for the fact this hardly fit the image they wanted to project, and the embarrassment involved, this would have provided excellent material for their act.

"Once we showed up at a cheap motel in Missouri at three o'clock in the morning and had to wake the desk clerk up," Dreesen says. "All of a sudden, he's looking at a black guy and a white guy who don't want separate rooms or adjoining rooms, but the *same* room. He said, 'Do you want one with a king-size bed or one of those . . . *queens*?' And we said, 'Just give us a goddam room with two beds!' We didn't care if they thought we were gay as long as they thought we were *mean* gay."

One night, after finishing their act in the glitzy surroundings of the New York Playboy Club, they discovered the nearby hotel they had checked into earlier in the day catered largely to prostitutes and their customers. "I've been in some scary places," Reid says, "but this one was terrifying. I remembered what somebody told me once—when you're in a really rough place, sleep with the door open and the lights out because nobody with any sense would walk into a dark room at night. We did that more than once."

Getting places could be equally nerve wracking. There was the gig in Nebraska in the fall of 1971 where the pay was $600 for a couple of nights' work. They drove Reid's company car and made the round trip of more than 1,000 miles in two nights. A month later there was the date in Bloomington, Indiana, to which Dreesen's friend Sammy Eubanks, a card shark whose street name was Champagne Sammy, drove them in his big black Cadillac, but only after making a couple of stops along the way. "He was one of the smoothest, most soft-spoken hustlers, black or white, I've ever met," says Reid. "When we started this trip, he drove around to the house of one girl after another. I thought, 'Oh my God, he's going to take these girls with us to Bloomington. How is that going to look?'"

But as the women came out to the street to greet Eubanks, it was clear he had a different agenda.

"Sammy, you haven't been around," they would say. "When am I going to see you?"

"It's not that I haven't been thinking about you, baby," he would answer. "Listen, I just need a few dollars."

"They would go back in the house and come out with $20 or $30," Dreesen says. "Then we'd go on to the next one. None of them ever asked if he was going to pay them back. And that's how he got the money to drive us to Bloomington. The women just adored him."

There was the last-minute offer of a week at the Boston Playboy Club in November 1971 that would pay them $375 apiece for six shows a night if they could be there in two days. They rented a Pinto, promised the man behind the counter they would not leave Chicago, borrowed a fake credit card from Eubanks, and set off. In the Pennsylvania hill country near Pittsburgh, they ran out of gas and decided that Reid should hitchhike to the nearest gas station.

"After four cars went by at about 100 miles an hour, I said, 'Wait a minute. Nobody's going to stop for *me* out here,' so Tom got out on the road and, sure enough, the first car picked him up." Dreesen returned with a can of gas, drove to the station and said, "Fill 'er up."

"Those were the days when you filled in the number on the credit card slip by hand," Dreesen says. "One of us would distract the guy at the pump and the other would change one number and sign the slip. We'd been doing that the whole trip, but we were tired and not thinking so I talked to the guy while Tim signed. The guy looked at the card, looked at Tim and said, 'This says your name is Jaworski. You don't look like a Jaworski to me!' We jumped in the car and got the hell out of there. Then, about half an hour outside of Boston, the car exploded, just blew up. Now, I've got to call the guy in Chicago and tell him the car we'd promised not to take out of town was a piece of junk in Boston."

Several weeks later, they found themselves at a pre-Thanksgiving gig at the Missouri State Prison in Jefferson City. "You never get used to hearing that big door close behind you," Reid says, "but the prisoners seemed to appreciate us and they always wanted to talk afterwards." After this performance, a young pimply-faced white inmate—no more than five-foot-five and 110 pounds—approached Reid and asked him what it was like to be a comedian. As they were talking, Reid noticed one of the guards ease over and stand close by.

"You had nothing to worry about," the guard told Reid after the inmate returned to his cell. "I was right there watching."

"What do you mean?" Reid said.

"Don't you know who that is? He's one of the most notorious serial killers in the United States. He murdered eight people."

"*What?!*"

Always looking to save money on hotels, they accepted the

invitation of a farmer moonlighting as a prison guard to stay with his family that night. But Reid's gratitude turned to trepidation as they drove through the darkness to their destination. "Here I am, the only black guy for miles around and I'm going to a house that looked like something out of *Nightmare on Elm Street*," he says. "The guy was trying to express his liberalism—a lot of people overcompensated that way—but his kids looked at me like I was some kind of alien. They put us in bunk beds, but I didn't sleep a wink, thinking somebody was going to chop me up in pieces in the middle of the night."

In the morning, they were served newly laid eggs and raw milk fresh from the cow as Reid, desperate to get home for the holiday, thought, "The glamour of show business. This has to be the bottom." Later in the day, Reid's Volkswagen broke down near Springfield. "The part we needed was in St. Louis and of course they couldn't get it to us on Thanksgiving," Reid says. "So we spent the day in Springfield, waiting for the part to arrive on Friday. *That* was the bottom."

There was another trip to Missouri where, feeling pleased with themselves after a well-received performance at a showcase for college booking agents at Northeast Missouri State, they pulled off a rural road onto the gravel approach to Jim's Cafe, the one spot nearby they'd been told they could get a late dinner.

"Now, we don't want any trouble," Dreesen said before they walked inside. "You never know who might be in there and what they might do. Let's just get something to eat and get out."

Reid, who had learned to be nonconfrontational when necessary, agreed. "We had that discussion a lot," he says. "No black and white man traveling the country at that time would think of going into a place like that without talking about it."

But as they ordered dinner, they heard voices from a table in the corner that indicated Reid wasn't the problem so much as Dreesen.

"Well, look what we've got here," said a man with long thin

sideburns who was wearing a John Deere cap. "That boy needs a goddam haircut. I wish I had my sheep shears, I'd cut that goddam boy's hair off."

"They were talking about spade this and spade that, too," Dreesen says, "but I had long hair and I'm the one they wanted, calling me a hippie son of a bitch and all kinds of things."

And now it was Reid's turn to tell Dreesen to stay calm. "Let's be cool and not have any problems here," he said as their food came, but soon the men in the corner began trying to top each other.

"Long-haired weirdo son of a bitch bringing his bullshit down here . . ."

"Somebody ought to whip his fucking ass and cut his fucking hair . . ."

"Send him home to his mama where he belongs . . ."

"Maybe he's going to suck that nigger's dick . . ."

Dreesen's days on the street had taught him to recognize when someone was just mouthing off and when there was going to be trouble and he knew this was the real thing. "Go get the car and pull up to the door," he told Reid. "I'll be out in a minute."

Dreesen took his time, finished his dinner, walked up to the counter, and paid the bill. Then, seeing Reid drive up, he walked to the door, turned around, and interrupted the men, who were still discussing the proper use of sheep sheers.

"You know something," he said, looking at the ringleader. "You chicken-shit motherfuckers are right. I came down here just to suck that nigger's dick. And do me a favor. If you ever come to my neighborhood in Chicago, bring all your sissy-ass redneck friends and we'll whip your fucking asses."

Chairs and tables went flying as the men chased Dreesen out the door where he jumped in the car and shouted, "Go!" The gravel hitting the plate glass window of Jim's Cafe sounded like bullets as the car accelerated out of the parking lot. "We might have hit one of those mothers in the face with a rock, too," Dreesen says. "I hope so."

"The menace was always there," Reid says. "There were some parts of the country where there weren't many places we felt comfortable going in. But we had to eat."

After driving eight hours in the dead of winter from Chicago to Chadron State College through northwest Nebraska in wind so strong it nearly blew the Volkswagen off the road, they stopped in a roadside diner. Better not eat anything strange, Reid told himself, and he ordered soup. Hmm, that's odd, he thought as he saw the waitress and the chef peering out at him from the window into the kitchen. They had barely gotten back on the road when he had to pull over and throw up everything he had eaten.

"I don't know what they put in that soup, but I almost died," Reid says. "I'm just glad Tom was there. If I'd been alone, I probably would have been taken out in the back. I was a bit more comfortable in those kinds of situations because he had proven that if anything happened I wasn't going to be alone. But I guess that's one time when I got *too* comfortable."

The receptions they received while performing could be terrifying, too. Opening for George Clinton and Funkadelic at Cobo Hall in Detroit in the summer of 1971, they were all but booed off the stage by a young crowd that had no patience for the traditional progression favored by many producers: a comedy act before the headliner. "When we came out there was dead silence," Reid says. "We were the last people anyone in the audience wanted to see. And when we went into the act, they started booing and wouldn't stop."

They were treated even worse later that year when they were booked as the opening act for Sha Na Na at the Arie Crown Theater in Chicago. "You guys do seventeen minutes," the vintage rock group's promoter told them backstage. "Don't do sixteen minutes and don't do eighteen minutes. I go get them in their dressing room when you hit twelve minutes and five minutes later they're on stage. Got it?"

As Dreesen and Reid looked at each other in confusion—seventeen minutes *exactly?*—they heard the auditorium announcer say, "All right, we've got a comedy team" only to be interrupted by five thousand white teenagers who didn't want to hear it.

"Fuck the comedy team!" they shouted. "We want Sha Na Na!" And they started to chant: "Sha Na Na! Sha Na Na! Sha Na Na!"

"They were throwing things at us," Reid says. "You could hear them land, bing, bing, bing, across the stage."

"They would not let us perform," Dreesen says. "They were booing us so hard, and chanting so loud you couldn't even hear us. Eight minutes went by and I thought we'd been out there an hour. I was sopping wet and I looked at my watch. Nine more minutes to go. Somehow we got through it and all I could think of was the time we opened for Bread at a college and five or six guys in the audience were talking while they were singing one of their quiet songs — 'If a picture paints a thousand words . . .' Their road manager went up to the guy who ran the venue and said, 'Either you quiet them down or I'm going to go out there and break their fucking heads.' I thought, 'I want this guy to manage *us*.'"

On other occasions the fact they were not headliners created situations that were more comic than threatening, such as when the Dells hired them as their opening act at a Black Expo in Indianapolis in 1971. "We were in the dressing room after a show getting our picture taken with Jesse Jackson and Ralph Abernathy, and people started leaving," Dreesen says. "There were crowds in the corridor waiting for the big acts to come out and they had to get security to lead the way. One of the guards said, 'It's a little rough out there, so we'll do this one at a time.' Smokey Robinson went first and you could hear them yelling, 'Smokey! Smokey!' and the security guards shouting, 'Get back! Let us through!' and fighting their way through the crowd to get him outside the building and walk him to his limousine.

"They did the same thing for Marvin and the Dells and then one of the guards said, 'All right, Tim and Tom, your turn. Stay close to us and keep your arms in or they'll grab you and pull you away. OK, ready?' They opened the door and there were hundreds of people there, yelling, 'Who is it? Who is it?' Then somebody saw us and said, 'Oh, it ain't nobody,' and it was like the parting of the Red Sea."

"We felt pretty silly bunched up next to the security guys and nobody else around," Reid says. "We followed them outside and one of them just grinned and said, 'Well, I guess you're safe now.' I'll never forget that: 'Who is it? Who is it?' 'Oh, it ain't nobody.'"

Performing in the South could raise the tension on and off stage to an even higher level. In May of 1972, as they were checking into a cheap hotel in the New Orleans French Quarter, one with a Confederate flag hanging in the lobby, they heard someone say, "George Wallace has been shot."

"Oh, God," Reid thought. "Please let it be a white man." Wallace's would-be assassin was indeed white, but Reid and Dreesen were worried as the updates came in all day on the condition of the South's favorite son.

Before their performance at the Playboy Club that evening, a nervous young bunny came into their dressing room with a warning: "There's a guy out there saying some bad things and waiting for y'all to come out." As they took the stage, Dreesen passed the message to the club's manager who promised to watch for trouble.

"Hi, we're the comedy team of Tim and Tom," Dreesen said, swinging into the act, "and . . ."

"Hell, we don't give a damn who you are," said a heavyset man sitting with a woman at a table in the front of the room and working on what was clearly not his first drink. Then, turning around to the audience behind him, he said, "Any of you people give a damn who they are?"

"Sir, if you promise not to interrupt our act," Dreesen said, "I'll promise not to come down to your job and tell you how to use your shovel," Dreesen said.

"I've got a whole bunch of shovels, boy. I'm in construction in Calhoun, Alabama. You know anything about Calhoun?"

"Wasn't he Amos and Andy's lawyer?"

"What was that? What'd he say?"

"He said they named your town after Amos and Andy's lawyer," the woman next to him said.

"Are you insulting the fair state of Alabama?" the man yelled.

"No, sir," Dreesen said. "I'm not insulting anyone. I'm . . ." and he looked around to see he was alone. Reid had left his side and backed into the darkness at the rear of the stage.

"I think you're insulting my state," the man said, more belligerently now, and the crowd began to grumble in agreement.

"No, I'm not insulting . . ." and he sensed his partner stepping out of the shadows.

"I think he's right, Tom." Reid called from behind him. "You *were* insulting the fair state of Alabama."

"No, I'm not," Dreesen said, as the audience began to laugh at the notion of Reid taking the side of the heckler. "I'm just . . ."

"Yes, Tom, I think you did insult him," Reid said. "You owe the man an apology."

At this, the room broke up, laughing hard at Reid and at their antagonist. Realizing he was being mocked by his own people as well as the two uppity Northerners, the man got up, scattering drinks and members of the audience as he moved toward the stage. He had almost reached Dreesen when the manager of the club and several security guards grabbed him and pulled him over to a flight of stairs leading down and out of the building, trading punches all the way.

"The guy was tough," Dreesen says. "He fought all the way downstairs and then, when they thought they had finally thrown him out, he came back up and they had to drag him down again."

With the room still buzzing with excitement and their own adrenaline pumping, the rest of their performance was a triumph. "That was one night we went out front afterwards where everybody could see us," Dreesen says, "and I swear one guy came up and said, 'Tell the truth. That's guy's part of your act, isn't he?' I said, 'Do you think we'd stage a fight going up and down stairs five shows a night?' The guy wanted to kill us and he thought we put him in the audience as a shill."

"It was a gut reaction," Reid said of pretending to agree with the heckler. "In a fight, you have two options—fight or flight. But comics have a third option—fight, flight, or make it funny. I could feel the tension in the room, the audience getting nervous. If you can inject humor into a situation, you can exercise power over it."

The remainder of their two weeks in New Orleans was among the most pleasant they ever spent together. When a bunny mentioned that the bar where they liked to drink after closing time had recently burned down, Dreesen and Reid recommended the Club Car Lounge, which they had discovered the night before.

"By the third or fourth night, there were about fifteen bunnies hanging out there, along with the band from the Playboy Club, and dozens of guys who were always searching for bunnies after hours," Dreesen says. "It was standing room only and the owner loved us so much he wouldn't let us spend a dime. He was a former diver on an oil rig who used his retirement money to open the club and I think he must have lost some oxygen because he wasn't playing with a full deck. A couple of guys started fighting one night and he shouted at them to stop. Then he pulled out a pistol and fired it into the ceiling. Everybody went, 'Holy shit!' and it got very quiet as he stood there with a smoking gun. A minute later, a guy walked in wearing pajamas wanting to know what was going on. He lived upstairs and the bullet had gone right up through his floor."

"The guy was cool, though," Reid says. "He spent the rest of the night at the bar drinking with us, still in his pajamas."

After the bar closed, the entire Playboy Club contingent would wander over to Lucky Pierre's, which had once been a French Quarter horse stable and was now a restaurant catering to those who had no sense of, or interest in, what time it was. "Hookers, pimps, waiters, all the night people went there to have breakfast," Reid says. "If you were an entertainer, you could perform and if they liked you they would pick up your tab. Some nights, we'd stumble out of there and just sleep in the park and wake up with the winos because we didn't want to be in that fleabag at night. In the morning, we'd get a piece of fruit at the market and then go back to the hotel and sleep some more."

Late one night at the Club Car, Reid found himself in earnest conversation with a young white bunny named Cathy, who wanted to know how he'd felt dealing with the heckler from Alabama. "You know," she said after they talked for a while, "I've never met a spade before."

"You haven't?" Reid said. "Well, let this spade buy you a drink."

"I just fell out laughing," he says. "She said it so innocently. That really endeared her to me. Then she told me her brother was a member of the Klan in one of New Orleans' parishes."

At six in the morning, after breakfast at Lucky Pierre's, Cathy invited Reid back to her place, a small basement apartment in an antebellum home near the French Quarter. "It was a neighborhood with huge mansions, beautiful gardens, and streetcars running by," Reid says. "I couldn't help thinking that my people had served many a year there." About noon the next day, they left the apartment and climbed the stairs to the sidewalk where an elderly white woman watering a small flower smiled at Cathy. Then she saw Reid and her mouth dropped open as she stood rooted to the spot, the hose in her hand forgotten. "Remember, now, it's 1972," Reid says.

After a long pause, Reid looked down and said, "Madam, you're drowning your begonia," and he and Cathy walked to her car.

On another night, the door to the Club Car flew open and a young man drove a motorcycle inside. "You son of a bitch!" the owner yelled and he jumped over the bar and attacked the driver. After landing a few punches, he hopped on the back of the motorcycle and the two men drove out onto the street. "We didn't see him the rest of the night," Dreesen says. "So we went behind the bar and started mixing drinks. The people that came in thought we owned the place and we closed up the bar for him that night. It was some of the most fun I've had in my life. I've never forgotten it."

Their stay ended with Cathy kissing Reid goodbye at the airport while Dreesen received a fond farewell from the lovely black singer who had been their opening act at the Playboy Club. "There was a convention from Chicago on our plane," Dreesen says. "I often wonder what they thought when they saw us kissing our wives at the gate when we landed."

It wasn't only in the South that working before white audiences could be cause for concern, as Dreesen learned in the early days of the act when he announced he'd arranged a gig at the International Polka Music Hall of Fame in a Polish section of Chicago.

"Have you lost your *mind?*" Reid said.

"What?"

"Black folks don't go to those neighborhoods. They don't even drive *through* them. Didn't you read about the black couple who had a flat tire near there and a mob attacked them? They *killed* them, Tom."

"Oh, come on. That's not going to happen."

"Tom, you have no idea. Let me tell you about the time I drove out to a plant in Cicero when I was working for DuPont. There were two Italian guys there who looked at me like they couldn't believe what they were seeing. They just couldn't fathom the idea that a black man was in their town. One of them said to me, 'You're not from here, are you?' I said, 'No, I'm from Virginia. I've only been here a few months.' And he said, 'All right, this is what I want you to do. I want you to get in your car and drive as quickly as you possibly can and leave Cicero and don't ever come back.' And then he shook my hand. I drove back to my office and I said, 'You give that territory to somebody else. I am not going into that neighborhood again.'"

"Well, maybe we can figure out a way to disarm them," Dreesen said. "Just go right in there and start talking about it." Against his better judgment, Reid agreed to take the job.

"I'm sorry we're late, folks," Dreesen said as they began their act that night. "We had to stop off on the South Side for some soul food."

"Yeah," Reid said. "We had pierogi, kielbasa, golabki, ga-lunki, czarnina . . ." The stiffness in the room dissolved into a huge laugh.

"We did the Dating Game routine and the one about Tom taking me to meet his Italian father, and they loved it," Reid says. "We were smart enough not to do the bit about me teaching him to be black, though."

Appearing in front of black crowds on the Chitlin' Circuit in the North offered its own set of challenges. "When you worked the black clubs, you had to *work*," Dreesen says. "Their attitude was they had worked hard all week and when they came to see a show, they wanted to see a long one. You had to leave it all out there. James Brown's famous bit where he sings until he falls down and doesn't have an ounce of strength left and then he's up again singing, 'Please, baby, please,' that's the kind of thing black audiences love."

Nor were black audiences shy about expressing their opinions. "If a white audience didn't like us, you'd hear them whisper, 'I thought they were awful,'" Dreesen says. "But a black audience would just yell, 'That's bullshit, man! Get off the goddam stage!' Then, maybe later they'd yell, 'Now, *that's* funny! I like that!'"

"It wasn't really heckling," says Reid, "more like the call and response you heard in a black church and you had to learn to deal with it." And following the pattern they had established earlier—testing material that went right up to the edge of racism and stepping back when they saw they had crossed over—Dreesen and Reid worked to bring the audience response into their act.

Trying out new material one afternoon as they sat in their hotel room before a performance at the 20 Grand in Detroit, Dreesen said, "How about this? When we're working in front of a white audience and we get interrupted by a heckler, what if I said, 'Hey, go get your own. He's mine. After all, you know how hard they are to train?'"

"Gee, Tom, that's kind of on the racist side, don't you think?" Reid replied.

"You're right. I'm sorry."

"No, no, don't be sorry. I understand. We're just practicing. I don't want to block your creativity. Let's keep trying."

At the 2 a.m. show at the 20 Grand that very evening, someone in the crowd shouted out, "Hey, white boy, what are you doing here?"

Reid stepped forward and said, "Hey, brother, go get your own. He's mine. After all, you know how hard they are to train." The audience erupted in laughter.

"You know, Tom, that line *is* pretty funny," Reid said later.

"Well, how come it's not funny when I say it?" he said.

"Tim was right, though," Dreesen says. "It's a basic lesson in comedy Charlie Chaplin taught years ago. A pie in the face of a banker is funny. A pie in the face of a homeless man is not. There were things he could say to me that wouldn't be funny if I said them, and vice-versa. But we didn't know it until we tried it out."

The fact that the Chitlin' Circuit had been the home to so many great black entertainers over the years gave Tim and Tom a legitimacy with black audiences they might not otherwise have had, but they always had to be mindful of their surroundings. As Dreesen discovered one rainy afternoon as he wandered through the downtown Detroit neighborhood where the 20 Grand was located while Reid occupied their hotel room with a woman he had met the night before. This was part of an agreement they had. "If one of us got lucky, the other guy took a hike," Dreesen says.

As he was walking, two black plainclothesmen drove up and said, "Hey, white boy, what are you doing here?"

"I'm working at the 20 Grand," he said. "I'm a comedian."

"A white boy working the 20 Grand? Get in the car." And they drove him to the club where Bill Kabush, its mob-connected owner, vouched for him.

"You have to understand," one of the policemen told Dreesen as they drove back to the hotel. "If we see a white man in this neighborhood, he's buying either pussy or drugs."

Dreesen returned to the room and knocked on the door only to hear Reid say, "Hey, man, give me a little more time," and he wandered back out into the rain. "Just a little more time," Reid said again when Dreesen knocked half an hour later. When he was finally allowed in the room, he saw Reid and the girl had been using his bed.

At the club that night, they got into an argument and Reid said, "That's the racist part of you talking there."

Dreesen exploded. "I walk around in an all-black neighborhood in Detroit, I'm soaking wet, the cops pick me up, you're banging a white girl in my goddam bed, and I'm a *racist*?"

Reid thought a moment. "Well, maybe I was a little hasty," he said, and the two men had a story they've laughed about for more than thirty years.

During a later gig at the 20 Grand, the picture on the television set in their hotel room began flickering on and off. They removed the back cover to see what the problem was and several large stacks of money fell out. "Tens, fives, twenties, and a lot of singles," Dreesen says. "There must have been $2,500 or $3,000. It was more money than we had made all year. We knew what we had to do, though."

"Can you tell us who was in our room before us?" Reid asked the front desk clerk.

"Some drug guys," he replied. "The cops came and got them."

"Well, we found some money in the room, and we're turning it in," Reid said.

"You're *what?!*"

"Here it is. Now give us a different room."

"It's a good thing we were both street kids or we might have tried to keep the money," Reid says. "But we were pretty sure they'd get bailed out and come back for it. And sure enough, we could hear them arguing from our room across the way. I don't know if they got their money back or not. All I know is we didn't have it."

Whether performing in the North or South, in front of black, white, or integrated audiences, their education about race continued. There was the constant realization that who they were meant as much as what they did, that their listeners' reaction was based on something beyond the jokes they were hearing. It was as if they were constantly taking their own temperatures, responding to Tim and Tom, and then responding to their responses.

"Everywhere we went, people came up to us after the show to talk about race," Reid says. "They were using us to work through their concerns, to prove there was nothing racist about *their* attitudes. They'd buy us drinks and open themselves up in very personal ways when sometimes all we wanted to do was get away. We weren't psychologists, we were comedians. How were we supposed to respond?"

"Hot damn, boys! I just love y'all!" a slightly inebriated man said after a performance at the Atlanta Playboy Club in 1972. "We've got this old colored gal, Flo, who's been with us for thirty-some years now and she's like one of the family. We sit on the same toilet and everything. I even drink out of the same glass she does."

"Do tell," Reid said.

"Is that your drink?" the man asked, pointing at the glass on the bar in front of him.

"Yeah."

The man picked up the glass, drank from it, and put it back down.

"I was waiting for Tim to say, 'Get away from me,'" Dreesen says. "But all he did was push the glass away and order another drink."

"Being cynical was my protection in situations like that," Reid says. "I didn't allow what he said to touch me. I kept it outside. But there was no way I was going to play the happy Negro for him. I was anything but happy then."

While taking a cab that afternoon to Underground Atlanta, the city's big shopping district, Reid was startled to see the driver had a gun strapped to his side in a holster. And when he arrived, he saw the shop where Lester Maddox was selling ax handles and racist memorabilia. "It was right out there in broad daylight," he says. "I couldn't believe it. My attitude about America and racism was bleak then anyway. And Nixon, Watergate, the mood of the country, it was all really getting to me. Tom didn't pay much attention to it—his head was in show business 24/7—but I was just a few years removed from the civil rights struggle and my antennae were up wherever we went. I'd been thinking I might want to move to Atlanta because I'd heard it was a good place for blacks. But that trip changed my mind. The atmosphere was really charged and I felt in danger. I couldn't wait to get out of there."

Confrontations with audiences in other cities could be upsetting, too. "If we worked an all-white club where there was a redneck who hated black people, he wasn't mad at Tim, he was mad at me," Dreesen says. "I was a nigger-lover and he didn't mind calling me that name. And if we played a black club and there was somebody who hated white people, he wasn't mad at me. To him, Tim was an Uncle Tom."

Most painful of all was when the threat Tim and Tom represented to deep-seated prejudices struck close to home. One of Dreesen's friends was a lawyer he had met in the Jaycees and had considered having handle their business affairs. "We were talking one day," Dreesen says, "and he said, 'How are you guys doing? Are you still delivering those *messages?*' He didn't want to know if we were making people laugh, only if we were doing racial material. I was really hurt by that."

But it was not always race that caused these divisions. Sometimes, when they least expected it, they were made to understand they could never escape who they were and where they came from. Walking into the Wooden Keg in Midlothian, a town adjacent to Harvey, one night in the summer of 1972, Dreesen ran into Tommy Johnson, one of his closest friends from the days they had set pins and shot pool. "We literally grew up on the streets together," Dreesen says. "Tommy lived with his mother above the pool hall and she had a new boyfriend every six months. Every time somebody new showed up, he would pray the guy was going to be his daddy, but usually they just beat him. He grew up to be a really tough guy."

After being sent to a juvenile detention center, Johnson's luck changed when a local judge gave him a choice between more jail time or the army. Thriving on the discipline his life had lacked, he qualified for the 101st Airborne. "I was so happy for Tommy," Dreesen says. "We both came home after the service and met each other at parties and joked around. It was like we had never been apart and would be buddies for life."

Johnson had been among Tim and Tom's protectors at the Golden Horseshoe after the night Reid was attacked so Dreesen was startled when, after a night of drinking at the Wooden Keg, Johnson began making snide remarks about his "black friend." "I could see he wasn't just talking, that he was looking to hit somebody," Dreesen says. "So I eased out the back door and was getting in my car when he ran outside and grabbed me. Just as he was going to throw a punch, I moved in real close so he couldn't put any power behind it and I said, 'Tommy, don't do this.' I didn't want to hit him, but I didn't want him to hit me, either."

Just then, Mike Cravens, a policeman they had known since childhood, pulled into the parking lot, jumped out of his car, grabbed them and said, "What the hell is this? You guys are friends. Cut it out." His eyes still glaring with anger, Johnson released his grip on Dreesen and returned to the bar. The following morning, sober now, he appeared at Dreesen's house.

"I came to apologize, Tommy," Johnson said. "It's just that I'm so jealous. When you and Tim became a comedy team, I knew you were going to make it. You were going to become a success and leave Harvey and I'd never see you again. And I couldn't stand that. I wanted it to be you and me. Why couldn't *we* be the comedy team? Tommy, I almost hit you. I would cut my arm off if I ever did that. From now on, I'm your biggest fan. You know that, don't you?"

Dreesen grabbed his friend and held on. "You're my buddy, Tommy," he said. "You're my childhood buddy. You'll always be my buddy."

Years later, when Dreesen played Las Vegas for the first time, he invited a number of friends from the old neighborhood. Goochie Nicholson, Tutu Brackens, Champagne Sammy Eubanks, Mike Crowder, they were all there, along with Tommy Johnson. As they walked outside Caesars Palace several hours before the show, they stopped at the marquee and Dreesen again saw tears in the former paratrooper's eyes.

"Tommy, what's the matter?" he said.

"Don't you get it?" Johnson said, and he pointed up at the sign that said "Sammy Davis Jr. and Tom Dreesen." "If your name is up there, all of our names are up there. Everybody in Harvey is on that marquee. The whole neighborhood is riding with you."

And then the tears were in Dreesen's eyes.

**6**

Vince Sanders was the first to say what they both knew was true.

"Tom's into it and you're not," Sanders, who was still lining up jobs and taking them to black clubs around Chicago, told Reid.

"What are you talking about, Vince?" said Reid, whose arguments with Sanders were becoming more frequent as the frustrations over how little money they were making continued to grow. "Maybe if you found us a gig that actually *paid* something once in a while."

"That's bullshit," Sanders said. "You're getting work, but the only way to take it to the next level is to be totally committed. Tom's got the passion. He's put everything he's got into it. He's got no alternative. Look what he's done. He's screwed up his entire life. But you're holding back. You've got a job. You've got a college degree. You've got money. You're living in a nice house. Your half of the act isn't doing its share."

"What are you telling me?" Reid yelled. "That I should quit my job, too?"

"I'm telling you that's the only way you're going to know," Sanders shouted back.

"Godammit, Vince, do you know how much money we made last year?" Reid said. "Not even $10,000. To *split*. I've got a house, a car, a child, and another one on the way. And you're telling me to quit a job any black man in America would kill for so I can go out on the road and beat my head against the wall? Are you *insane!?*" And he stomped out of the room.

"It was getting to the point where I couldn't take the disappointments any more," Reid says. "I kept thinking this was not the way it was supposed to be, that we should have *happened* by now. I didn't have the passion for stand-up that Tom did—I was always more interested in acting—and I didn't like nightclubs. I didn't like going into a room full of people drinking and smoking cigarettes and sitting there saying, 'Make me laugh.' Maybe my father losing his club had something to do with it. It really began to bother me."

Nor was he able to match Dreesen's optimism, which at times seemed to border on the delusional. While in the navy, Dreesen had begun reading self-help books that stressed the importance of tenacity, willpower, and maintaining an upbeat attitude in the face of adversity. Norman Vincent Peale's *The Power of Positive Thinking*, Napoleon Hill's *Think and Grow Rich*, W. Clement Stone's *Success through a Positive Mental Attitude*, and Joseph Murphy's *The Power of Your Subconscious Mind*—Dreesen read all of them and more. Their messages, which became a part of his outlook on life, were summed up in a mantra he would repeat to himself over and over: if it is to be, it's up to me.

"I started noticing a pattern," says Dick Owings. "We would meet backstage after a bad performance and try to figure out what had gone wrong, and Tom would somehow change every defeat into a victory. He'd say, 'Well, that bit killed,' or 'They really liked that part,' and I'd stand there thinking that was not what had happened. I'd been in the audience and seen the reaction, people going back to their conversations and just ignoring the act. It was one of the things that kept him going. Tim was much more realistic, and much more pessimistic."

Dreesen hadn't been able to help himself, had never even considered trying. Barely a year after he and Reid had started performing, he walked into his boss's office and said he was quitting. "How you can do this?" asked the president of Columbus Mutual, who flew to Chicago expressly to see him. "You're a member of the Million Dollar Round Table. You have vested renewals in your pocket. You've laid the foundation for a great career. How can you give it up for something as precarious as show business?"

Dreesen had no answer, certainly none that made sense. "The only thing I could say was that I had the bug," he says. "The first time I wrote 'professional entertainer' on my income tax form, it hit me. This is what I wanted to do, what I *had* to do."

So while Reid drove them to out-of-town jobs in his own car or his company car, and often paid more than his share of expenses, Dreesen became the engine that kept Tim and Tom running. He chatted up managers, agents, club owners, and local television producers. He wrote thank you notes, went to parties, frequented restaurants and bars where entertainers hung out and discussed upcoming auditions and potential bookings. He searched the papers to find which black headliners were coming to town, then called the clubs where they were appearing to ask if they needed an opening act. "I was always selling the act," Dreesen says. "As far as I was concerned, everybody was somebody who might book us. To this day, when I'm on an airplane I'll ask the guy next to me, 'What do you do?' If I'm in first class, it might be somebody who runs a company and will need a speaker for a corporate event some time. Before the flight is over he knows exactly how to get in touch with me."

"I don't talk to people on planes," says Reid with a laugh. "I won't even talk to my wife. Tom could walk into a room full of strangers and twenty minutes later he'd be introducing them to someone like he'd known them for a year and a half. I could be in a room full of strangers for four days and walk out not having spoken to one of them. I don't know what it was in my past that made me that way—being an only child, maybe—but I regret it. There are people I've met in show business I would have liked to know better. But I only returned the friendship I was offered to a few."

And so Dreesen became the act's manager/agent/publicist/promoter. Tim and Tom was his twenty-four-hour obsession, one that overwhelmed every other aspect of his life. Maryellen's angry reaction when he quit his job was followed by weeks of sullen silence and then, one day in the dead of winter, an announcement she was leaving. It was the first of more break-ups than he could count over the next twenty-five years — some lasted a few days, some much longer — and he called the one person he knew would understand.

"I picked up the phone and heard him say, 'Tim . . . Tim . . . Tim . . . It's Tom . . . Tom . . . Tom . . .'" Reid says. "I said, 'Where the hell are you? In an echo chamber?' He said, 'The bitch . . . bitch . . . bitch . . . took everything . . . everything . . . everything . . .' I said, 'I'll be right over.'"

"Look at this," Dreesen said as they walked through the empty house. "She even took the toilet paper."

"I couldn't help it," Reid says. "I just started laughing. There was nothing in that house, not a toothpick. She'd cleared it out so completely that everything you said echoed off the walls."

"What am I going to do?" Dreesen said.

"Let's throw a divorce party," Reid said. "We'll tell everybody to bring a piece of furniture."

Dreesen's friends showed up with whatever household items they could spare. "I brought a lamp, other people brought furniture and dishes, and so on," Reid says. "But nothing matched. Every item in the house was different. There were no two chairs alike, no two plates, no two forks. It was a great party, though."

Later that week, Reid was driving them back from meetings downtown where they had tried to scare up some work when he noticed something. "Where's your coat?" he asked.

"I don't have one," Dreesen said.

"What?" said Reid, who was bundled up against the subzero temperature in a heavy coat, scarf, and gloves. "You don't have a *coat*? Here, take this one. I've got another coat."

"I wore it for a long time," Dreesen says. "It was warm, and nice looking, too."

Some time later, Dreesen moved into his brother Glenn's attic. Reid began calling him Cinderella. And he became affected by Dreesen's plight. "I was feeling some of his hopelessness, too," he says.

Reid's immediate supervisor at DuPont was Jack Boyd, who had the charm and the looks of a young Sean Connery and soon became his friend as well as his boss. Sitting in Boyd's office one day, Reid pointed to a picture on the wall and asked, "When was that, Jack? I didn't know you played the guitar."

"Yeah," Boyd said, a dreamy tone coming into his voice. "I used to be pretty good. Remember *Hootenanny,* the television show? I was on it a few times. I really thought I was going to have a decent career as a folk singer."

"No kidding?" Reid said.

"Yeah, I had to make a decision . . . I often wondered what my life would have been like if I'd followed my dream . . ." and the room grew silent.

"I saw the pain in his eyes," Reid says, "and I remembered Rita's father's regrets about not going to New York to see if he could make it as a drummer. He would play his drums once a year, on the Fourth of July in the backyard, and he would beat on them until he was exhausted. It was the only time his wife would allow him to play them. He did it every year until he died. I said to myself, 'I'm never going to say that. I'm never going to wonder what it would have been like if I had followed my dream.'"

Slowly, Reid began to make up his mind. He had his family, his home in the suburbs, his well-paying job with a bright future. He had the peace and security of the middle-class existence he had longed for. And he was still bored. Show business, for all its frustrations, was thrilling. The emotions it created were so raw and intense. If his experiences so far had shown it to be more a dream than reality, the potential payoff could make it all worthwhile.

"It was a fantasy without any boundaries," Reid says. "Everything was possible, whereas in my early life so little was possible. And I still had that fear of abandonment I'd felt as a child. I think one of the reasons I stayed beyond any rational limits is I didn't want to throw away the one opportunity I had. For both Tom and me, it was our backgrounds that kept us going as much as anything else. We had both struggled so much. If we'd been raised in the middle class, we probably would have quit. There were so many times when I thought, 'Maybe this is it. Maybe we'll never work again.' But then somebody would call and we'd get a job and for a little while I would forget the pain."

But even beyond the excitement of show business, and the desire to see if it could somehow be made to work, Reid came to understand there was another factor at work. "I realized that Tom was not only the first white friend I'd ever had, he was my first major friend, period," he says. "We shared everything— the pain, the success, the failure, the glee—all the things you share with a brother or a sister, a wife or a lover. We'd seen each other at our worst and at our best. We'd seen each other in ways nobody else had ever seen us. And when we went out on the road, we created a different world, with our own rules. When it worked, there was no greater feeling in the world, on stage or off."

If only, Reid thinks, he could have taken more pleasure in those moments when they came. "I didn't enjoy it as much as I should have," he says. "I didn't always allow myself to appreciate the good times. I spent too much time anguishing over the failures. We really did have fun—I see that now—but at the time I was too caught up in the frustrations. It makes me angry at myself."

"I wish he could have enjoyed it more at the time," Dreesen says, "but I think one of the things that kept us going even in the lowest moments was the fact that we could share it. I remember coming off stage when we bombed more than once and it looked like the end of the road. Had it been just me, I might never have gone up there again."

"Hey, would you look at this?" Dreesen said one day about a year after they began performing. "There's a blurb about us in *Jet* magazine."

"Never mind that," said Reid. "Look what I've got here, a letter from Craig Tennis."

"Craig Tennis at *The Tonight Show* wrote you a letter?"

"I sent him a tape. He says, and I quote, 'Enjoyed your material. If you're ever in New York, stop in and see me.'"

"Any reason we can't be in New York tomorrow?"

"None that I can think of."

They took a Greyhound Scenicruiser, sitting upstairs in front of a group of nuns who farted throughout the trip. "They stunk that bus up all the way to New York," Reid says. "Everybody thought it was us and we wanted to say, 'Hey, it's the penguins back here.' I never really did like nuns."

A day later, they left their cheap hotel and walked to NBC's imposing headquarters at Rockefeller Center for their appointment with Tennis, a senior producer for *The Tonight Show*. But as they sat in the waiting room, they realized they had arrived in the midst of some sort of crisis—worried faces, raised voices, hasty phone calls, people running back and forth between offices. Finally, after half an hour, somebody said, "Craig's got a problem. It'll be a while before he can see you," and hurried off.

"What do you think's going on?" Dreesen whispered.

"Damned if I know," said Reid, and they sat watching the flurry of activity.

"Thank you, guys, sit down," Tennis said when, after another half hour, he called them into his office. "Ah, that damned woman."

*That damned woman? What?*

"Tell me," Tennis said, looking at Reid. "What is going on with your people?"

*My people? Uh-oh . . .*

"Nina Simone just walked off the set," Tennis said. "She said she wouldn't do the show because we didn't have any black production people on the floor. We've got nobody to replace her and it's on me because I'm the one who booked her. Shit . . . All right, you're a black and white comedy team. Make me laugh."

*Make him laugh? Now?*

"We had no chance," Dreesen says. "We went into our routine and he looked at us like we were morons. He had his head in his hands and it just kept slumping farther and farther down. By the end of the bit, his head was on the desk."

"Guys, you're not ready," Tennis told them.

It was a long, silent trip back to Chicago.

Television was the holy grail. For all the times they had appeared on shows in Chicago, they knew they needed to get noticed nationally if they were going to move onto a larger stage. Was having their own show—a situation comedy or a variety show—out of the question? Diahann Carroll, Bill Cosby, and Flip Wilson had been given their own television series one after another between 1968 and 1970 and the world had not come to an end. Though those performers seldom dealt with any challenging material about race relations—the sort of thing that was Tim and Tom's bread and butter—they proved that things were changing. Or was there something different between a show starring a black performer and one built around a black man and a white man working together? Was what they represented another kind of taboo?

And so they kept trying, returning to New York again and again, going to auditions they had heard about, or simply showing up at studios on the off chance something might be available.

"Now if she asks us what we're doing in town," Reid said before a meeting early in 1971 with Ann Jackson, who booked acts for *The Merv Griffin Show*, "we'll tell her we're doing a gig and thought we'd stop in."

"Why don't we just tell her the truth?" Dreesen asked.

"We can't do that. It doesn't sound professional."

"Well, what if she asks us what gig?"

"She's not going to ask us that. They don't do that to professionals. Look, never mind. I'll handle it. You just be quiet."

No sooner had they sat down with Jackson than she asked, "So what are you guys doing in town?"

"We're doing a gig," Reid said.

"Really? Where?"

"Um, a college."

"A college? What college?"

"Um, um . . . what college, Tom?"

"Um, um, um . . . ," Dreesen said. "Um . . . Hofstra."

"That's *right*," Reid stood up and shouted as Jackson looked at him dumbfounded. "*Hofstra!*"

"Where did you come up with that?" Reid said when they were back out on the sidewalk.

"I was in the navy with a guy from Long Island who went to Hofstra." Dreesen said. "I had to say something, didn't I?"

Occasionally, Vince Sanders would drive to New York with them, hoping he could use his contacts to find them work. "Here, look at this," Sanders said one morning in the spring of 1971, reading the paper as they sat in the hotel lobby. "It says here my man Gene Ammons is playing at Small's Paradise. Maybe he'll let you work a night or two up there with him." Reid and Dreesen were skeptical but they had worked with Ammons, a top jazz saxophone player, at several Chicago clubs and had even done a show for him at the Joliet prison where he was sentenced to hard time for possession of a small amount of marijuana.

The famous Harlem nightclub was rocking that evening as Ammons led his group through one up-tempo number after another. Sanders sent word they were there and soon they saw Ammons motioning them to a table in the front of the room. "We've got a couple of funny guys here tonight," he told the audience between songs. "Tim and Tom, take a bow."

"Hey, this is going to work," Reid thought, and he sat back and enjoyed the rest of the show.

"How you doing, Vince?" Ammons said when he joined them after the set. Then, turning to Reid and Dreesen, he said, "I'm so glad to see you guys again. Listen, do you think you can get me any work?"

They met with managers who brushed them off. They tried out at the Improv in New York, one of the first of the comedy clubs that were about to become popular around the country, where they found the facilities appalling and were shocked when other comedians heckled them. "Maybe they thought we were trying to take advantage of being an interracial act, that we were using race as a gimmick," Dreesen says. "But we didn't run away. We stayed and watched them work. We were jealous that New Yorkers had a place to try out material. There was nothing like that in Chicago."

"Today, there are comedy clubs in every city," Reid says. "There are guys making $150,000 a year working little clubs nobody's ever heard of. There was none of that back then. There was no place for us to be bad."

But for all the failures, there was always one more tantalizing glimmer of hope to keep them going. Walking down a street in midtown Manhattan late in 1971 after yet another rejection by *The Tonight Show*, Reid looked up and saw a sign that said *The David Frost Show*.

"Ready to be a salesman?" he asked.

"Let's make a cold call," Dreesen said, and they went inside.

"We'd like to meet the talent coordinator," Dreesen told the receptionist as if it were the most natural request in the world. "We're the comedy team of Tim and Tom."

"Do you have an appointment?"

"No, but they'll want to see us. We're from Chicago."

"Chicago!" came the voice of a black man who happened to be walking through the far end of the room. "Really? I'm from the South Side. I'm Ken Reynolds and I'm the talent coordinator. What do you do?"

*A black man from Chicago was the talent coordinator for one of the top daytime talk shows on television!*

"Um, we're a comedy team."

"A black and white comedy team from Chicago? You're kidding me. Are you funny?"

"Yeah, we're funny."

"Come on back to my office and do a quick something."

"He made the mistake of letting us get close to him," Dreesen says with a laugh. "There was no way we were going to let him get away."

After a bit of old-home week ("You know the Dells? Really? How's Marvin doing?") Reid and Dreesen did a few routines until Reynolds stopped them, said, "I think they're auditioning for the show right now" and picked up the phone. "Yes, they can come down," he told the stage director. "Come on, guys. Let's go." Fifteen minutes later, they were auditioning in front of a live audience and shortly thereafter performing before a studio audience for a show that would air a month later.

It was a euphoric ride home in Reid's company car as they took turns telling each other how well they'd done, how hard the audience had laughed, how receptive Frost had been when they sat next to him on the set and chatted after their performance. Everyone who saw the show—agents, scouts, club owners, bookers for other television shows—was bound to see them. This was it, the break they'd been waiting for. They began discussing places to hold a party celebrating their first appearance on national television.

When they got home, Reid made the decision he had been moving toward—he quit his job. "I had to," he says. "I was supposed to be working and there I was in New York, where I'd driven the company car, on national television. Somebody at DuPont, or one of their wives, was bound to see me and they'd have to fire me. I hated to admit it but Vince was right. Either I was in or I was out. I couldn't have it both ways."

Rita's parents were outraged. "They came up to Chicago to try to convince me not to quit," Reid says. "Our daughter Tori had just been born and Rita couldn't work for a month. They were sure I was taking their daughter into poverty, especially her mother." His own father thought he had lost his mind, too, and his mother, who was living with him at the time, was furious.

But we're going to make it, he told them. We're on our way. You'll see. "I wasn't frightened because I knew that after *The David Frost Show* we were going to be big stars," he says. "I felt like I was making a brilliant decision. My personal fear of failure was absolved because we were going to be on national television."

The only member of the family who supported his decision to leave DuPont was the only one who really mattered. "If that's what it will take to fulfill your dream, then you have to do it," Rita said. "I'll be back at work soon. We'll have enough to live on. We'll be fine."

"She had that old-school upbringing, that stand-by-your-man attitude," Reid says. "Looking back on it now, it amazes me because I was giving up so much for something that had such little chance of success. I can never repay her for that."

Reid and Dreesen spent the intervening weeks making lists, calling people, mailing cards with the details of their appearance on the show to everyone they knew in show business. They sent out pictures, planted blurbs in the Chicago papers, did everything they could think of to spread the word. Finally, they thought. This is it. As the air date approached, they were almost delirious with anticipation.

And then nothing. No phone calls. No job offers. No difference in the response of club managers and TV bookers. *The David Frost Show* had come and gone. It was as if nobody had seen it, as if they had never even been on it. They were devastated.

Though he was now without the job that had paid him more in a year than he would make in the entire five-year collaboration of

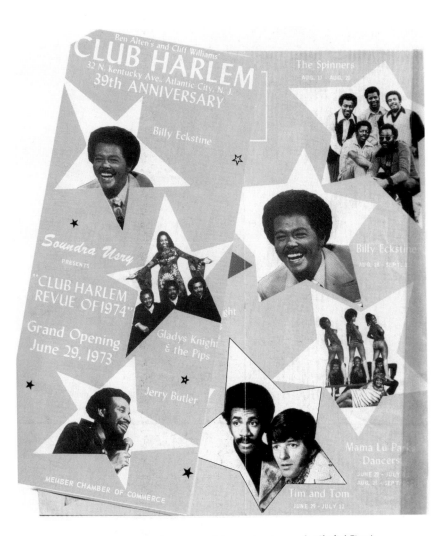

Club Harlem in Atlantic City was one of the premier stops on the Chitlin' Circuit, a loose confederation of black owned and operated nightclubs around the country. Tim and Tom were thrilled when they were booked there in 1973.

Tom Dreesen, age ten in this picture, was one of eight children who lived with their alcoholic parents in a cold-water shack near the railroad tracks in Harvey, Illinois. "We were raggedy-ass poor," Dreesen says. "To this day, some of my brothers and sisters can't talk about it."

Tim Reid, shown here at thirteen with his mother and a neighbor's child in Baltimore, was shuttled from the home of his heroin-addicted stepfather to his grandmother's boarding house, to his aunt's whorehouse, and finally to his father's home in Norfolk, Virginia. "I was a bastard child," Reid says. "I always had a fear of abandonment."

Taking their Junior Chamber of Commerce anti-drug campaign to Ascension
Catholic elementary school in Harvey, Dreesen's alma mater, in 1968.
After one presentation, a student said, "You guys are so funny. You ought to
be a comedy team."

At one of their first performances near Chicago in 1969. As Tim and Tom worked before black, white, and integrated audiences, they could never be sure whether the reaction would be a standing ovation, a racist heckling, or worse. Those dinner jackets are powder blue.

Performing before 10,000 people at the first Black Expo at the Union Stock Yards in Chicago in 1969. Tim and Tom went on after Stevie Wonder and before Howlin' Wolf. "You could just see people thinking, 'Who are these guys?'" Reid says.

With Jesse Jackson, Ralph Abernathy, and the singing group the Dells at the 1971 Black Expo in Indianapolis where crowds mobbed the celebrities as they left the hall. "When they opened the doors for us," Dreesen says, "people yelled, 'Who is it?!' Then somebody saw us and said, 'Oh, it ain't nobody.'"

Performing at Mr. Kelly's in Chicago. Those leisure suits can mean only one thing: it was the '70s.

Their "Dating Game" routine was always a big hit, particularly in prisons. Dreesen played the woman—if no wig was available, a mop would do—trying to choose between three men, all played by Reid.

Dreesen's big break came in 1975 when he was booked on *The Tonight Show*.
During subsequent visits, he would sit next to Johnny Carson and think it was as
if God had said, "Tommy, I'm going to put a load on you the first half of your life,
a real load. But if you survive, the second half is on me."

After Reid's star turn as Venus Flytrap on *WKRP in Cincinnati* made him a household name, he suggested Dreesen for a part in an episode in 1982. "It was like being at the finish line of a race we hadn't run," Reid says.

Dreesen was Frank Sinatra's opening act from 1982 until the singer stopped performing fourteen years later. Here they are at Bally's in Las Vegas in 1988.

Reid and his wife, Daphne Maxwell Reid, surrounded by the cast of *Frank's Place* in 1987. Set in a fictional New Orleans restaurant, it was a critical hit but was cancelled after only one season. It regularly appears on lists of "shows too good for television."

Tom Dreesen today. He works more than 200 days a year as stand-up comedian, toastmaster, host of corporate and charity functions, and motivational speaker. "You can drop Tom out of a helicopter anywhere in the world," David Letterman says, "and as soon as he hits the ground he'll quickly assess the situation and do a top-notch show."

Tim Reid today. As an actor, producer, and director, he has for decades been
at the forefront of black artists breaking out of the roles they have traditionally
been assigned in the movies and on television, on and off the screen.

The bright lights of show business.

is guaranteed success in this business," Reid says. "I don't care how talented you are. It's very whimsical."

"We just didn't know what it took to make it in show business," Dreesen says. "And you know what? All these years later, I still don't know. I was once on a plane with Suzanne Somers to Canada where we were going to do a show and she said, 'Tommy, you're a comedian. Look at this script and tell me if it's funny.' I read it and I said, 'This is probably the most unfunny thing I've read in years.' It was *Three's Company*. So maybe we shouldn't have been so hard on ourselves. Somebody once said success is an idea whose time has come. Nobody really understands it."

But there was something else, too, something they were slow to pick up on: the one thing they were counting on to propel them to stardom wasn't enough. "Every act has to have something different about it, some uniqueness," Dreesen says, "and who was more unique than we were? What we didn't realize was that you had to have talent to go along with it. That was a shocker. We saw that saying it was just the racial nature of the act that was holding us back was the easy way out. It was harder to say that maybe we just weren't good enough."

As they agonized over what was lacking, they developed new routines, worked on their timing, pushed for greater consistency. "I just wish we had been able to afford some writers," Dreesen says, "a few old pros who could have helped us turn the racial turmoil that was going on in the country into better material, something more socially poignant. If we'd had real hot material when we were on David Frost, we might have made more of a splash. We were too green to do it by ourselves. But suppose we had made it as a team. Suppose we had gotten a regular show on television. Can you imagine what our take on the O. J. Simpson trial might have been? Or Jimmy the Greek's rant about black athletes being genetically superior to whites? Or Michael Richards's racist tirade that night at the Laugh Factory?"

"I look at what has happened in show business in the last thirty years and it amazes me that there aren't two young guys out there today making a fortune doing what we did," Reid says. "Look at the comedy movies they've made with a black man and a white man. Gene Wilder and Richard Pryor; *48 Hours*, which launched Eddie Murphy's movie career; *Rush Hour* and all the others. They keep making them over and over again and it works. Audiences have become used to the idea by now. So why isn't there a comedy team doing it? You'd need talent and good writing and exposure, of course, but the upside would be unbelievable. It's just one more thing about show business I don't understand."

Reid got a glimpse of what the future might have held for Tim and Tom years later when he became a regular contestant on ABC's *Battle of the Network Stars* and became friendly with its host, Howard Cosell. One show was taped shortly after one of the biggest crises of Cosell's career—his calling Alvin Garrett, a black running back for the Washington Redskins, "a little monkey" during a *Monday Night Football* game. My God, he looks terrible, Reid thought as he spoke with Cosell while the camera crew set up. It's as if he's aged ten years. "Nobody said anything about it on the set, though. It was like the elephant in the room."

Finally, the shot was ready and Cosell said, "I'm here with Tim Reid, who will be running the obstacle course in today's competition. How are you, Tim?'

"I'm fine, Howard," Reid replied. "You little monkey."

"I thought he was going to spit out his dentures," Reid said. "He'd gone through all the criticism, now he needed somebody to laugh with him about it. Every time I saw Howard after that he would come up and we'd laugh some more. It was a small thing, but it was positive. I think that's the kind of thing Tom and I could have done more of if we'd stayed together."

Their inexperience also kept them from understanding that while club owners and audiences could see the unique nature of their act at a glance, they did not always know what to make of it. Was Dreesen supposed to be a hip, ultra-liberal white person or a racist? Was Reid a militant black man or an Uncle Tom? Maybe they'd go over better if they *did* conform to easily recognizable stereotypes. Maybe the very equality they were trying to project was holding them back. "They couldn't pigeonhole us," Dreesen says. "That hurt us, I think."

There were also times when age-old reactions to who they were overcame any understanding of what they did. Once, before an appearance on a cable television show, Dreesen visited Reid in the makeup room to go over their routine and was astonished at what he saw. "The woman kept making his face darker and darker, until it was completely black, at least three shades darker than his skin," Dreesen says. "I never saw anybody made up like that."

"All you could see were my eyes and the rouge she put on my lips," Reid says. "Red lips and eyes, that's all. I looked like a pickaninny. I said, 'Damn woman, I know I'm black, but what is *this* about?'" And he got up, walked over to the sink and washed his face.

"Sammy Davis Jr. explained it to me years later," Dreesen says. "He said he used to wear black face, that the black acts in vaudeville had to pretend to be white men pretending to be black men. It was the only way white people would accept black people doing comedy."

In the end, perhaps the most important thing that kept them going was Chicago. The city gave them regular employment, a reasonably high profile, and, more and more often, good notices. "Watching Tim and Tom work is like watching a great Ping Pong match," one critic wrote in a tribute to the timing they had worked so hard to master. They almost cried when they read it. "Café comedy delights of the year," wrote another. "Bring them back as headliners," said a third. And "This team will be around for a long time." Bruce Vilanch, an entertainment writer for the *Chicago Tribune* who would later go on to a sparkling career as a comedy writer and actor, also gave them glowing notices and they continued to receive regular mentions in Irv Kupcinet's column in the *Chicago Sun-Times*. Increasingly, they became part of the entertainment fabric of the city and continued to work in every possible venue with every conceivable type of performer. All of whom seemed to have something to teach them.

Late in 1971, sitting in the makeup room at the studio where Kupcinet's television show originated, Reid was suddenly aware that Jack Benny was in the chair next to him. "Two people brought him in and carefully put him in the chair," he says. "He was so pasty-faced and frail he looked like a ghost, as if he had an hour to live. He kept slumping down in his chair, napping, and they had to hold his head up to put on his makeup. I felt so sorry for him."

"Listen, Tom," he said, "we have to be respectful of him during the show, make sure we give him the time he needs to talk to Kup."

Dreesen agreed and a little later, as Benny was led slowly into the studio and sat asleep in his chair, the set grew quiet. "Shhh, don't wake him," somebody said, and a painful silence lasted until the director started his countdown and the band began to play an opening theme.

"Welcome to Kup's Show," Kupcinet said into the camera. "My guests today are the Moondog and Muledeer Medicine show, Chicago's own comedy team of Tim and Tom, and the legendary Jack Benny."

Reid turned to look at Benny and could not believe what he saw. "It was like someone else had possessed his body," he says. "He looked to be about fifty years old. As soon as the introductions were over, he immediately told a joke and everybody laughed, including us. Then he told another one and people cracked up again. This went on and on until Kup said, 'We'll be right back,' and we realized we had not said a single word. His energy had filled up the entire segment. During the commercial, I said, 'Damn, Tom, we've got to say *something!*' Luckily, it was an hour show and we were able to get in a few words. Then when the show was over, Benny slumped back in his chair until the two guys came and led him out of the room. It was one of the most amazing things I ever saw."

But for every Jack Benny they worked with, there was a Billy Falbo to show them the other side of the show-business coin. A comic who started in burlesque, Falbo scuffled to make a living for years and left no more enduring legacy than appearances in *The Adventures of Lucky Pierre* and *Living Venus*, two early sex-farce movies in the 1960s. Dreesen and Reid ran into him on one of Kupcinet's Purple Heart Cruises on Lake Michigan.

"Just before the boat docked, Billy started putting towels, ashtrays, all the leftover box lunches, and everything else he could find into a suitcase," Dreesen says. "It looked as if it would take two guys to carry it. He saw me looking at him and he said, 'This may be a benefit for you guys, but it ain't a benefit for me.'"

"You know what you need?" Harry Breen, a veteran Chicago agent who occasionally found Tim and Tom local bookings, told them early in their career. "A song."

"A song?" Dreesen said. "Harry, we're a comedy team."

"Lots of comics have songs," Breen said. "You come out, you sing something to break the ice—something like 'I want to be happy but I can't be happy till I make you happy, too'—and then you go into your routine."

Dreesen and Reid looked at each other. They were the novices, Breen was the old pro. What did they know?

"Here," Breen said, writing a name and an address on a piece of paper. "This guy writes special material. Go see him and tell him I sent you."

Arriving at an old apartment building in a run-down neighborhood, Dreesen and Reid knocked on the door and introduced themselves to the disheveled-looking man with nervous mannerisms who answered. "Harry Breen sent us," Dreesen said. "We're a comedy team and he thought you could write a song for us."

"Come on in," the man said, and he ushered them into a room that had dusty stacks of newspapers piled on every available surface and cobwebs hanging from the walls.

"Show business," Reid whispered as he looked around in disbelief.

This guy doesn't look right, Dreesen thought. Something's wrong here.

"Now, what is it you want?" the man said, sitting down at a beat-up piano in the corner of the room with a wild look in his eyes.

"Harry thought we needed a song to open the show," Dreesen said. "We're thinking that Tim's black and I'm white so maybe something about that, how we're comedians and we have a lot of fun together."

The man doodled on the piano a bit and then said, "How about this?" He played a bit of a tune, then stopped, stood up, waved the palms of his hands in front of his face, shook his head up and down and back and forth, and began to sing: "Niggers are fun to have around."

"We just about died," Dreesen says. "I'm not sure I've ever laughed harder in my life. And God bless Tim. Another brother might have killed the guy, but he just said, 'Thanks, but no thanks.' I think we both knew something was wrong with him. Later, we learned he'd been a performer and had suffered two nervous breakdowns."

Not long afterwards, they attended a publicity event where Dreesen sat at a table with Vince Sanders and a few other people. Looking up from his own conversation across the room, Reid caught his partner's eye and, mimicking the songwriter, waved his palms in front of his face, shook his head up and down and back and forth, and pretended to mouth a few words.

"We both came unglued," Dreesen said. "We couldn't stop laughing and nobody knew what it was about."

"What's that?" Sanders asked, looking puzzled. "Something from your act?"

"It could have been," said Dreesen.

"So you're from Chicago," Lee Magid said to Dreesen not long after he and Reid had returned from New Orleans in 1972. "Have you ever worked at Mr. Kelly's?"

"No," Dreesen admitted. It was the city's best-known club, located in the heart of the Rush Street nightlife district, and drew the biggest stars and hippest crowds. "We keep trying, but that's one place we can't get in."

"Well, I'm going to book you there in August," Magid said. "You'll open for Della Reese. And let's talk about cutting a comedy album. I've had some success with them lately."

Dreesen could hardly believe their good fortune. God bless that girl singer he'd met at the New Orleans Playboy Club for giving him Magid's card. And God bless Magid, who had started as a song plugger in New York and gone on to become one of the top managers and promoters in the music business, for thinking they were funny. A pat on the back for himself, too, if you please, for following up on the lead as he had on all the others, for writing Magid and selling Tim and Tom to him. And now Magid was not only going to book them into Mr. Kelly's—wait until the boys in the neighborhood heard about *that*—he was going to have them open for Della Reese, who had long been one of the top jazz singers in the country. This was good, very good.

"Let me ask you guys one thing," Magid said. "What are your vices?"

"Vices?" said Reid, startled by the question. "What are you talking about? We don't have any vices."

"Oh, yeah, that's right," Magid said. "You're nobody. As soon as you get some money, we'll find out."

If being on the same bill with Reese was exciting, watching her work was an education. "The crowds at Mr. Kelly's were mostly white, but there were black folks, too, and they all just adored her," Reid says. "She had a very clever way of maneuvering through the differences in the audiences. I really admired the way she appealed to everybody."

Reese herself was a delight. A dozen years older than Dreesen and Reid, she was friendly, funny, smart, and full of show-business stories, particularly about her early struggles, that both men could relate to. After many years of success as a singer, she was beginning to branch out, making guest appearances on television shows and even hosting her own syndicated variety show. This would prove to be the start of an entirely new career that would result in her starring role in *Touched by an Angel*, one of the longest-running hits on television, two decades later. Clearly, she was somebody they could learn from.

There was also a down-to-earth quality about Reese that made it seem like the most natural thing in the world when, discovering a tear in her dress one night, she asked Rita Reid if she had a needle and thread and made her own repairs between shows. And when she asked Dreesen to accompany her to a publicity luncheon.

"Chicago's your town," she said. "You can show me around."

"Great," Dreesen said, looking at Reid, who smiled and all but winked as if to say, "Good career move."

The first hint of a problem appeared after lunch when Reese and Dreesen went back to her suite at the Ambassador East. Relaxed and suddenly amorous, Reese made one suggestive remark after another and there was no doubt about what she was suggesting. The second hint came when Reese rolled a joint.

Though feeling uncomfortable, Dreesen tried to act cool, and not to insult her, by taking a few hits. Big mistake. "One thing I can't do is smoke grass," he says. "I've done it half a dozen times in my life and all it does is make me paranoid. I should do a bit about it in my act. 'Whenever I smoke grass I only know three words: *What was that!?*'"

Dreesen soon left the suite, feeling more than a little embarrassed and hoping Reese wasn't too angry at him. What could he say? She just wasn't his type.

An American Comedy in Black and White     *139*

"How did it go?" Reid asked before the show that night.

"Nothing, man," Dreesen said, feeling more uncomfortable than ever. "Believe me. Nothing went down."

A whole lot more than nothing, Reid thought, as he saw the tension between Dreesen and Reese. "Whenever they were together, you could sense the negative energy," he says. Reid, on the other hand, continued to find Reese fascinating.

"We were up till three or four in the morning," he told Dreesen the next day of his dinner with her at Papa Milano's, an Italian restaurant on State Street that was a late-night hangout favored by show people. "We have a lot more in common than I thought."

"Oh, really?" Dreesen said.

"Yes, really. She has a lot to teach us."

"Right," Dreesen said.

"Nothing *happened*, Tom," Reid said. "All we did was talk."

Sure, Dreesen thought, and let it go.

One of the things about Reese that appealed to Reid was the energy she devoted to her career and her ability to take it in new directions. "I had always really wanted to know a top entertainer, find out what makes one tick," he says. "And Della had done so many things. Starting as a gospel singer, moving on to jazz and rhythm and blues, acting on television, becoming the first black woman to host her own TV show. That's what my initial interest was in her, not romantic, but as somebody who had information I needed. She was one more strong woman in my life. I know she was a thorn in Tom's side, but she was a mentor to me."

Reid and Reese stayed in touch in the coming months. Just to be able to talk to someone who was having the kind of success he envisioned for Tim and Tom was comforting somehow. Her description of her life in Los Angeles, of the opportunities there and the contacts he could make, were particularly fascinating. If he was really interested in acting, she said, he should come out and visit her. It was not a bad idea, he said. He would think about it.

In the meantime, Reid and Dreesen continued working around the country and returning to Chicago where they often appeared at Le Pub on Clark Street, which Dreesen had convinced the owner, Henry Norton, to turn into the city's first regular comedy club on Monday nights. Along with their own routines, they took turns as emcees, introducing the other acts and telling jokes on their own. Le Pub soon became a magnet for other local comedians and Norton was pleased that as Dreesen and Reid talked up their comedy nights on the radio and in newspapers, the audiences grew. He was particularly delighted when, after a performance of her own one night, Della Reese appeared in the audience.

"You know what," Reese told Dreesen as they sat together while Reid was on stage. "*He's* funny."

"I know," Dreesen said.

"Yes, *he's* funny."

"I know. He's my partner."

"No, no, honey. He's *really* funny." And she turned back to watch Reid perform.

Dreesen's heart sank. "It suddenly dawned on me," he says. "She was saying, 'He doesn't need you.' She was saying what Marvin Junior had warned us somebody would say one day. That one of us didn't need the other. That one of us was holding the other back."

Reid's complaints about their lack of success began to occur more frequently now, and were more insistent. And Dreesen's positive attitude, his determination to soldier on, was becoming less effective at overcoming Reid's impatience. As he saw Dreesen continue to tinker with the act and develop as a comedy writer as well as performer, he realized yet again there was something he lacked. "The focus he had, the passion, it just wasn't as strong for me as it was for him," Reid says. "And after all we'd been through, I couldn't see us succeeding or making any money at it. Whatever it would have taken to move beyond where we were, I just didn't have it any more. I realized that I no longer believed in our dream."

The fact that Rita continued to be so patient as he and Dreesen struggled, and that she continued to provide the bulk of their income, made it seem worse somehow, made him feel like less of a man. "I couldn't take the failure and I couldn't adapt," he says. "I was angry all the time. I was not a nice person."

In June 1973, Reid received a telegram saying his father had died. He was fifty-six. His grandmother had died a few months earlier and he realized he had now lost two of the people who had meant the most to him growing up. "They were my rock, the ones I depended on," he says. "My grandmother died at a time when we were not working, when everybody in the family except Rita was still mad at me. Then, just as we were getting excited about landing the gig at Club Harlem we'd been after for so long, my dad died. I felt like I was on a roller coaster, and abandoned all over again."

During the gloomy trip to Norfolk, he realized there were practical matters to consider. How was he going to handle his father's funeral? Sit with his mother, who had raised him as best she could? Or with his father's wife, who had accepted him when William Reid took him in and gave him his name? Would he even be able to mourn in the midst of so much tension and emotion? He didn't know the half of it.

"As soon as we got to the church, two other women came up to me crying hysterically, and I remembered them from when I was nine or ten years old and my father would take me to dinner at their houses after church," he says. "The way they carried on made it clear to me that they still loved him." Then, during the funeral service, a grief-stricken young member of the choir — she appeared to be in her twenties — fell to the floor as three young children screamed "Mama!" and several men in the choir carried her out of the room.

"I started counting, there were one, two, three, four, five distraught women in that room, and the only one who wasn't crying was his wife," Reid says. All the women appeared to respect the position of Novella Reid, however, and there were no further outbursts, no confrontations, no recriminations. "Somehow, the ladies kept it together and paid their respects without crossing the line. I felt like a grief counselor."

Outside on the sidewalk, the emotion welled up again. "Yeah, it's all right, I understand," he told the two women he had visited as a child, trying to comfort them while at the same time looking for a ride for his mother to the cemetery and keeping an eye on his stepmother with whom he would make the trip. "The only one I couldn't talk to was the young girl in the choir, the one I was most worried about," he says.

Emotionally exhausted, Reid boarded the train for Atlantic City and reflected. He was making no real money, traveling around the country in pursuit of a dream, chasing women, not fulfilling his responsibilities, becoming someone he didn't want to be. He was becoming his father. He was traveling down the same road, making the same mistakes, causing the people he loved the same heartaches. The very thought of it made him even more depressed. He was going to have to make some changes, he thought, changes in his career and in his life. The only question was what those changes would be and when he would make them.

A few hours later, he joined Dreesen onstage at Club Harlem where they put on the show of their lives.

"Of course, you've got to do it," Rita, ever trusting, told Reid when he first mentioned visiting Reese in California. "She'll show you around, introduce you to people. It's a wonderful move for your career." And so Reid began traveling back and forth between two worlds. One of struggle and failure and a modest home in suburban Chicago, and one of almost unimaginable opulence and opportunity, and a gated estate on a hilltop in Los Angeles.

"To get to Della's house in Bel-Air, you had to drive past Sly Stone's house," Reid says. "Around the bend was the house where they shot *The Beverly Hillbillies* and then you'd go up the road past Johnny Carson's house to the top of the hill where she lived. Her place was beautiful, and huge—it had an indoor swimming pool—and was like nothing I'd ever seen. Suddenly, I was in Hollywood and it was everything I had imagined it to be. I fell in love with it."

Reese seemed to know everybody—actors, singers, musicians, agents, producers. They were at her pool parties and the glamorous events he accompanied her to, such as the NAACP Image Awards, which drew the biggest names in the black entertainment community. "I'd be sitting with Della and people would come over to talk to her—Sammy Davis Jr., Sidney Poitier, Diahann Carroll, and younger actors like Greg Morris of *Mission Impossible*," Reid says. "I had never thought I'd have the opportunity to meet any of them and here I was *talking* to them. Immediately, I began picturing myself doing what they were doing, becoming an actor more than a comedian. I was also being exposed to the business end of things, learning how they managed their careers, which was fascinating to me."

"It was all he talked about when he came back," Dreesen says. "Meeting Ed McMahon, going to places with Della. He had a whole new world opened up to him and it gave him a whole new attitude."

Reid and Dreesen continued working together, but as Reid returned to Los Angeles many times in the ensuing year, his very surroundings proclaimed what seemed more obvious with every trip. He had to start making the changes in his life and his career that he had started thinking about at his father's funeral. "I'd seen all the temptations now, all the pleasures," Reid says. "I was being exposed to things I had only dreamed about and I couldn't imagine going back to what I had. I had to make the sacrifices, take the ultimate risk. And I had to do it now."

The pressure and confusion he felt was compounded when, after a party one night, he and Reese began a brief affair. His flings with Playboy bunnies and the occasional woman who approached him on the road were one thing—they seldom lasted more than a night or two, or perhaps the length of an engagement—but this was different. A relationship with Reese would mean the end of his marriage because there could be no hiding it from Rita, who was loyal but also proud and certainly not stupid. How long would it take for her to realize what was happening?

Deciding to split with Dreesen was hard—how do you tell your best friend, your *only* friend, it's over after all they had been through together?—but the thought of leaving Rita was excruciating. "It was the abandonment thing all over again," Reid says, "but I didn't want to put Rita through what my father had put Novella through. I didn't want us to live that lie. And I made the decision that no matter how difficult it was I was going to have a relationship with my kids."

The last straw for Tim and Tom was an engagement at the Los Angeles Playboy Club early in 1974. "Once again, we had such high hopes," Reid says. "We had fought for it and fought for it. It was the one Playboy Club they wouldn't give us because they kept saying only the big acts worked there. We thought we'd go out there and just kill, that Hollywood would discover us. Then they finally let us in and we bombed every night. To me, that was the final trumpet call. I didn't know what else we could do, where else we could go."

The day after the Playboy Club gig ended, Reid, frightened and depressed, drove up to Reese's hilltop mansion, whose very luxury seemed to mock him, while Dreesen returned to the gloom of a Chicago winter. They still had a few contracts to fulfill, but they were for more of the same—low-paying gigs, with no promise of anything better down the road.

"What are you going to do?" Reese asked him.

"I don't know, Della," Reid said. "I just don't believe in the act any more."

The next day, she presented him with a poem she had written. "Dear Clown," it said in part. "You have what it takes to be a star. You have the humor and the manner to reach your dream.

There is a dressing-room door out there with your name on it."
He could only hope that it was true.

The bitter winter wind Chicagoans call the Hawk was flying
the day Dreesen took the train into the Loop from Harvey. His
car had broken down and he couldn't afford a cab so he shiv-
ered in the twenty-below wind chill as he walked more than
a mile from the Randolph Street station to a building at Rush
and Oak. It was completely dark when he arrived at five thirty
in the afternoon and found Alan Curtis, one of the agents who
occasionally found them jobs, alone in his office at the end of a
business day.

"Tim and I need some work, Alan," Dreesen said. "What
about it? Do you have anything for us?"

"I don't know, Tom," Curtis said. "You know I've always liked
you guys. I'll try to see what's out there, but I can't promise
anything."

Curtis interrupted the conversation to answer the phone.
"OK," he said. "Uh-huh. All right, I'll see what I can do." And
he hung up.

"Go get yourself another partner, Tom," Curtis said.

"What are you talking about?"

"Get yourself another partner."

"Are you crazy? I don't want another partner. Tim's my
partner."

"That was Tim on the phone. He wants me to look for work
for him in LA. For him alone."

It was all Dreesen could do to keep from crying. "I felt as if
somebody had punched me in the stomach," he says. "Walking
back to the station in the freezing cold, I felt all my dreams were
just flying away. It was like a marriage had broken up."

What was surprising about the last dates they were contractu-
ally committed to was how well they went. The breakup seemed
to remove the pressure from their performances, to absorb

the tension that had been building for so long. The warmth was gone from their relationship but they were civil to each other. Reid was already auditioning for acting roles and hanging around the Comedy Store in Hollywood in an attempt to establish himself as a solo comedy act. He still disliked doing stand-up, but Reese had said he could be her opening act once his split from Dreesen was final and he had to be ready. Lee Magid, with whom he had been squabbling over the failure of the Tim and Tom comedy album he had produced, was not happy about it, but Reese had insisted.

The end came in November 1974, at the Hyatt Hotel in Houston, and it was a disaster. Reese came in from Los Angeles for opening night—"It was as if she was making sure I wasn't going to talk him into staying together," Dreesen says—and Reid quickly got into an argument with the manager of the hotel.

"There are only four people here," Reid said as he looked at the audience for their first show. "You don't really expect us to go on, do you?"

"You guys have got a contract with me and, dammit, you're going on," the manager said.

"It was awful," Dreesen says, "although it did get a little better the next few nights. And that was it. We were through."

Immediately after their final performance, Reid and Reese flew to Los Angeles while Dreesen, defeated and depressed, went home. A few days later, with no place to go, nothing to do, Dreesen decided to follow them. Maybe there was something out there for him, too, he thought. Who knows?

**7**

True to her word, Reese booked Reid as her opening act at clubs in New York and New Jersey, and at a particularly rewarding gig at Mr. Kelly's in Chicago on New Year's Eve, 1975. Exactly six years earlier, before he'd had any idea of becoming a performer, Reid read in the paper that Richard Pryor was performing at the club and he and Rita drove downtown. Rush Street was mobbed with New Year's revelers, many of whom were braving the sub-zero temperatures in the line outside Mr. Kelly's.

"Now I'm a country boy and I don't know you're supposed to have reservations," Reid says. "The show had been sold out for six months and most people had reservations from *last* New Year's Eve. So we just walked past everybody in line, went in the exit door as somebody was coming out, and asked the maitre d' for a table for two. He looked at me like I was from outer space. 'You see that line?' he said and was about to give me a lecture and tell us to get lost. But just then the entrance door opened and people came rushing in and he got busy so we just stood there as the club filled up. Pretty soon, every seat was taken and I was pissed and wanted to leave, but Rita said, 'No, no, let's see what he says. Maybe he'll find us a table.'

"Finally, the maitre d' came over to us looking really angry and started giving me an education. He said 'Let me explain something to you,' and just then we heard off in the bar a loud slap and a woman cursing out a guy. He said, 'Baby, no, it's not like that,' but she grabbed her purse and walked out of the room and the guy followed her. The maitre d' said, 'Sir, are you going to be staying?' and he said, 'I guess not,' and left. The maitre d' glared at me and said disgustedly, 'Go sit down.' So we went in and sat at the elevated bar where we had a perfect view of the stage. True story."

Pryor's performance left Reid helpless with laughter—"When he gave birth to himself on one leg, I thought I was going to die"—and with a dream that seemed more like a fantasy. "I want to do that," he told Rita. "I want to do it on that stage on New Year's Eve." And now, opening for Reese, he was on the stage for Mr. Kelly's last New Year's Eve. The venerable club, which for years had hosted many of the top music and comedy acts in show business, closed its doors the following August and was replaced by another of the singles bars that were taking over Rush Street.

A series of concerts in South Africa that followed was a triumph for Reese, who insisted that blacks be admitted into auditoriums where she performed, as well as for the handsome, assured young black man who introduced her. "We were all honorary whites," Reid says, "which was certainly strange. So much of life in South Africa seemed so odd to me, in fact, that I worked it into my act. When we were in Johannesburg, for instance, they took me to what they said was the world's largest shopping mall, but it turned out to be no bigger than a department store. And although you could buy a television set, they didn't have any television *broadcasts* yet because the apartheid government was worried they might undermine its authority. And they had never seen an Afro like mine so I did a bit about how hard it was to find an Afro pick."

"The surprise of the evening," one critic wrote, "was young Tim Reid, who gave us a wonderful look at ourselves." Even Lee Magid, who hadn't thought he was ready to emcee such a big event, had to admit he had acquitted himself well.

Back in Los Angeles, there was also the excitement of his

first job in television, an appearance on the sit-com *That's My Mama*, although it brought with it a lesson of what lay ahead. At the audition, Reid was told he was not right for the part because he looked too much like the show's star, Clifton Davis. Disappointed, he returned to Bel-Air and was startled to find Davis among a group of visitors sitting by the pool.

"I just left your show," Reid said. "They had me reading for the part of Reverend Armbruster."

"No kidding," Davis said. "How did it go?"

"Pretty well, I think, but they said it probably wouldn't happen because you and I look too much alike."

"What?! You're kidding me. Hold on a minute," Davis said and he walked into the house and picked up the phone.

"I understand a young fellow named Tim Reid read for a part today," Reid heard Davis say. "How did he do? . . . Well, if he did well, are you going to hire him? . . . A resemblance? That shouldn't have anything to do with it. We do *not* all look alike, you know . . . All right, good."

Once Reid got the part, though, he had to play it and the prospect terrified him. Acting had been his goal for so long now, but he had not done any since college. Reese patiently helped him, going over his lines word by word until he was able to conceal his nervousness on the set. "It was not my finest hour, but I got through it," Reid says. His relief was tempered by the fact that, as had been the case with Tim and Tom, the breakthrough didn't lead to anything. He would not work in television again for two years, which was particularly galling because Reese was making sure he was getting to the right places and meeting the right people.

One night they went to a party at the home of the actor Darren McGavin where he was surrounded by celebrities and was seated at dinner between Cubby Broccoli, the producer of the James Bond movies, and Fred De Cordova, the executive producer of *The Tonight Show*. "I sat there thinking either one of these people could snap their fingers and change my life," Reid says. "But I didn't say a word. I didn't say, 'Mr. De Cordova, I've tried out for your show.' I didn't even say I was an actor. I mumbled a few things and hoped the subject would come up, knowing that Tom would have been all over them. As far as they were concerned, I was just Della's date, some young stud. I could see some of the wives looking daggers at me, as if to say, 'What is she doing with *this* guy?' It was the most depressing, painful evening I've ever spent."

How long could this go on? Reid wondered as he stood in line at the unemployment office. How long could he sponge off Reese, whose patience and kindness only exacerbated the guilt he felt about leaving Rita and the kids? The breakup, when it finally came, had been particularly traumatic because Rita had always been so trusting, so insistent that he follow his dream. He could never repay her for that. Rita had cried and cried, and taken to her bed for a week. "When Tim said he needed to be single and that he was moving to California permanently, I was just devastated," she says. "And I was so surprised. I thought everything was fine, that we had a great life."

Dreesen, who stayed in touch with Rita, was equally upset. Fooling around on the road was one thing. Who could resist the Playboy bunnies who came on to them as if they were rock stars? Aside from being gorgeous, most of them were bright, hip, and fun to be with. Talk about living the American dream. But leaving someone as loyal and supportive as Rita was a mistake he was sure Reid would regret. "It broke my heart," Dreesen says. "She was everything any man could want and more. I kept hoping they would get back together. I guess I was thinking of all the times Maryellen and I broke up and started over."

Reid pleaded with Rita to allow their two-year-old daughter, Tori, to live with him and his mother in Hollywood, where he rented a small apartment to use when he wasn't staying with Reese. But with Reid traveling and Tori crying to Rita on the phone every day, it didn't work out and she returned home. "I had sworn I wouldn't abandon my kids," Reid says, "but I didn't know how hard that would be."

He spent much of his time taking walks, staying high, and

feeling sorry for himself. To do something, *anything*, he would occasionally drive to the Comedy Store, the only place in town where unheralded comedians could get work, to try out new routines with Paul Mooney, John Witherspoon, and other young black comics he had become friendly with. "We always went on last, about 1 a.m," Reid says. "We called it the nigger hour. I would get out of bed a little bit high and drive down the hill in Della's powder blue Mercedes, go on last or next to last, and then drive back up the hill. I was living in the lap of luxury, but I felt homeless."

At the bottom of the hill, Dreesen felt homeless as well, and there was nothing luxurious about it.

"You can't stay here any more, Tommy," Pat Hollis told him. "It was fine while I was out of town, but I'm back now and my boyfriend is jealous."

"Pat, I've got no place to go," he pleaded. "Isn't there something we can do? I think I might be making inroads at the Comedy Store. I just need a little more time."

"He'll kill us if he finds out you're here, Tommy," Hollis said. "Look, I've got this little room in the back of the house by the alley. All it has is a mattress and a lamp. You can stay there, I guess. But if you see Gene's car out front, you can't come in. All right?"

"I'll be careful, Pat. Thanks. You don't know what this means to me."

Hollis, a singer he had met on the road, was a good friend, especially after he'd put her in touch with some club owners who had hired her. "You're coming to LA?" she said when he told her of his plans after his final performance with Reid in Houston. "I'm going to be out of town then. Why don't you house-sit for me until you find a place?"

"I'd never heard the term," Dreesen says. "In Harvey, if you were sitting in a house, you were burglarizing it."

But after three weeks, Hollis returned and nothing was happening. He had very little money, no job, no car, nothing to occupy himself other than walk from Hollis's small home in Brentwood to Sunset Boulevard and hitchhike into Hollywood where agents and managers had their offices. There, he would pass out his picture and his bio, schmooze the secretaries, and try to grab a minute with their bosses. Occasionally, he would see a few glimmers of hope—Herb Karp, a William Morris agent he met playing softball at a park in Sherman Oaks, liked him and his act—but nothing came of them.

"I didn't realize how *slow* things would be," Dreesen says. "I learned that when somebody in New York says they'll help you, they mean within the next sixty seconds. In Chicago, they mean sometime that day. In Los Angeles, they mean in the next couple of years. Maryellen and I had been talking about getting back together and I told her that as soon as I found something I'd come back for her and the kids. I was desperate."

The scene at the Comedy Store was particularly grim. There were so many comedians hanging around, most of them frantic for bookings, and the stakes were as high as the odds were long. The fact that scouts from all the major late-night and daytime talk shows were often in the audience only added to the tension. "Everybody would be whispering, 'Don Kane is here from *The Merv Griffin Show*,' or 'Vince Colandro is here from *The Mike Douglas Show*,' or 'Les Sinclair is here from *The Dinah Shore Show*,'" Dreesen says. "We knew all the names and when they were there."

ABC, CBS, and NBC also sent scouts looking for comedians to perform in situation comedies they were developing, and every once in a while somebody might show up representing the greatest showcase of all: *The Tonight Show*, which Johnny Carson had moved from New York to Los Angeles in 1972. Even performing at Open Mike Night, which was reserved for unknowns, could lead to bigger things. "We would all wait in line on Monday nights, hoping to get picked," Dreesen says. "Sometimes, a big car would pull up and Jimmy Walker would get out, or Freddie Prinze, who had been given his own TV series after just one appearance on *The Tonight Show*. They'd be there to see a friend perform and we'd all feel very small. David Letterman and I used to joke about Open Mike Night at the Comedy Store. He called it Pud Night."

Occasionally, Dreesen ran into Reid at the Comedy Store, where he told him about his own after-midnight struggles for recognition. "Go back to Chicago, man," Reid said. "It ain't going to happen. They're looking for eighteen-year-old comics now, not guys like us." Reid did introduce Dreesen to Kris Kenney, the assistant to Mitzi Shore, the club's cofounder who booked every act personally and could make or break a comedian's career simply by deciding whether or not to put him on stage. That was one thing a friend could do for a friend, at least.

Dreesen wandered the streets, nursed a bowl of oatmeal at Schwab's, the Sunset Boulevard restaurant that had once been a drugstore where legend said Lana Turner had been discovered. He hung around a nearby apartment belonging to the Burskys, the parents of a fledgling comic he had become friends with. Though they were hardly affluent, Helen Bursky always had a cup of tea for him, and perhaps a cookie. A few other comedians lived in the same building and they traded stories, read the trades, killed time. In the evenings, they went to Canter's, the famous "we-never-close" delicatessen on Fairfax Avenue, or Theodore's on Santa Monica Boulevard, where they would trade the latest gossip about which variety shows were looking for comedians and which sit-coms were hiring.

Afterwards, Dreesen hitchhiked back to Hollis's house and made sure her boyfriend's car was not parked in front before going in. If it was, he would walk to the gas station around the corner and wait for him to leave. Thank goodness he seldom spent the night. Maybe something would break tomorrow.

And then, in forty-eight hours, it all fell apart.

There was the letter from Maryellen. "This is your dream, not mine," she wrote. "I will never come to California. This is it, Tom, the final goodbye."

There was the visit to the office of Irving Arthur, an agent who had gotten Tim and Tom work in Playboy Clubs around the country. Julie, his sweet, chubby secretary, liked him and would turn her back when he stuck his head in Arthur's door to ask if he had anything. But this time Arthur was on the phone and was furious at being disturbed. "Get out of here!" he shouted. "Don't ever come in here unannounced again!" And he shoved him out the door.

Humiliated, and knowing he had gotten Julie in trouble, Dreesen walked to the elevator feeling sick to his stomach. A month of hitchhiking and sponging off people. Sleepless nights agonizing over a life without his family. One of the few agents in town who liked his work yelling at him. Things couldn't possibly get any worse. Could they?

Late that night, Dreesen returned to Hollis's house and though the block was lined with cars—somebody must be having a party, he thought—her boyfriend's wasn't among them. He went around to the back and let himself in.

"Who's that?!" somebody shouted from the front bedroom. "Pat, call the police!"

"Oh, Tommy, no!" Hollis said when she saw Dreesen, and she started to cry.

"Pat, I didn't see his car, I'm sorry."

"The block was parked up. He had to park three blocks away . . . Gene, he's just a friend. He's been staying here. He was house sitting . . ."

"A *friend*?! House sitting?!"

"It's not what you think," Dreesen said. "She's just a friend. She was trying to help me."

"Bullshit. If you're a friend, why didn't she tell me? I'm going to kick your ass."

"Listen to me, dammit! I'm a married man with three kids. It's the truth."

"The truth, my ass! And I'm going to kick *your* ass!"

"I keep telling you! She's just a friend trying to help a friend. She's a decent person. You're lucky to have her. But you don't want to hear it. You want to kick my ass? Fine, let's go out in the alley and see how tough you are."

"I lost it," Dreesen says. "After all that had happened, I was mentally and physically exhausted. I'd have killed him if he'd followed me out to the alley. I think he knew it, too, because he stopped yelling."

The door slammed behind him, then opened again long enough for Hollis to yell, "God damn you, Tommy!" and throw his clothes out into the alley. It was three in the morning.

All but weeping with frustration, Dreesen saw an old Nash Rambler up on blocks behind a house a few doors away. He had noticed it before while taking out the garbage and he walked over, opened the back door, and put his belongings inside. Then, remembering something about this particular make of car, he tried the front door. There it was, a lever under the seat that allowed it to fold down flat. He climbed inside, closed the door, and sobbed. How much lower could he go? He was thirty-two years old, not a kid anymore, and he was hitchhiking around town, begging for work. And he was sleeping in a *car!*

"I was so distraught I literally prayed," Dreesen says. "Some of the books I was reading then said that when you're at your wit's end, you should turn things over to God. And that's what I did. I said, 'I've done all I can do. I don't have a place to live. I can't get anybody to book me. So I'm going to sleep now and I'm turning it over to you. You'll have to manage my career.' At that moment, I felt a tremendous sense of relief, as if somebody had taken a boulder off my chest and help was coming. I slept like a baby that night."

For the next month, the Nash Rambler in the alley was Dreesen's home. "I'd clean up in the gas station and hitchhike to the Burskys or the Comedy Store," he says. "I'd eat once a day at Kentucky Fried Chicken where you could get two pieces of chicken and two small ears of corn for ninety-nine cents. They called it corn and cluck for under a buck and it kept me alive. To this day, when I go by KFC I genuflect."

Unaware of just how desperate his former partner's living arrangements had become, Reid invited Dreesen to Reese's house for Thanksgiving, where his surroundings, and his hostess, did nothing to lighten his mood. "Here I am with a bunch of celebrities, eating dinner in a house with an indoor swimming pool, and Della is coming around smiling and asking Tim, 'Is there anything else you need, darling?' I felt what she was really saying was, 'He's here and you're there and you're no longer a team.' Divide and conquer. I smiled and kept my mouth shut, but I took it very personally."

"All right, Tom, we've got a five-minute spot on Open Mike Night next Monday," said Kris Kenney whom Dreesen had tried to befriend without coming on too strong. "You know Mitzi likes to see how comedians do there before she thinks about booking them on other nights."

"I'll be there," Dreesen said, trying to hide the mixture of excitement and dread he was feeling. Five minutes at the only place in town where he had any chance of working. Five minutes that would determine if he would have to give it all up and return to Harvey. He hitchhiked back to the alley in Brentwood, and sat in the car, going over and over the routine he'd been working on until he had it down cold. All he could do now was wait.

Not a bad crowd for a Monday night, he thought, as he took the stage. But he was really performing for an audience of one, wasn't he?—Mitzi Shore, who stood in the back of the room. A sense of calm came over him then, a feeling of positive energy and confidence he hadn't felt in a long time. Maybe it was all the self-help books, or maybe it was his own natural optimism that had somehow survived the last five years. Or maybe it was the fact he no longer had anything to lose. He looked out at the audience, forced a smile, and launched into his routine.

"My name is Tom Dreesen and I'm originally from a suburb on the south side of Chicago called Harvey, Illinois," he said. "I was raised in what they called a changing neighborhood. It's really easy to tell when a neighborhood begins to change because McDonald's starts selling things like Chitlins McMuffin. The Big Mac becomes the Big Leroy. To me, it was like growing up anywhere else in America. You get up in the morning, you open up the window, you listen to the sound of little children talking to one another: 'I'm gonna break your face.' 'Oh, yeah. I'll cut you four ways, turkey—long, deep, wide, and repeatedly.' And that's just the girls jumping rope."

People were laughing now, laughing hard. Was there a sweeter sound in the world than an audience laughing at your jokes? There was not.

He told more stories—about Goochie, about going to Catholic school and the nuns there. About the kids in the neighborhood doing the dozens. It was amazing how many jokes you could tell in five minutes. Just as amazing as listening to people laugh the entire time.

". . . I said, 'That's right, I'm talking to you, Batman's wife.' She went, bam, bam. I said, 'Damn, baby. I was only fooling . . .'"

And then he was done, saying "Thank you very much," acknowledging the laughter, and walking off the stage. Where Mitzi Shore was waiting for him.

"You've worked before, haven't you?" she said. "You've got real stage presence. Maybe we can find something for you during the week."

"Thank you, that's great," Dreesen said, trying not to show his excitement. And then, almost instinctively, he raised the stakes. "You know, I've emceed before. I can do that—introduce other acts, do it on a regular basis."

"That's an idea now, isn't it?" Shore said. "We'll see."

His heart jumped at the thought of steady work. Of the chance to be a Comedy Store regular, one who could call in for a booking rather than just hang around hoping to be noticed. Of the chance to work his way up from the after-midnight shows to prime time, 8 to 10 p.m., and then to weekends, the most prestigious spots of all. It would all be for no pay, of course—nobody at the Comedy Store ever got paid—but you never knew who might be in the audience. It could be the break he had been waiting for.

Standing on the sidewalk outside the club chatting with a friend a few weeks later, Dreesen felt a tap on his shoulder and heard someone behind him say, "I enjoyed your act very much, young man. You're very funny."

"Why, thank you very much, sir," Dreesen said, turning around. "That's very kind of . . ."

*Holy shit! It's Carl Reiner!*

". . . very kind of you. That really means a lot to me. I'm such a big fan of yours."

"Well, good luck to you," Reiner said, and he turned away to talk to someone else.

"I'm Estelle Reiner, Carl's wife," said a woman standing next to him. "I think you're just adorable, and very funny."

"Oh, thank you," Dreesen said. "I really appreciate it."

"How long have you been working here?" she asked.

"Oh . . . a little while now. I'm trying to get established."

"And do you have a family?"

"Yes, a wife and three kids. They're in Chicago. I'm trying to get enough together to bring them out here."

"In *Chicago!* Carl, come here. I want you to hear this."

Reiner rejoined them and his wife said, "This boy has a wife and three children and they're living in Chicago and he wants to bring them out here so they can all be together. You've got to help him."

"I did help him, Estelle. I told him he was very funny."

"That's not helping him. He needs work. He needs a job. You have to *help* him."

Reiner laughed, put his arm around her, and then reached in his pocket. "Here's my card," he told Dreesen. "Give me a call tomorrow."

"I don't know how to thank you, Mrs. Reiner," said Dreesen after Reiner returned to his conversation.

"Don't bother," she said with a smile as she squeezed his arm. "Go see Carl tomorrow. He's working on a new television show. He plays an angel who comes down from heaven to answer people's prayers. They're filling some smaller parts. He'll have something for you." And she moved off to join her husband.

An angel who answers people's prayers, Dreesen thought, as he stood alone on the sidewalk. Imagine that. He walked a few blocks down Sunset until he was certain nobody in front of the Comedy Store could see him. Then he stepped off the curb and put his thumb in the air.

He was the old Tom Dreesen now—self-confident, organized, thinking ahead—and his mind was racing. The one-day shoot on Reiner's new sit-com *Good Heavens*—he and Rob Reiner, branching out from *All in the Family,* played softball players rushing their pregnant wives to the hospital—gave him his first paycheck as an entertainer since his split with Reid.

"Mr. Reiner, is there any way I could be paid right away?" Dreesen asked at the end of the day.

"Let me see what I can do," Reiner said, and Dreesen left the studio with a check for $500. "It might just as well have been $5,000," Dreesen says. "I was still living on a dollar a day."

At Theodore's, everybody seemed to be talking about *The Tommy Banks Show* in Edmonton, Canada, which flew in guest performers, many of them unknowns, first class and paid $500. He called Banks's wife, who booked the acts, and pretended to be an agent representing a bright young comedian named Tom Dreesen: "Yes, he's very funny. He's a regular at the Comedy Store and has been on *The David Frost Show* and he's just taped a sit-com with Carl Reiner."

He got the booking along with an agreement to fly him to Chicago instead of back to Los Angeles. He would see Maryellen and the kids, show her how well he was doing, try to talk her into coming to Los Angeles. He called Paul Wimmer, the manager of Mr. Kelly's.

"You're a single now?" Wimmer said. "Look, Tommy, I've got Fats Domino coming in for two weeks. You can open for him. But I've got to level with you. I can only give you $750 a week."

Seven-fifty a week for *two weeks!* It was a fortune, certainly enough to keep up appearances around town, to take the family out while he worked on Maryellen, and to see how Goochie, Tutu, Sammy Eubanks, Tommy Johnson, Mike Crowder, and the rest of the guys were doing. This was one road trip he was really going to enjoy.

"How are things in Hollywood, Tommy?" Doll Franks asked him one night in the Junction Lounge. "Are you doing OK?"

"I'm doing good, Mrs. Franks," he said. "I'm a regular at the Comedy Store now. TV scouts come by there all the time. You might see me on one of the late-night talk shows sometime."

"You'll let us know, won't you?"

"You know I will, Mrs. Franks. You'll be the first to know."

The kids were thrilled at the prospect of going to California, but Maryellen was wary.

"Where will we live?" she asked. "Do you have a place for us?"

"Oh, there are apartments all over," he said, not breathing a word of his current accommodations. He had a few dollars now. He would find something. How hard could it be? He piled their belongings in his brother-in-law's pickup truck and with Tommy Jr. sitting next to him headed west followed by Maryellen, Amy, and Jennifer in an orange Volkswagen. They were a family again.

Finding a place to live was brutal—he had no credit and who knew there were so many places that didn't accept children?— but finally the wife of an apartment manager in North Hollywood took pity on him. "Damn it, Harold, have a heart!" he could hear her yelling at her husband. "He has three kids!" Harold relented and said he could have a three-bedroom apartment for $225 a month. The money was going fast, especially after the nights they had spent in a hotel, but now that he had an address and a record of working in California he could apply for unemployment insurance. It would be tough for a while, but it was a start. And he had a manager now, too, Dan Wiley, whom he had met in Edmonton where he had accompanied his client, the singer Johnny Ray, to *The Tommy Banks Show*. Call me when you're back in LA, Wiley had said, and given Dreesen his card. They would remain together for more than thirty years on the strength of a handshake.

"You'll put me on as often as you can, Mitzi, won't you?" Dreesen begged Mitzi Shore, no longer even bothering to assume the air of casual confidence he tried to project with people who could help him. "I need all the work I can get."

"I know you do, Tom," said Shore, who, tough as she was, had a soft spot in her heart for young comedians so desperate to succeed. "Keep calling in. We'll have work for you. I promise."

He could feel it now. His act was getting better and better, and he was becoming more methodical, almost scientific, in his approach. He taped his performances and began counting the laughs. When he had a five-minute routine that received between twenty-two and twenty-six laughs, he would type it up and go over it again and again, polishing his timing. On stage, he would slowly work in new material. If he could get a laugh out of one new line, he would be thrilled.

"I can't do what you do, Tommy," Shecky Greene, the veteran comedian whose work he adored, told him one night. "I can't go out there and just go bing, bing, bing. It takes me five minutes to say hello."

Often Dreesen stood in the wings to see what he could learn from other comedians. It didn't hurt that other comedy clubs were beginning to open around town, including one in North Hollywood called Showbiz, where on any given night an audience might see Robin Williams, Jay Leno, David Letterman, Elayne Boosler, Gallagher, or Michael Keaton, and where one of the waitresses was an aspiring young actress named Debra Winger.

Dreesen was particularly fascinated by Letterman, whose material was so fresh and funny ("You know how toothpaste gets stuck in the sink and hardens? Well, it makes perfect after-dinner mints"), but who seemed oddly uncomfortable on stage. It was only later, when he saw Letterman on television, that he thought, "My God, he's home!"

"Dave cut his teeth as a TV weatherman and he's totally at ease there," Dreesen says. "But he doesn't really like stand-up. He's been offered tons of money to work Las Vegas or Atlantic City the way Jay Leno does, but he won't do it." Tim Reid was the same way, he thought. There are some comedians who just don't like doing stand-up comedy.

Dreesen was playing third base for the Comedy Store softball team at the park in Sherman Oaks one afternoon when he looked up and saw Craig Tennis in the coach's box for the team from *The Tonight Show*. "Um, Craig, it's Tom Dreesen," he said, reaching out to shake hands. "Tim Reid and I tried out for the show a couple of times."

"I remember," said Tennis, who had been promoted to head talent coordinator and was now in complete charge of booking guests. "How are you doing?"

"Fine, Craig," Dreesen said. "I'm a single now. I'm working at the Comedy Store a lot. Maybe I'll call you sometime."

"I'll keep that in mind," Tennis said noncommittally.

Several innings later, Paul Bloch, a *Tonight Show* producer, hit a long double to center field but, trying to stretch it into a triple, was thrown out on an excellent one-hop throw to Dreesen at third.

"You're out!" said the umpire.

"Out?!" Tennis shouted. "Bullshit! He was safe! He missed the tag!"

"All right," the umpire said. "He's safe."

"Safe?!' screamed Gabe Kaplan, the star of the popular new sit-com *Welcome Back, Kotter* who was pitching for the Comedy Store, as he rushed over from the mound. "What are you talking about?! You called him out!"

"He was safe, dammit!" Tennis yelled, and, as the argument continued, Dreesen wandered away.

"Tommy, what the fuck is wrong with you?" Kaplan hollered

at him after the argument was lost. "Why didn't you say something? He was out by three feet. He slid right into your tag."

"I know he was, Gabe," Dreesen said. "But you're already doing *The Tonight Show*. You're going to guest-*host The Tonight Show*, and that's Craig Tennis. So I don't care if he was out or safe."

A week later, sitting in the audience as Kaplan was substituting for Johnny Carson, Dreesen handed a note to an usher and asked him to give it to Tennis. "Dear Mr. Tennis," the note said. "My name is Pop Williams. I'm 88 years old and my vision is almost totally gone. I was sitting in the stands the other day when Paul Bloch slid into third base. Even from where I was sitting, I could see he was out by 30 feet."

Moments later, Tennis stuck his head out from behind a curtain and peeked into the audience. Dreesen gave him a little wave, and Tennis pointed at him and laughed. Dreesen grinned back, feeling more than a little proud of himself. He had made a connection.

"My God," Dreesen thought as he pulled up to the Comedy Store. "Who *are* all these people? There must be 150 of them. We never draw a crowd like this on a Tuesday night. Wait a minute. That's Norman Lear. And Carl Reiner. And all the network scouts. And there's Craig. What is going *on*?"

Tennis hadn't promised anything when Dreesen called to ask if he would come by and look at his act. "When I get a chance, Tom," was all he said. "Stay in touch." But then, a few weeks later, he called. "All right, I'm coming over there. I'm looking at three acts—you, a team named Baum and Estin, and a new comedian named Billy Crystal. He's supposed to be very funny."

Dreesen soon discovered that the size and prominence of the crowd was the work of Rollins and Joffe, the powerful management company that was putting all its resources behind Crystal, convinced he was on the verge of stardom. Still, he thought, the bigger the crowd, the better chance he had to get some energy going in the room. It wasn't the first time he had performed for an audience that had come to see somebody else. His luck really was turning now. He could feel it. And then he walked out onto the stage in a room that contained twenty-two people.

"They didn't bring all those people there to see another act, Tommy," Mitzi Shore told him. "They want all the emphasis to be on Billy. So they're keeping everyone outside until he goes on."

But by then he didn't care. Small crowd or not, his performance went well enough and there was only one reaction that really mattered. "Come see me in my office tomorrow," Tennis said when he came off the stage. "Let see what we can do."

"I liked your act, Tom," Tennis said the next day. "You did, what, twenty minutes? Show me the five minutes you would do for us."

Dreesen suggested a bit and Tennis said no. He suggested another one and Tennis said yes. And that one, too, he said. That was funny. Then, after a little more back and forth, Tennis said, "Good. You're on the show next Tuesday."

"I was on cloud nine," Dreesen says. "I went to the Comedy Store every night and worked on my routine. I called everybody I knew in Chicago, everybody I knew in show business, to tell them I was going to be on *The Tonight Show*. I couldn't sleep for a week."

He was living a dream now. A parking spot at the studio in Burbank with his name on it. A dressing room with his name on a little card on the door. ("I brought it home," Dreesen says. "I still have it.") The makeup room. The green room where the other performers and their friends hung out. The nervousness as the time approached. A good nervousness, though, the kind he had before every important performance. He was as ready as he'd ever be. And then . . .

"We're sorry, Mr. Dreesen. We're running out of time. Come back next week, OK?"

The deflated feeling on the way home. The calls to friends to say he wouldn't be on the show after all. The trips to the Comedy Store to polish the material to a razor's edge. The drive back to Burbank the following week. The parking spot. The dressing room. The makeup room. The green room. The nervousness.

Bumped again.

"That's the guy who got bumped," he heard someone say as he was leaving the studio for the third time. He looked up and found himself face to face with Johnny Carson.

"I'm sorry," Carson said. "But remember this. Flip Wilson got bumped five times and look what happened to him. Maybe it will happen to you."

"Hey, Tommy, Mrs. Franks has pulled the plug on the jukebox again," Tutu hollered over the phone from the Junction Lounge. "She says you're going to be on *The Tonight Show,* but it just started and they didn't mention your name. Are you going to be on that goddam show or not?"

"No, Tutu," Dreesen admitted. "I got bumped again."

"Hey, Tyrone!" Tutu yelled. "He got bumped again! Play E14!" And he hung up.

Thanks for the sympathy, you sons of bitches, Dreesen thought, and he laughed long and loud for the first time in weeks.

"I've got bad news for you," said Fred De Cordova, the producer of *The Tonight Show,* as Dreesen sat in the makeup chair for the fourth time. It was December 9, 1975.

"What?" Dreesen said, not sure he could bear to hear the answer.

"You're going on tonight," De Cordova said with a laugh. "Good luck."

He went back to his dressing room, sweating. A few minutes later, the door opened.

"How are you doing, Tommy?" Ed McMahon asked.

"Fine, Ed," he lied. "I'm doing fine."

"Remember to have fun" McMahon said. "If you're having fun, the audience is going to have fun."

"I'll have fun, Ed. Thanks."

He could hear Doc Severinsen's band playing as he made the long walk from the green room around to the back of the stage. This is like going to the electric chair, he thought. He could hear stagehands whispering, "First time. It's his first time," as he walked past them. He could see Tennis standing with Irv, the stagehand who had opened the curtain ever since *The Tonight Show* began.

"You ready?" Tennis asked.

"I'm ready."

"OK, babe. Break a leg."

"God, what's my first line," Dreesen thought as he paced back and forth. "Oh, yeah, right. I come out and I say . . . I've got it."

The music stopped, which was the sign the show was coming out of a commercial, and his heart stopped, too. Later, he would make a joke out of it: "All of a sudden you feel something nudging your Adam's apple, and you realize it's your asshole trying to get out."

He could hear Carson's introduction—so warm, so wonderful, all he could have asked for.

"We are back. Thank you, Doc. It's always fun to introduce somebody new to *The Tonight Show*, especially comedians because they are probably the hardest commodity to find. And I'm glad that you're in such a good mood tonight because this is his first national television appearance. Will you welcome him, please . . . Tom Dreesen."

The curtain opened and he blinked in the glare of the lights, which made him feel as if he was in an operating room preparing for surgery. He looked down to find the green T painted on the floor where he had been told to stand and, as the applause died down, he walked to the mark, smiled at the audience, took a breath, began.

"I didn't realize what a warm show this is. Just before I came out, three guys rushed up and said, 'Hey, have a good show,' and they all hit me on the rear end. Isn't that nice? Men do that all the time. Did you ever watch a football game? A guy 6-foot-9, 280 pounds scores a touchdown, the whole team gets around him and (turning away from the camera and patting himself on the behind) says 'Way to go.' What if women did that? Imagine the girls at the office. 'Gosh, Alice (patting his behind again) you type a great letter.'"

Hearing the initial laughs felt like being tackled for the first time in a football game, or being hit for the first time in the ring. They told him things were going well, gave him confidence, made him feel that, yes, he *was* having fun. Thank you, Ed McMahon.

He started talking about Harvey, bringing the audience into his world, getting laughs of recognition from people who knew all about changing neighborhoods and racial tensions.

"Did you ever watch little white girls jump rope with one rope? (A slow schoolgirl's cadence now) '*Down* in the *valley* where the *green* grass *grows*.' It's far more exciting watching black girls jump rope. They jump with five ropes all going at the same time. (Talking very fast now) "You know I'm alive, I'm jumping with five, got a bald-headed momma, that ain't no jive."

He had to wait now, wait for the laughter to stop so he could go on with the routine. It was happening, he thought. It was really happening. Stay calm, he told himself. Wait. Don't rush it.

"I was the skinniest kid in my neighborhood so I used my head. I made friends with the toughest guy, a black guy named Goochie Nicholson. Goochie was tough and he was smart, but some of the guys in my neighborhood weren't very smart because they thought I was a Chinese guy named Say Foo. Every day I walked by, they go, 'Say, Fool!' Because of that neighborhood, my mother was terrified I'd end up in prison. So she decided to send me to Catholic school. Which I think is great training if you plan on going to prison. They're tough there. If you talk in class, they beat your hands with a ruler. And if you cheat in bingo, too."

And then he heard the sweetest sound of all. Not just the audience laughing, but *Carson* laughing, too, laughing hard. He was telling the crowd that he thought Dreesen was funny, that he approved. "Thank you, God," Dreesen thought, and he waited again for the laughs to die down, and went on.

"I was always in trouble, especially with a friend of mine named Frankie O'Brien. Frankie was a poor kid and I kind of felt sorry for him. His whole family was wiped out when automatic pinsetters came in. Sometimes Sister would be up at the blackboard and I'd whisper in Frankie's ear and make him laugh out loud. Then Sister would beat him with a ruler. I loved them days. One day, she caught me. She said, 'Oh, is that funny? Well, come up here and tell everybody what you said.'

"Sister, I'd rather not."

"Get up here, Milton Berle."

"Sister, all I said was Mary Jo Feldes doesn't have any underpants on."

"Go to confession!"

"Bless me, father, for I have sinned. Mary Jo Feldes doesn't have any underpants on."

"What are you telling me for?"

"Sister told me to tell you."

"Oh? Where does she sit?"

It was time to wrap it up now, to wait one last time for the laughter to subside, to give them something to remember him by.

"You've been a marvelous audience. This is my first *Tonight Show* appearance and I've got to ask you a favor. Show business is a tough life, as some of you know. So if you like me and you're Protestant, do me a favor and say a prayer for me. If you're Catholic, light a candle. If you're Jewish, somebody in your family owns a nightclub. Tell him about me, will you?"

He stood for a moment, smiled, acknowledged the laughter and the applause, then walked back through the curtain and saw Tennis running toward him.

"Go back!" he said.

"Go back? Go back where?"

"Go back and take a bow. Don't you hear what's happening out there? Johnny just called for you. Go back! Now!"

He walked back out into the lights. He smiled, waved, looked appreciatively over to Carson, who was still applauding. He stood there for one more moment, willing himself not to get emotional. As he walked through the curtain for the second time, Dreesen realized that Carson wasn't letting it go. Famous for his generosity to young comedians, he was delaying the cut to a commercial to tell the audience it had just witnessed a classic show-business moment.

"You probably don't realize it," Carson said. "But you don't know how happy you just made a young man. Tom has been booked on this show four times. And three of the times we ran out of time and he did not get on. It's a tough spot for a young comedian because you mentally get all set in your rhythm and what you're going to say and all of a sudden it's like shutting the floodgates at Hoover Dam. So it's nice to see him score."

Backstage was a madhouse. Tennis hugging him. De Cordova pounding him on the back. Severinsen's manager, Bud Robinson, applauding. His own manager, Dan Wiley, saying "Bravo." The stagehands applauding. The production people applauding. Irv, who had lifted the curtain for every performer who had ever walked through it, applauding. At that moment, he understood a basic truth of comedy. It can be the highest of highs and the lowest of lows. He thanked everybody, said goodbye, walked out of the building into the parking lot and the sweet night air. And then he wept.

"I swear this is true," Dreesen says. "When I got in the car that night and drove home, the first person I thought of was Tim. I wanted that to be *us*. All the hard work we had done, all the dues we had paid. That was *our* dream. I wasn't thinking, 'Boy, I hope you saw this.' I was thinking, 'I wish we could have shared this.'"

And now, telling the story more than thirty years later, there are tears in his eyes again.

Lying in bed at the top of the hill watching television, Reid felt as if someone had kicked him in the gut.

"He wasn't so good," Reese said as Dreesen walked off the stage the second time.

"No, Della," Reid said. "He was great. Just great."

This is as low as it gets, Reid thought. He was working too little—if he weren't opening for Reese, he would hardly be working at all—smoking dope too often, scoring at the Comedy Store too seldom. He had quit his job, walked out on his family, and now he had nothing. And Tom had made it through to the other side. All the dreams they'd shared, all the hopes they'd had, were gone. Tom was on his way now. On his way without him.

I'm lost, Reid thought. Lost. I've got to do something.

**8**

"Hey! It's you!"

The man in front of Dreesen in the line at the Van Nuys un-employment office looked as if he'd seen a ghost.

"I saw you on *The Tonight Show* last night, didn't I?" he insisted.

"Yeah," Dreesen said. "That was me."

"I thought so," he said, talking so loud everybody else in the crowded room could hear him. "Hey, look at this guy. He was on *The Tonight Show* last night."

"He wasn't on no *Tonight Show*," somebody else in the line said. "He's bullshitting you. What would he be doing here if he was on *The Tonight Show*?"

"It's him, I'm telling you," the first man said. "I saw him last night. Come on, man, what are you doing here? Don't they pay you enough money on that show?"

"Well, it's my report date," Dreesen said, embarrassed at all the attention, and not about to tell anybody he had received only $212 for his performance.

Nor did he have any idea that back home all hell was break-ing loose.

Goochie called. Tutu called. Tommy Johnson called. Cham-pagne Sammy Eubanks called. Doll Franks called. His sisters and brothers called, and many of his old classmates. For a while, it seemed as if everybody in Harvey was calling, including people he hadn't heard from in years. His navy buddies called. Mitzi Shore called. Estelle Reiner called. Almost all the comics at the Comedy Store and Showbiz called. Thanks, oh thanks, he said. Yeah, it was great. Very exciting. Yeah, thanks.

Agents called, too, agents who wouldn't see him before, wouldn't talk to him, wouldn't give him the time of day. "I just got a call from the New York office," said Herb Karp, his softball-playing buddy at the William Morris Agency. "Lee Curlin, a big executive at CBS, said he saw you on *The Tonight Show*, but he didn't catch your name. He wanted to know if I know who you are."

"Herb, they were never interested in me," Dreesen said. "You know that. You tried."

"That's what I told them, that we were friends and I had told them all about you and they didn't want you. Well, they want you now. They're telling me to sign you quick. Look, Tommy, I'm going to tell you the truth. You don't need us. There's a deal waiting for you at CBS right now. You can go with anybody you want, or you can do the deal yourself."

"You're a good guy, Herb," Dreesen said. "I'll sign, but on one condition. You have to be my agent."

Two days later, he had a check for $10,000, the first payment on a $25,000 development deal with CBS. He held it in his hand and did the math. More than $2,000 a month for a year. Enough to pay for everything—rent, groceries, gas, clothes, whatever Maryellen and the kids needed. Enough to pay back the friends he'd borrowed money from. And enough to buy the most precious commodity of all—time. Time to develop new material, time to work on the act, time to look for new places to work. Time to breathe without worrying about tomorrow.

The CBS contract was a crapshoot, he knew that. The networks were signing all sorts of comics to development deals, hoping to build sit-coms around them, and only a few ever led to anything. And to tell the truth he wasn't really that interested in sit-coms anyway. Stand-up was what he cared about, becoming the best stand-up comedian he could be. But he would play CBS's game, and he would certainly take CBS's money. If they came up with something for him, fine. If not, that was fine, too.

The work came flooding in now, more than he could handle. Dinah Shore wanted him. Merv Griffin wanted him. Mike Douglas wanted him. *Hollywood Squares* wanted him. *American Bandstand* wanted him. *The Midnight Special* wanted him. *Don Kirschner's Rock Concert* wanted him. Everybody, it seemed, was booking comics now, even the music shows. It was as if comedians were rock stars themselves. There were offers from nightclubs, too, prestigious clubs around the country that, unlike the Comedy Store, paid and paid well. And there were a few unexpected offers, too, that reminded him of his past, reminded him that his comedy must always be fixed in where he came from.

"How you doing, man?" said Don Cornelius, who had put Tim and Tom on his WVON radio program back in Chicago and was now producing *Soul Train*, the syndicated television show that was hugely popular with black audiences around the country. "I didn't know you were out here."

"I'm doing good, Don," Dreesen said. "Real good."

"My partner called me the other day and said there was this white boy on *The Tonight Show* talking about niggas and he was very funny," Cornelius said. "I told him the only white boy I know who did that is from Chicago and his name is Tom Dreesen. He said, 'That's him and I'm telling you that white boy made it funny. We should book him.' How about it? You want to do *Soul Train?*"

"Are you sure, Don?" Dreesen said. "You don't have white comedians on your show."

"Well, then it's time we did," Cornelius said. "You aren't prejudiced, are you?" and they both cracked up.

Many times over the ensuing months and years, Dreesen would return to *The Tonight Show*. He would take the long walk from the green room to the curtain backstage and the stagehands who had whispered, "First time. It's his first time," would now yell out, "Hey, Dreesen, how you doing? How's your Cubs?"

He would do his routine, then walk over and sit next to Carson, who would tell him how funny he was, treat him like an equal, and announce where he would be performing next. He would think how calm he felt, how relaxed, how different from that first appearance on *The Tonight Show*, which had changed his life. He would listen to Carson talk to the other guests, look out into the audience as Severinsen's band played during the commercials, and think that it was almost as if God had said to him, "Tommy, I'm going to put a load on you the first half of your life, a real load. But if you survive, the second half is on me."

Reid's breakup with Della Reese was almost peaceful. There were no arguments, no recriminations, no bitter words over whose fault it was. She hadn't believed him when he said he was moving out, but one day she returned from an out-of-town engagement and he was gone. Gone from the hilltop to the city down below.

"Let me get this straight," the manager of the apartment building in West Hollywood said as he noticed Reid's current address. "You're living on Bel-Air Road and you want to move *here?*"

"Show business," Reid told him, smiling weakly. "Sometimes you're up, sometimes you're down. Right now, I'm down."

"All right, man, hang in there," John Witherspoon, his pal from the Comedy Store, said after helping him move his few belongings. Reid looked around at the four bare walls of the room he would come to call his cave and then it hit him. For the first time in his life, he was alone. No wife, no children, no girlfriend. No mother, no father, no grandmother, no aunts, no uncles. No support system of any kind. Tom is opening for Sammy Davis Jr. in Las Vegas, he thought, and nobody cares if I live or die.

Reid slept on the floor that night and when he woke in the morning, he couldn't move. For a moment, he thought he was paralyzed, but as he started to crawl across the floor he realized his back had gone out. It took him twenty minutes to get to the bathroom, ten more to get to the phone and call the only person he could think of for help. Reese arrived an hour later with some soup and a heating pad, but little sympathy. "Uh-huh," she said as she looked at him lying on the floor of the small room. A few minutes later she was gone, out of his life forever.

"This is it," Reid said as he ate the soup. "This is where I find out what I'm made of."

He bought some wood and built a bed, a sofa, a dining-room table, and a coffee table. He read books, hundreds of them, about religion and mysticism and eastern philosophy. The Bible, the Koran, the Bhagavad-Gita. Books about Buddhism, Confucianism, and Hinduism. He tried to take something away from each of them, tried to find something he could apply to himself. Moderation in all things, they taught him. Seek balance in your life. Enjoy a wealth of experiences, but reside in none of them. It all made perfect sense and brought a feeling of peace.

He began to paint and write poetry and stream-of-consciousness essays. He took lessons and learned to play the flute. He gave up red meat and sugar and began cooking large quantities of chicken, potatoes, and green vegetables, which he put in small bags and froze to eat later. He stopped buying over-the-counter medicine and began using herbs. Camomile tea for his headaches. Dandelion root tea for the pain of the stomach ulcer he had developed. Herbal poultices to ease the aches and pains in his joints and muscles. He preached the gospel of organic foods and herbalism to his family and friends, who started calling him the herb doctor.

He cut back on marijuana, until he was hardly smoking at all any more, and he became celibate. Though he still saw a few friends, he often stayed in his cave for two or three days at a time, reading, meditating, thinking. None of these changes, he was surprised to discover, was difficult to achieve. He found himself becoming less concerned with failure and more confident in his ability to survive on his own. He was breaking bad habits, replacing the quest devoted to his ego with a spiritual one, emptying all that was destructive out of himself, starting over.

He asked Rita for a legal separation, but convinced her they should wait to get a divorce. His reading of the Talmud taught him that Jewish law commands a man who divorces his wife to continue supporting her. So they should wait until he was back on his feet and earning a living. Fortunately, money was not a problem, as long as he lived frugally. He had his unemployment checks, and the gold coins he had bought several years earlier after reading a book that had correctly predicted a forthcoming devaluation of the dollar and the skyrocketing price of gold that would result. When his rent was due, he would sell one coin. When his car payment was due, he would sell another. When he was feeling guilty about Rita and the kids, he would sell one more. Richard Nixon's decision in 1971 to devalue the dollar had devastating short-term effects for the U.S. economy, but it helped keep Reid alive. "The one thing the book recommended that I didn't do, which I regret to this day, is get an off-shore account," he says with a laugh. "Not many people were doing that then and I could have really cleaned up."

One day as he wandered through the Bodhi Tree, a bookstore on Melrose Avenue devoted to spiritual literature, Reid realized how complete his transformation had been. He was more interested in what was on its shelves than he was in reading the trade papers and magazines and looking for work. Though he continued to take acting classes, to go out on auditions for television shows, and to work the after-midnight shows at the Comedy Store, he was no longer consumed by the fact that his career had stalled. It was enough to know that he was continuing to develop as a comedian, that his routines were becoming more polished and the audiences were reacting positively. He would never develop a real love for stand-up, but it was the one thing he knew, the one thing that gave him any professional satisfaction. And he was proud of himself for staying with it, for not running away. He had done enough quitting in his life. No more.

If Dreesen's emergence from the depths of despair began with five minutes on *The Tonight Show*, Reid's started with an eight-week engagement at a topless restaurant in Washington, D.C. It was not the $1,200-a-week job in Las Vegas he had been promised by Lenny, the promoter who showed up at the Comedy Store one night, but it was something.

"Are you going to do this?" asked Jay Leno, the young comedian he and Dreesen had met hanging around the Boston Playboy Club and who was now performing at the Comedy Store.

"I've got to, Jay," Reid said. "I need the money. I haven't had a paying gig in over a year. Lenny said he'd give us apartments in Vegas and we'd take turns as headliners in the showroom."

"Be careful, Tim," Leno said. "My manager checked on the guy. There's some shady stuff in his background."

And sure enough, the deal in Las Vegas fell through. Just his luck, Reid thought. He had found someone who wanted to hire him and he was all smoke and mirrors. Or was he?

"Look, I'm really sorry," Lenny said. "But I'll tell you what. I've got this topless place in Washington called the Boardroom that needs entertainers. The biggest crowds are at lunch so it's not exactly what you're used to, but I think you'd like working there."

Has it come to this? Reid wondered. To working in a place that sounded almost as depressing and embarrassing as not working at all? But when Lenny said the pay was $800 a week for eight weeks, plus room and board, he grabbed it. What did he have to lose? He left his cave and flew to Washington where he did three shows a day, six days a week for government employees, many of whom worked at the Pentagon. "I'd come out and do my act," Reid says, "but what they really wanted to see was tits."

The length of the engagement gave him a luxury he hadn't

had in a while, time to work on new material and see how it was received from one day to the next. He began to think through his approach to humor based on race more carefully and realized he was becoming less interested in making comparisons between white and black people, which always seemed to make blacks less intelligent and whites less hip. Rather, he viewed the world through the ironic lens of being black in America.

"Hello, are you ready for some Negro humor," he would say, and the crowd of white government employees would titter. "You know what Negro humor is, right? Let me give you an example: 'Tell me, sir, can you identify your assailant?' 'I don't know, but he was Negro.' 'In that case we know what he looks like.'"

Since he was working in a town consumed by politics, he brought the latest headlines into the act. He began telling more stories, too—he had always loved the way Bill Cosby created humor out of everyday situations—and working the room in a way he had never done before, bringing in the audience, improvising, having fun. He began to see repeat customers, including some who were there to see him and not just the girls. Late at night, he loosened up even more, got a little racier than he was used to and enjoyed it. The audiences did, too, and so did Lenny. "These are horny guys, Tim," he said. "You've got to be a little blue once in a while."

"I'm so sick of you young guys today," Reid would say. "You've got it so good. You know what we had to go through to get laid when we were kids? Looking like a hoodlum didn't make it back then. Take just the act of trying to put your hand on a woman's crotch. The girdles they were wearing were made out of steel-belted radial tires. They could snap back and break your finger. Today, they don't wear anything at all." But he stayed away from four-letter words and the disturbing new trend among black comedians of denigrating black women.

When the Boardroom closed at night, he went to after-hours clubs with some of the girls. They were fun and bright—one was working her way through law school—and each one seemed more beautiful than the last. They would sit in the clubs and laugh as they openly discussed which one of them was going home with him that night to the nice apartment Lenny had arranged, which was five times the size of his cave. After being celibate for a year, it was one hell of a coming out party. Sometimes, though, they would all just sit and talk until sunup and he would go home alone and sleep all day.

There was no sense in kidding himself, of course. The Boardroom wasn't *The Tonight Show* or the main showroom at Caesars Palace, but working there was a good creative experience, one that gave him the old feeling of self-confidence that had been missing for so long. He began to feel as if he was walking around in his own little cocoon of accomplishment and contentment, that he could perform anywhere now and be successful. Isn't this strange? he thought. To be working at a topless joint, nothing more than a high-class dive really, and to feel better about himself, and his craft, than he had in years. Though he went home eight weeks later with a feeling of optimism and possibility, and with enough money to keep him from having to sell any gold coins for a while, he was almost sorry the gig had ended. Not when he discovered what was waiting for him, though.

Reid's breakthrough into television was so easy, so painless, he didn't know whether to laugh or cry. The day after he returned to Los Angeles—he hadn't even unpacked—he got a call for an audition for a summer replacement series called *Easy Does It . . . Starring Frankie Avalon* that needed a black man to fill out its comedy troupe.

"So what should I do?" he asked John Moffitt, the show's director, after regaling the production team with his tales of working at a topless restaurant. "Do you want me to read something?"

"You don't need to audition, man," said Moffitt, who was still laughing. "You've got the job."

And soon he was working on a variety show with guest stars like Bob Hope and Phyllis Diller, not to mention Annette

Funicello. "Boy, did I have a crush on those tits," Reid laughs. He was working with excellent writers now, too, real pros who took their comedy seriously and used his presence as a way to stretch the show's boundaries.

"Sammy Davis was catching a lot of heat for hugging Nixon around that time," Reid says, "so we did a bit where I came out loaded down with so much jewelry you could barely see what else I was wearing. I started hugging everybody and taking off one chain after another, and when I took off the last one I levitated out of the scene. I ran into Sammy a few years later and he told me he laughed like hell when he saw it."

*Easy Does It* lasted only a short time, but it was a godsend. He had been seen on national television several times now. He had shown what he could do. Producers and casting directors knew his name. And with shows looking for young black actors and comics he was suddenly in demand. He had a recurring part as a songwriter on *The Marilyn McCoo and Billy Davis, Jr. Show*, in which Leno also had a featured role. He was cast in episodes of *Rhoda*, *Fernwood 2Nite*, *What's Happening!!* and *Maude*. They were small jobs that didn't pay much, but they gave him steady work acting in comedy sketches, which is what he'd always wanted. They also gave him a glimpse of some of the difficulties he would face in the future.

"Here's your problem," an oh-so-hip young white producer told him after he read for a part. "You're not black enough."

"Excuse me?" Reid said.

"Really, you're not."

"Why don't you show me."

"Well, the black dudes I played basketball with in Harlem act like this," the producer said, and he began walking with an exaggerated strut and saying, "Hey, bro, what's happenin'?"

"You know what?" Reid said. "You're better than I am. I think you should take the part." And he walked out of the room.

Not long afterwards, Reid was hired to be on a show called *Looking Good* in which he played the owner of a hair salon on a street in Los Angeles that marked the dividing line between

a wealthy white neighborhood on the north and a less affluent black one to the south. "The idea was that we were on the
corner of 'Ro-*day*-o Drive,' which was what they called it in
Beverly Hills, and '*Road*-eo Drive,' which was how black folks
pronounced it," Reid says. "Whenever I had a white client, I'd
be all continental—'Hello, so good to see you again'—but when
a black woman walked in I'd say, 'Yo, baby. What 'cha want? To
get yo' wig done?' I thought I could have some fun with it."

But as they shot the pilot, the script began to change from
an equal division between standard English and street talk to a
cartoonish overuse of the latter. "In the original script, it was
50-50," Reid says, "but on the first day of rehearsals they took
away a few lines of me talking normally to white people. The
second day, it was 65 percent 'Yo mama,' and the next day it was
up to 80 percent."

"What's the point of this?" Reid asked the show's director. "I
thought we were trying to do something different here, to show
a black man with a little class. This is just the same old shit."
Soon he was in a shouting match and a day later he was fired.

"Thank God," he thought, and then he was struck with a
feeling of panic. Had he ruined things again? Was word getting around town that he was a troublemaker? Why didn't he
just shut up and read the lines they put in front of him? If he
couldn't perform that simple task, what was he doing in show
business anyway? It was some consolation, though not much,
when *Looking Good* didn't get on the air.

The first thing Reid saw when he entered the waiting room was
what appeared to be every young black actor in Hollywood auditioning for the same part—the overnight disc jockey on a new
sit-com on CBS. The second thing he saw was a script open to a
page that said, "Black man enters room wearing a coat with an
ermine collar and a big hat cocked to the side."

"Not again," Reid thought. "I got fired four days ago because
I wouldn't do this kind of crap and now this. You're testing me,
God, right?" His anger built as he quickly read through the

script. "This is insane," he thought. And then he heard somebody call his name.

He knew he shouldn't have done it. He should have told
them what they wanted to hear. That it was a wonderful part in
what was going to be a great show, and that he was just the one
to play it. But as he felt the tension in the room, as he saw the
judgmental attitude of the men on the other side of the table—
were they trying to scare him?—he couldn't help himself. So
what if he was sitting with Grant Tinker, the powerful head of
MTM Enterprises, Jay Sandrich, the director who had helped
turn *The Mary Tyler Moore Show* into a television franchise, and
Hugh Wilson, the creator of this new show. They had asked him
what he thought of the part and he was going to give them an
answer.

"The character is a stereotype," he said. "It seems so one-
dimensional. And I'm not sure I want to be walking down the
street when I'm sixty years old and have somebody refer to me
as Venus Flytrap."

"All right, if that's the way you feel," said Sandrich, who,
along with Tinker, was shocked by Reid's effrontery. "Let's call
in the next guy."

"Wait a minute," said Wilson, in a soft southern accent that
sounded like home to Reid. "Give me your view of the part. Tell
me how you think this character should be portrayed."

"Look," Reid said "the black disc jockeys I grew up listening
to in the South had larger-than-life personas when they were
broadcasting, but when they were off the air they were real people with real lives. They didn't look or act or talk anything like
the way they did on the radio."

"I agree with you," Wilson said. "That's what I had in mind
for this character, that he's multidimensional, not the same
old stereotypical stuff. This is just the pilot, something to get
him established. Why don't you read for us? Let's see how you'd
do it."

"Hugh told me later that he was the only one who wanted
me," Reid says, "but they figured Venus Flytrap was not an

important character anyway so they let him have me. I owe Hugh for that. I owe him for a lot."

On September 18, 1978, a cast that included Gary Sandy, Gordon Jump, Loni Anderson, Howard Hesseman, Richard Sanders, Frank Bonner, and Jan Smithers debuted in *WKRP in Cincinnati*, a show about a struggling radio station that changes its format from easy listening to rock 'n roll. In the pilot episode's final scene, Venus Flytrap makes his first appearance wearing a purple suit and hat, a full-length white leopard-spotted coat, and a towering Afro.

"It's the hour of darkness, children," he says as the closing credits begin to roll, "and Venus is on the rise in Cincinnati. The moon is high (he hits a gong and winces) and so am I. So let's get *down*, pretty brothers and sisters. Let's prowl and *howl*. After this word from Shady Hills Rest Home."

"I guess we didn't get away from any stereotypes in the pilot, did we?" Reid says with a laugh. But he was on his way now. The show was going to be huge. He could feel it. Who knew where this might lead?

They were off on their separate paths now—Dreesen into the life of a stand-up comedian he had always dreamed of, Reid into one that would lead from acting to developing, producing, and directing his own projects for the movies and television. Later, they would come to see that they had not only chosen different careers, they had chosen different *sorts* of careers that reflected how show business was changing in some very fundamental ways.

Somewhat to his chagrin, Dreesen would discover that he had become a part of an era that was beginning to disappear. "When I first went to Las Vegas, every hotel had a singer and a comedian on the bill," he says. "The same thing was true for Atlantic City and Lake Tahoe and Reno. Performers like Frank Sinatra and Sammy Davis played there three or four times a year. The hotels were always what they called loading in and loading out. They'd load Sammy out and load Frank in, load

Dean Martin out and load Tom Jones in. I thought it would go on forever. But today they load in Celine Dion or Wayne Newton, who stay for ten years. I still work Las Vegas occasionally, but it's not like it used to be."

The reason for this change in the casinos' policies was simple enough. "In the old days, they thought they needed the shows to attract people to come and gamble," Dreesen says. "But then they saw gamblers would come if there was no show at all. When the first casinos in Atlantic City opened, there were lines around the block and people learned that if they bought tickets for the shows they could get in faster and start gambling. They didn't even *go* to the shows so there was no reason to keep changing the acts. High-paying gigs for comedians began drying up, which is why a lot of them took their acts to television and built sit-coms around them."

Over the years, Dreesen learned to adjust, taking his act to venues where comedians hadn't commonly performed in the past. He appeared at private corporate events, often for some of America's largest companies, as executives increasingly began hiring entertainers to provide a break from long hours devoted to business. And he went to motivational and self-help forums where his own experiences, and his humor, offered a message audiences could relate to. He also performed more and more often at charities and as toastmaster of numerous dinners, many of them related to golf. "I figured I worked about twenty days out of every month this year," Dreesen said late in 2007. "I don't know how those other ten got away from me." The wide variety of audiences he appeared before forced him to tailor his act to vastly different surroundings. "You can drop Tom out of a helicopter anywhere in the world," David Letterman once told his television audience, "and as soon as he hits the ground he'll quickly assess the situation and do a top-notch show."

But if Dreesen had become a part of the entertainment business's past, Reid was moving into its future—a period when the struggle for racial equality was beginning to manifest itself in new and challenging ways. The portrayal of blacks in movies and on television was changing radically, opportunities for black artists to break out of the roles they had been traditionally assigned on and off the screen were opening up as never before, and Reid found himself at the forefront of those trying to capitalize on this transformation.

"Bill Cosby, Flip Wilson, and one or two others were the real pioneers, the first ones who weren't just performers but producers, too," Reid says. "They got into the boardrooms, the rarefied air where things are really decided—who should be hired, what characters can say, what they can wear. I followed in their wake and wound up in hand-to-hand combat with mid- and lower-level guys who had a lot of control over what got to the boardrooms. They fought just as hard as rednecks in a bar, too, but instead of putting out a cigarette in my face they would do things under the table."

There were times when Reid felt as if he were back in his college battling for civil rights all over again. "The surroundings and the weapons were different," he says, "but the fight to be treated equally was the same. When Hugh Wilson and I did *Frank's Place,* the network wasn't sure about having a black executive producer. Hugh said, 'Hey, we created this thing together, what's the problem?' and they finally said OK. But it was always a struggle."

Later, when he did gain a measure of creative control, Reid's determination to hire black stagehands, technicians, and other behind-the-scene employees also raised some eyebrows. "I had executives say, 'Tim, you should focus more on the creative elements of your show and less on trying to get your people work because the network will think you're more committed to a cause than the show itself.' They were probably right—I did create a lot of friction for myself—but the more they warned me the more I pushed back."

The life of a pioneer had its rewards, though. "A black Hollywood trade association invited me to a function once," Reid says, "and the woman running it said, 'Everybody who has ever worked on a show Tim Reid was in charge of, please stand.'

There were a couple of hundred people there and it brought tears to my eyes when 20 or 30 percent of them stood up."

But even as they were moving in different directions, there would always be reminders of how much their shared struggle as Tim and Tom had prepared them for life on their own.

**9**

"I saw your jokes about black people on *The Tonight Show*," the producer said. "You can't do them here."

"What?!" Dreesen said. "You've got to be kidding. That's what I do. Jokes about growing up in a black neighborhood, about our families, our basketball teams, the cheerleaders, the differences between the two cultures. That's why Johnny Carson keeps asking me back. He loves that stuff."

"Tom," the producer said, "Johnny Carson is white. Sammy Davis is black."

"No, shit," Dreesen said. "Why do you think I've been trying so hard to get on this show? Sammy is going to love these routines."

"Well, if that's what you want to do, then go ahead and do it," the producer said, and he turned and walked away.

"I knew what he was thinking," Dreesen says. "That it was a taped show and they'd just cut me out. But I knew in my heart that Sammy would like my routines. He'd grown up in show business, where blacks and whites ran into each other all the time. My routines were tailor made for him."

Getting on *Sammy and Company*, Sammy Davis Jr.'s new variety show, hadn't been easy. It was the one television show Dreesen wanted more than any other, one that featured many black performers and where he would feel at home, but he couldn't seem to make any headway. Keep trying, he would tell Debbie Miller, the William Morris agent who, along with Herb Karp and Dan Wiley, was finding him work in clubs and on television. It's just the right show for me. We *are* trying, Tom, they would say, but the show is not doing well in the ratings and they only want big names.

Then one day the phone rang. Bill Cosby had cancelled and they needed somebody fast, Miller said. Could he get to Lake Tahoe, where *Sammy and Company* was shot, right away? Damn right, he could. He was right about Davis's reaction to his act, too.

"You're a funny man, my friend," Davis told him when the show was over. "You're coming with me."

"Coming with you? Coming with you where?"

"On the road. I'm playing some theaters in the East in a couple of months. And you are going to be my opening act. OK?"

*OK?!* Go on tour with *Sammy Davis Jr.?!* Hell, yes, it was OK. It would be his first real taste of performing live in the big time. The highest production values. The classiest audiences. The top venues like the Front Row Theater in Cleveland, the famous Oakdale theater in the round in Wallingford, Connecticut, and—how about this?—the Mill Run Theatre in Niles, just north of Chicago. That was where all the top touring acts played—Bob Hope, Jack Benny, Lena Horne, Tom Jones, you name it. What a homecoming that would be.

But if the anticipation of working with Davis was exciting, the reality was astonishing. What a lesson in show business, Dreesen thought, as he stood in the wings night after night. Davis could sing as well as anybody else, tell jokes as well as anybody else, dance and do impressions *better* than anybody else, and play the piano, the trumpet, the drums. And the energy level night after night! He's a one-man parade, Dreesen thought. He had never seen anything like it.

Dreesen was gratified to see his own act accepted and appreciated by the large black audiences who came to see Davis. It was the first time he had performed in a truly integrated setting—not just a few blacks in a largely white crowd or vice-versa—and there seemed to be a comfort level on both sides of the divide. "This white boy obviously grew up around the brothers," reviewers from the black press would write, and not once did he hear any complaints about the nature of his material. I wish Tim could see this, Dreesen thought. We could be doing this together.

While telling his stories about growing up in Harvey at the Mill Run one night, Dreesen waited for one laugh to subside and then said, "By the way, let me introduce you to my friend, Everett Nicholson. Stand up, Goochie." And as his old pal shyly rose from his seat, Davis came running out from the wings, shouting, "Goochie's here?! Where is he? Let me get a look at you, man," and the audience cracked up.

"It's great to meet you," Davis told Goochie in his dressing room after the show. "Tommy talks about you all the time." And as they stood having their pictures taken, Davis turned to Dreesen and asked, "Have you ever worked Las Vegas?"

"No, Sammy. I never have."

"Well, you open there for me on January 15. You come, too, Goochie. We'll have a ball."

Dreesen thought Goochie might never stop smiling. They were standing no more than thirty miles away from Harvey, but it seemed like all the distance in the world.

The more he moved around the country with Davis, the more Dreesen had the sense of traveling back in time. He was reminded yet again that there was a line he couldn't cross, that as much as he might be accepted in the black culture he would never be a part of it. But as he sat in Davis's suite late into the night—did the man ever sleep?—and listened to his stories about the enormous dues he had paid for acceptance in a segregated America, he realized that the struggle to succeed created a bond that people outside show business could never truly understand. And for Davis, that bond brought a sense of responsibility.

"When we go out for dinner after the shows, Tommy, I want you to sit next to me," Davis told him. "The theater owners and the promoters will be there and you have to meet them. These are people who will be important to you down the line. You can't stay with me forever. Two years, three at the most, and then you've got to move on. I'm just part of your progression."

Was there any end to the kindness of some of the biggest people in show business? Dreesen wondered, thinking back to how handsomely Johnny Carson had always treated him. And indeed there were times when Davis's benevolence seemed without limits. When they played Harrah's Lake Tahoe, Davis insisted that Dreesen stay in the house on the lake that was one of the headliner's perks and came with a cook, a maid, a butler, and a yacht. "I don't like living in houses, Tommy," he said. "I'm more comfortable in hotels. Maybe it's because I grew up sleeping in dresser drawers. Bring your wife and kids. I'll fly them in. It's on me."

As for their date in Las Vegas, Davis's insistence that Dreesen's name go on the Caesars Palace marquee, a rare acknowledgment for an opening act, was particularly sweet. "Your names are on a huge billboard on Sunset Boulevard," Maryellen excitedly reported over the phone one day. "I've got a picture of it."

"Thanks, sweetheart," Dreesen said, not bothering to tell her how many times he had hitchhiked up and down that very street.

Dreesen was still getting used to the opulence of his surroundings—the beautiful hotel room, the limos, the huge private dressing room that was so different from the dingy rooms and basements where he and Reid had waited before performing—when he sat down with Davis and Nat Brandwynne, the Caesars Palace orchestra conductor.

"The show lasts an hour and a half," Brandwynne said. "Tom, you'll do twenty minutes and Sammy will do an hour and ten."

"No, Nat," Davis said. "This is Tommy's first time in Las Vegas and all the critics are going to be here. So I'll come out first and do three songs and then I'll bring him out and introduce him. Tommy, you take as much time as you want and when you feel like you've scored, I'll come out and finish up."

"What you have to understand," Dreesen says, "is that all during the opening act they're serving drinks and dinner. People are eating, dishes are banging, the comic never stands a chance. But when the headliner comes on, the waiters and waitresses go around and snatch up all the plates. So if Sammy went out first, people who hadn't even started eating yet were going to see their food disappear."

After their first rehearsal, Dreesen stood on the stage and looked out into the silent room and the empty seats. "My God!" he thought. "Caesars Palace!" His reverie was interrupted by Davis, who had been watching him. "You know why they call a stage 'boards,' Tommy?" he asked. "Because of the wooden boards it's made out of. Well, you earned every single one of the boards on this stage. You belong here because of what you can do. Don't let them take that away from you."

"I won't, Sammy. Thank you."

And, oh, did Davis lay it on thick, show after show, night after night, as he almost dared the audience not to like Dreesen's act.

"Ladies and gentlemen," he would say after his opening songs, "you've been very good to me throughout the years. I like to think of my audience as friends and when friends are good to you, you want to bring them a gift. Well, I've got a gift for you tonight. It's a young man I had on my television show and I know you're going to love him. This is his first time here in Las Vegas so please make him feel at home. Ladies and gentlemen, Tom Dreesen."

"He had the crowd all revved up, just waiting for me, thinking I had to be someone special," Dreesen says. "By then, I could do no wrong."

"All my life, I dreamed I would work in Las Vegas," Dreesen would say after walking out onto the stage. "And I always dreamed it would be Caesars Palace. But one thing I never dreamed was that Sammy Davis Jr. would be my opening act." The laughs for that joke, and for those that followed, were long and loud, and the reviews in *Variety*, the *Hollywood Reporter*, and the Las Vegas papers mentioned him prominently and favorably. After the fuss Davis had made over him, they couldn't ignore him, could they? Dreesen thought. How do you thank a man for a thing like that?

Soon, people were stopping him in the casino and on the street ("Saw you with Sammy—really enjoyed it") and he was hanging out late at night with Davis, for whom two shows a night never seemed to be enough. "We'd get in the limo and drive around town, see who was playing in the lounges," Dreesen says. "Sammy loved the Treniers, the wonderful veteran singing group, and he'd get up on the stage with them, sing a song or two, and then I'd do a few minutes. It was old-time show business, the way Las Vegas used to be."

Dreesen quickly learned he had to watch himself with Davis, though. The man had a devilish sense of humor and loved practical jokes, which didn't necessarily end when the show began. "Sammy used a teleprompter to break in new songs," Dreesen says, "and they used to start rolling it when I had five minutes to go, just as a reminder to start wrapping things up. One night, I looked down and there was a porno film in the teleprompter— two girls, a guy, and a donkey—and here I am talking about Catholic school and nuns. I was, 'buh-buh, buh-buh,' stumbling for words, and the band was cracking up. I looked over in the wings and there was Sammy laughing his ass off."

But for all of Davis's manic spirit and generosity, he had a depressive side, too, one that was easily hurt, remembered every slight, and was quick to take offense at any transgression, real or imagined. Dreesen got a close look at this part of his personality one night when Davis resolved his long-standing estrangement from Frank Sinatra. Sometimes in his suite late at night, or while traveling to their next engagement, Davis would talk about his days with the Rat Pack in the early 1960s, about the fun he'd had with Sinatra, Dean Martin, Joey Bishop, and Peter

Lawford when they performed in Las Vegas together. They had not only played an important role in turning the town into the huge entertainment mecca it had become, but also, by refusing to play at casinos that didn't treat black entertainers equally, had forced them to abandon their segregationist policies. There always seemed to be a wistfulness about these stories, though, because Davis and Sinatra had had a falling out and hadn't spoken in several years.

"Sammy adored Frank," Dreesen says. "He thought the sun rose and set with him and couldn't stop talking about how much Frank had done for him early in his career, about how he and Frank and Dean had been like brothers. But now Frank wouldn't have anything to do with him—I think the cocaine Sammy started using had something to do with it—and you could tell how much it hurt him."

So Dreesen was surprised when, several days before a Las Vegas engagement, Davis called with exciting news. "Hey, babe. We're going to go in a night early and catch Frank's closing night. Barbara Sinatra and my wife Altovise have been working on him. We're going to have dinner after his first show and then we'll stay for the second one. I need you in the audience, Tommy. I've got to have my peeps with me."

Davis was as excited as a kid on Christmas morning as he took his seat at a table in the front of the Caesars Palace showroom. "Frank and I are talking again, babe," he told Dreesen, draining his drink and reaching for another. "We're friends again." And he sat back to watch the show.

Will you listen to this guy? Dreesen thought as Sinatra, in superb voice, sang one song after another while the audience, high on his very presence, cheered and cheered. Has there ever been anyone like him? Then, as the orchestra played the opening bars of "The Lady Is a Tramp," he felt a tap on his shoulder and heard Davis whispering "Watch this" as he finished another drink.

As Sinatra sang the first verse for the second time, "She gets too hungry for dinner at eight . . ." Davis suddenly leaped out of his seat, jumped up on the stage, grabbed the microphone, and sang, "She loves the theater, but doesn't come late . . ." The rest of the song was swallowed up in the shrieks of the crowd as it witnessed the public reunion of two old friends who had been on the outs for so long.

Thrilled at how the number had gone, Davis returned to his seat and, after Sinatra performed his closing number, "New York, New York," and left the room, couldn't stop talking, or drinking. Finally, it was time to go and one of Davis's bodyguards said he'd be mobbed if he walked out of the showroom into the casino and suggested they return to his suite through the kitchen. Davis's entourage led the way and just as the kitchen door opened, Dreesen heard a black man in a white waiter's uniform yell, "Hey, Al, bring in the meat!" to someone standing beside a large cart filled with steaks on the other side of the room.

Instantly, Davis pushed through the people in front of him and shouted, "Who you calling Buckwheat?!"

"I didn't call you no fucking Buckwheat," the waiter said angrily, turning around, his eyes growing wide as he realized who he was talking to. "Mr. Davis, no. I didn't . . ."

Dreesen began to laugh—it was all a misunderstanding, they'd clear it up—until he heard a jumble of voices, each one angrier than the last, but none angrier than that of a very drunk Sammy Davis Jr. "He called Sammy Buckwheat . . ." "Motherfucker said Buckwheat . . ." And damned if Davis's bodyguards weren't reaching for their guns. This is ridiculous, Dreesen thought. I've got to do something.

"Sammy, he didn't call you that," he said. "I was standing right here and he didn't say Buckwheat. He said, 'Bring in the meat.'"

"Sammy didn't say anything but he gave me a very hard look with his one good eye," Dreesen says. "Then he turned around and walked away. Everybody else left, too, but you could still feel the tension in the room."

This was one night he wouldn't go to Davis's suite, Dreesen

thought, but as soon as he returned to his room the phone rang.

"Sammy wants you to come to the party, Tom," said Davis's assistant, Shirley Rhodes.

"I don't think I should go down there tonight, Shirley. That was a pretty hairy situation."

"No, it's fine. Come on down."

Dreesen sat quietly at the bar, talking with Davis's road manager, Murphy Bennett, while Davis held forth on the other side of the room. Everything looks cool, he thought, but half an hour later, as the crowd began to thin out, Davis came over and sat beside him.

"Let me see if I get this straight," he said. "I'm the nigga that pays you, but the nigga in the kitchen, who insults the nigga that pays you, you stick up for him. Maybe I'm missing something here."

"Sammy, I'm being honest with you," Dreesen said. "The guy didn't say . . . he didn't call you . . ."

Suddenly, he burst into laughter while Davis looked at him in disbelief. What was funny about this? the livid expression on his face asked, but Dreesen couldn't stop laughing. "I lost it," he says. "It was all so absurd. Every time I tried to say Buckwheat, I broke out laughing. I just couldn't get the word out. I had to just get up and leave with Sammy and everybody else in the room thinking I had lost my mind."

The next day, Dreesen avoided Davis as long as he could, but an hour before showtime there was a knock on the door of his dressing room.

"I was wrong, wasn't I?" Davis said. "I owe that guy an apology."

"Yes, Sammy, you do."

"Let's go find him."

The two men walked into the kitchen where Dreesen saw the waiter, motioned him over and said, "Sammy wants to talk to you."

"Oh, Mr. Davis, I couldn't sleep all last night," the waiter said. "When I heard you were coming here, I called my mother in Cleveland and she said you were the greatest entertainer in the world and I was lucky to be in the same room with you. For you to think I would call you, or any other brother, that name made me sick to my stomach."

"I'm sorry," Davis said. "I had kind of an exciting night and I drank too much. I apologize."

"Thank you, Mr. Davis," the waiter said, as the three men beamed. Thank God that's over, Dreesen thought.

The following night, Shirley Rhodes handed Dreesen a small gift box and asked him to give it to the waiter. Inside, to the astonishment of both men, was a Rolex watch. And now it was Dreesen's turn to confront Davis.

"Let me see if I get this straight," he told Davis in his dressing room. "If I call you Buckwheat, I get me one of them Rolex watches?"

"Yeah, you'll get one," Davis said. "And you'll need it to know what time it is so you can catch the next bus back to Harvey, because your ass is out of here." Friends again, they collapsed into gales of laughter.

**10**

The critics loved *WKRP in Cincinnati*. "A sitcom perfect storm," one called it. "Brilliant writing, colorful characters, an expert cast." The ratings, though small at first, consistently increased as the show developed a devoted fan base, and as disc jockeys around the country talked it up as an honest and enjoyable portrayal of local radio stations. The television industry admired the show, too, voting it ten Emmys during its four-year run and the prestigious Humanitas Award for "film and TV writing deemed to promote human dignity, meaning, and freedom."

The cast members enjoyed it so much that after work they often went out on the town together and ended up at one of their homes. This was something Reid had never seen in television before and would never see again. "We ate dinners together, we spent weekends together," he says. "When the show was picked up after we made the pilot we all came together and held hands—I think we knew it was going to be important to our careers—and looked at each other as if to say it's never going to be like this again. I know it's a cliché, but we really were a family."

The only people who didn't seem to care for the show, who never really understood its appeal and got behind it, were the executives at MTM Enterprises, who produced it, and at the network that put it on the air. "We were CBS's bastard child,"

Reid says. "They just never embraced the show. They didn't even allow us on the MTM lot. We shot at KTLA, a television station in Los Angeles. I think they viewed us as rogue characters with this rogue creator, Hugh Wilson, who were off in our own world."

This front-office discomfort was not hard to understand. On the one hand, *WKRP* had all the trappings of a typical 1970s sitcom—broadly drawn characters, slapstick comedy situations, snappy one-liners. More than three decades later, its "Turkeys Away" episode—the station director, not realizing turkeys can't fly, drops live birds out of a helicopter over a shopping center as part of a Thanksgiving giveaway, while shoppers run for their lives and the news director describes the scene as if it were the Hindenburg disaster—is widely considered one of the funniest half-hours in the history of television. But the show also had a social agenda that made it extremely daring for its time. Wilson and his staff wrote scripts dealing with war, racism, drug abuse, abortion, homosexuality, abandoned children, union organizing, and conniving politicians. At times it seemed as if he was almost daring MTM and CBS to put a stop to it.

The fact that Reid as Venus Flytrap and Howard Hesseman as Dr. Johnny Fever chose their own music for their disc jockey segments, and that much of it was the latest thing in rock 'n roll, also led the show into uncharted territory. "Howard was into the Rolling Stones and Pink Floyd and I was playing Earth, Wind and Fire and Marvin Gaye," Reid says. "Pretty soon record companies were begging us to play their songs and sending music to our homes. I ended up with thousands of records from all over the world. The irony is that when they finally brought the show out on DVD in 2007, they had to change all the music because they couldn't afford the rights to the songs we'd used."

This cutting-edge approach inevitably led to problems, and occasionally the disconnect between the KTLA sound stage and the executive suite could have been the basis of a sit-com of its own.

"I got a troubling call from CBS today," Grant Tinker told Reid one day after summoning him to his office.

"What is it?" Reid said, wondering what he had done now.

"They said you had slipped the F word into this week's show."

"The *F* word? You've got to be kidding."

"Tim, did you say mamma jamma when you were introducing a song? One of the executives in New York thinks that's a code word for motherfucker."

"Mamma jamma? Grant, that's the name of a song. 'She's a Bad Mamma Jamma.' It's a big hit by Carl Carlton."

"Oh," Tinker said, and both men burst into laughter.

"Do you mean to tell me executives are sitting in a room at Black Rock debating mamma jamma?" Reid asked. "I can just picture it: 'Gee, I don't know, Al. I think mamma jamma could mean motherfucker. What do you think?'" And he and Tinker laughed some more.

But occasionally, the network's worries were more serious.

"Were you wearing the Star of David in one episode?" Tinker asked Reid.

"I wear a lot of jewelry. It's part of the character—open shirts, jewelry. Why?"

"Well, they're trying to sell the show abroad and Jordan has refused to buy it because they think you're wearing a Star of David. They're offended and I'm supposed to ask you to take it off."

"Grant, it's the word 'LOVE' that a jeweler has created around six points. It's a beautiful piece. I wear it all the time. Here, look at it."

"OK, Tim," Tinker said with a heavy sigh. "I'll see you later."

Then there were the death threats. "I got ten or twenty a year," Reid says. "They always came when I was alone in the broadcast booth with one of the women. Loni Anderson kissed me on the cheek in a Christmas episode and that really set them off. In another show, Jan Smithers and I jumped up and down and hugged each other. I got so much hate mail the network had to increase security for a few days. Things are different now, I guess, but back then a show like ours could have a tremendous impact on the American psyche. Some people found what we were doing very threatening."

Though *WKRP in Cincinnati* was conceived as a star vehicle for Gordon Jump as the station manager and Gary Sandy as the program director—they were the only ones who received star billing in the opening credits of the first episodes—it quickly developed into an ensemble in which each of the characters played important roles and had episodes built around them. Hesseman as the spaced-out disc jockey; Anderson as the sexy, savvy receptionist; Richard Sanders as the bumbling news director; Smithers as the shy ingénue; and Frank Bonner as the libidinous sales director worked together in a way that led critics to use the word "seamless." And television insiders considered it remarkable that during the entire run of the show none of them was ever replaced or marginalized and no major new characters were added.

Reid's portrayal of Venus Flytrap quickly became something of a conspiracy between him and Wilson, two native Southerners who disliked the way people from their region, black and white, were so often typecast on television and who were determined to do something about it.

"The network doesn't think you're black enough," Wilson told him early in the first season.

"Not again," Reid said, starting to laugh. "You know it's a hell of a thing to be black your entire life but not be black enough for television."

"We can deal with it, Tim," Wilson said. "We can give them what they want and let the character develop, too, show that he's a human being and not just a one-dimensional street guy. Let's talk about yourself. What are you into? What is there in your life we can use?"

Before long, Reid's character was being portrayed as delving into meditation and herbalism. He was wearing the loose-fitting clothes with the far-eastern look that Reid had begun designing for himself and listening to reggae. He was also shown to be quite conservative on some social issues—against hard drugs and objecting to the sexual content of song lyrics—and worried that he might be losing contact with black culture. He was making it clear, in short, that there were really two Venus Flytraps, the glib on-the-air hipster and the more complicated man underneath. "Hugh began to write the yin and the yang into the character," Reid says. "It was a discovery for him as much as it was for me."

The complexity of Venus Flytrap would pay big dividends a number of times, as in "Venus and the Man," an episode during the third season in which, as a favor to the station's cleaning woman, he uses street language to explain the atom to her son, a gang member who wants to drop out of high school. Soon, physics teachers around the country were using clips from the show as a way of demystifying the subject.

"What do you think about Venus having a beard?" Reid asked Wilson one day after filming for the first season began in earnest. "He didn't have one in the pilot, but I think he should."

"Fine," Wilson said.

"How about an earring?" said Loni Anderson, who was listening to their conversation.

"An earring *and* a beard?" Reid said, thinking it over. "Nobody's ever done that on television before. But why not?"

"You'll need to get your ears pierced," Anderson said.

"That's a little extreme, isn't it?"

"Oh, it doesn't hurt, and it's the only way the earring will look authentic."

"There I was again," Reid says, "doing whatever a strong woman told me to do. And, boy, did she lie. It hurt like hell. I felt like they were driving a stick into my head."

For a time it appeared that Reid's suffering may have been in vain when CBS executives called a meeting in New York to discuss the matter. "Hugh Wilson stood by me again," Reid says. "He said, 'Has television come to this? Are we really going to lose ratings because a black man is wearing a beard and an earring?' Basically, he just insulted them and they probably figured what the hell, I wasn't going to be around very long anyway."

But they were wrong. After just a few episodes, Reid began getting applause from the studio audience as he came onto the set and by the end of the first season Venus Flytrap had developed a cult following. The candles he lit in the studio and the gong he played, the Bob Marley poster on the wall at a time when the Jamaican reggae star's fame was just beginning to spread in the United States, the clothes, the beard, the earring, the language all combined to make him a cultural touchstone. As the season wound down, it was clear that Reid was due for a big raise, and for the one thing he had yet to receive—an episode built around Venus Flytrap.

"What about it, Hugh?" Reid asked Wilson. "Everybody's had one except me."

"I wrote one for you, but the network isn't sure about it," Wilson said. "It's about Vietnam."

"*Vietnam?* In a *sit-com?* Whoa."

"I know. They said they'll let us do it on one condition, that we have military people on the set while we're rehearsing. If they don't like it, it's not going on the air. The season will have to be one episode short."

In "Who is Gordon Sims?" Venus Flytrap's real name is revealed for the first time. He is shown to be a soldier who, after witnessing Viet Cong prisoners thrown out of a helicopter and a buddy in his platoon intentionally walk into a propeller, goes into shock. Instead of reporting to an army base back home to receive his discharge, he disappears. Though it is clear Sims has served his country honorably, he is officially listed as a deserter.

"We had soldiers and marines sitting in the audience all day watching our every move," Reid says. "And Hugh was smart. He began talking to them, using them as consultants, and asking them what they thought. They really got into it. The network was still nervous, though. We didn't get the final go-ahead to air the show until the day before the final run-through."

The tension on the set as the episode was shot was such that Reid hardly noticed that the studio was filled with more spectators than usual and a number of MTM executives, including Mary Tyler Moore, Tinker's wife, for whom the company was named. After the final scene was shot—Sims appears before a military hearing and is given a reprimand and his discharge—Moore approached him. "You made me cry," she said.

The episode received glowing reviews—"a tour de force performance by Tim Reid," wrote a reviewer for *Variety*—and Wilson was nominated for an Emmy. It was the perfect end to the show's first season and a strong lead-in to the summer re-runs when it was discovered by more and more fans. By the first few weeks of its second season, *WKRP in Cincinnati* often ranked among the top ten in national audience ratings.

Reid's success on the show was a blessing in another way, too. Finally able to afford the divorce he and Rita had put off, he made a suggestion he hoped would reduce the friction between them and allow him to remain in the lives of his children. "You've always wanted to get a degree in gerontology," he told her. "There's a good school in San Diego. Move there, bring the kids. I'll support you and them—their college educations, everything."

Reid's mother, disabled after an accident and no longer able to work, moved west, too, and now his family was close enough to visit regularly. His relationship with Rita would never be what it once was, but after a while the tension eased and they were friends again. "I left the marriage but I didn't leave the family," Reid says. "My relationship with my kids is the one thing I'm proudest of."

As work on *WKRP in Cincinnati* progressed, Reid found himself becoming closer and closer to Wilson. Their southern backgrounds and their eagerness to move beyond established sit-com boundaries gave them a great deal in common and Reid also saw how much he could learn from Wilson about writing, directing, and producing. "Hugh is the most creative writer I've ever met," he says. "His take on life is so fresh and sharp that you just want to be around him. I'm nowhere near as talented as he is, but our sense of humor is similar. And Hugh gave me some great opportunities. He let me write some episodes and produce one so I learned what it takes to get a show on the air. I began to follow scripts as they were written, to sit down with the editors and watch how the shows were transferred to the screen, and to experiment with some short films of my own. My first real exposure to production came through Hugh."

But Wilson also had an anarchic streak, an us-against-them mentality that undermined him in his confrontations with network executives. His battles with MTM and CBS over the content of *WKRP in Cincinnati* and the way the show was shuffled around the network schedule grew increasingly bitter. He and the others involved in the show were particularly upset when, midway through the second season, it was moved from its prized position following "M*A*S*H*, the top-rated show on television, to an earlier time slot. This led to concern over what was appropriate for a show airing during television's "family hour" and was a harbinger of things to come. During its third and fourth seasons, *WKRP in Cincinnati* was moved around so often that the cast and crew often didn't know when it was on. This was, they thought, one more indication of how little regard the network had for the show despite its success.

Lacking the diplomatic skills to smooth the show's path, Wilson began feuding with CBS president Robert Daly, even taking shots at an unnamed network executive based on Daly in his scripts. So no one was truly surprised when the show was cancelled after its fourth season. "I'm convinced it was killed because Hugh and Bob Daly hated each other," Reid says. "That show should have run for ten years."

The point was proven when, after the cancellation was announced, the final episode was the seventh most watched show of the week and when *WKRP in Cincinnati* went on to become a huge hit in syndication. "It was the most profitable show MTM ever had," Reid says. "More than *The Mary Tyler Moore Show,* more than *Hill Street Blues,* more than any of the rest of them."

Many years after Reid and Daphne Maxwell were married, Dreesen showed them an ad in a fashion magazine they had made together in 1972 in Chicago. "We were wearing big hats, polyester clothes, and fur collars, and I was draped all over him," Maxwell says. "But I had no memory of shooting the ad, and at the time I didn't know who Tim was. He was just another guy I was working with."

They were thrown together once or twice more in Chicago but since it was always in a working environment, and since they were both married, their acquaintance was never more than a passing one. In 1979, when Maxwell came to Los Angeles to look for work as an actress, a friend from Chicago mentioned having seen Reid, who was then making a name for himself on *WKRP in Cincinnati.* "Tell him I said hi, give me a call," she said.

"We were supposed to meet for five or ten minutes for a drink," Maxwell says. "Five hours later, we were having breakfast and laughing our butts off. Twenty-eight years later, we're still together."

Maxwell's childhood could hardly have been more different from Reid's. Though her parents were far from well-to-do—they raised three children in a public housing project on Manhattan's west side on a soda jerk's salary of forty dollars a week—they made sure their smart, articulate daughter had all the opportunities Reid had been denied. She won admission to the Bronx High School of Science, one of the top public high schools in the country, where she was voted president of the senior class and earned a National Merit Scholarship to Northwestern University. In junior high school, she sang in an all-city chorus at Carnegie Hall. In high school, she acted in the Group Theater Workshop, the forerunner of the Negro Ensemble Company, with such luminaries as Robert Hooks, Douglas Turner Ward, and Moses Gunn.

She also had the kind of experiences with white people while growing up that Reid lacked. "Everywhere I went, starting with kindergarten, it was totally integrated," she says. "There were about forty blacks at the Bronx High School of Science and I was more comfortable with that than being in an all-black environment. My sensibilities were different from Tim's because of my background so I could balance out some of his reasoning."

"He only said no because I'm black," Reid would occasionally say when, over the years, an executive would reject one of his projects.

"No, Tim," Maxwell would say, "he said no because that's what people like him do."

But there were also times when she suspected Reid might be right, that racism could be involved. She might not feel it in her bones the way he did, but that was because she had arrived so late to the party. "When I moved into my freshman dorm room at Northwestern, a girl looked at me standing there with my suitcases and said, 'Oh, no. I'm not rooming with a nigger.' I turned around to see who she was talking about. I had never been called that before."

The feeling of being a black outsider for the first time in her life led to her involvement with the fledgling black power movement at Northwestern. "We took over the administration building and agitated for the creation of an African-American Studies department," she says. "I'd been in demonstrations in New York and gone to the March on Washington, but it was always for black folks down south. It was never for anything that happened in *my* neighborhood."

While still a freshman, Maxwell's picture appeared in *Seventeen* magazine, which led to a contract with Eileen Ford's modeling agency and, much to her surprise, to her election as Northwestern's first black homecoming queen her sophomore year. At the presentation ceremony, the president of the university wouldn't speak to her as they posed for pictures and, after the white princesses were applauded when they were presented at the exclusive John Evans Society, her appearance was greeted with silence. "They gave me a cup without my name on it," she says, "and they didn't put my picture in the yearbook. The editor said it wasn't important that year." The occasion was celebrated on the cover of *Jet* magazine, however, which made up for those slights and then some.

Maxwell had no plans to become an actress. She viewed the theater work she had done in New York as nothing more than a hobby because it seemed to offer no chance of earning a living. "There were so few examples of black women actresses," she says. "It was not something you could look to." But then one of her modeling jobs led to an offer to read for a commercial. "It happened to be a national spot and they started sending checks," she says. "I said, 'Hey, this *can* be a paying gig. Maybe I should keep my options open.'" Soon she was doing voice-overs for radio and television, though the bulk of her income continued to come from her work in Chicago and New York as a fashion model. In 1969, she became the first black woman to appear on the cover of *Glamour* magazine. "It just kept happening," she says.

Robert Conrad, the actor who was a fellow Northwestern graduate, gave Maxwell her first television acting job in his series *The Duke*, which was shot in Chicago. A year later, after a lucrative series of commercials for Cheer laundry detergent provided a nest egg, she moved to Los Angeles. "I thought it was time to jump into the big pond and see what I could do," she says. "I was divorced by then so there was nothing holding me back. Robert Conrad put me in another show, *A Man Called Sloane*, which helped me get an agent. People started calling and I kept working. I still am."

One of her early jobs was on *WKRP in Cincinnati*, where, visiting Reid on the set one day, she was asked to read for a part. Taking advantage of his new Writer's Guild card, Reid wrote her into several more episodes. Along the way, she began designing her own clothes and some years later formed a partnership with the McCall Pattern Company that produced a series of videos and a pattern kit titled, "Suddenly You're Sewing." Soon, the Daphne Maxwell Reid collection of patterns was on sale in fabric stores nationwide.

Along with her beauty, intelligence, and talent, Maxell possessed another quality Reid found fascinating. Her life was not wrapped up in her career the way his had become. "There are so many actors and actresses, actresses particularly, who invest everything they have in this business," Reid says. "Daphne couldn't care less. She goes with the wind. She's the closest thing to a Zen master I've ever known."

"It annoyed the hell out of him that I wasn't as consumed with acting as he was," she says. "I thought it was a hoot, something I enjoyed doing, but there were other things I liked just as much—raising my son, designing clothes and making patterns, decorating our home, and art, which I really love. I didn't have the drive Tim thought I should have, but that's just not how I'm built. He was driving the train and I was happy to shovel coal."

So though Maxwell compiled a lengthy string of movie and television credits—including a recurring role as Vivian Banks, Will Smith's aunt, in *Fresh Prince of Bel Air* in the 1990s—she was better equipped than Reid to handle the down periods. Particularly the one that came when he suddenly found himself out of work. "I was really upset when *WKRP* was cancelled because I was beginning to get some notice," Reid says. "I did a TV movie of *You Can't Take It with You* with Jean Stapleton, Barry Bostwick, and Blythe Danner, and I kept getting calls to go to parades—the Easter Parade and Thanksgiving Day Parade in New York, and the Rose Bowl Parade. I was the black guy they liked putting out there. So things were beginning to happen for me, and then, boom, the show was over and it all ended. That's when I started learning some big lessons."

One was that success in a television series was not necessarily transferable; casting rooms were full of out-of-work actors from cancelled shows. "We had an ensemble cast and we understood that only one or two people were going to break out," he says. "Everybody knew Loni was going to take off, and Howard, but what about the rest of us? I thought I've got to do something. I've got to create something for myself."

Another was that spending money as fast as it came in was fine—until it stopped coming in. "Daphne and I were talking marriage, but now I couldn't afford it," Reid says. "We got into some big fights because of that and at one point I just left. There I was again, abandoning someone I loved."

Reid packed up and went to Spain where Bob Guccione, the creator of *Penthouse*, sent him to adapt some of the magazine's features for cable television, which was beginning to show its potential as an outlet for programming the broadcast networks wouldn't touch. "He'd seen some short, sensual films I'd made from a book of my poetry and I was excited because it was my first real job as a producer," Reid says. "I was half way through it before I realized it might end my career because I was now producing soft-porn."

A further complication was the fact that Xaviera Hollander, the author of the best-seller *The Happy Hooker*, had no interest in working with a young inexperienced black director to turn her *Penthouse* sex advice column into material for television. "She was just horrendous," says Reid, who wanted nothing more than to finish his work and get back home.

"What am I doing?" he thought as he boarded the plane for New York. "I've got a good woman here. Am I going to make the same mistakes again?"

The badly overloaded 747 vibrated violently and needed every inch of the Madrid airport runway before finally leaving the ground. The plane dipped and scraped the tops of trees as passengers screamed and objects flew from the luggage racks before it stabilized. "Finally, everybody calmed down," he says. "I looked over at my photographer who was sitting next to me and he was looking down. I had gouged my fingernails into his fist and blood was coming from his hand."

A happier surprise was waiting for him at JFK Airport, though—Daphne, who had flown in from Los Angeles.

"Will you marry me?" he yelled impulsively when he saw her off in the distance.

"Yes," she shouted back.

"Better wait until I clear customs," he said, and soon they were hugging, kissing, and crying.

"Look," Reid said as they waited for a cab. "We have to make two things happen before we can get married. First, our kids have to agree to it. You know yours resents me as much as mine resent you. And second, I've got to get some work, a steady job in a TV series."

"Is that all?" she said with a laugh. "OK."

"As God is my judge, this is what happened next," Reid says. "We got to the hotel and a clerk said, 'Mr. Reid, you have an urgent phone call.' It was from my manager and all it said was, 'Call me.' I did and she said, 'Can you get here right away? NBC has a new series and they want you.' I said, 'I just thought I was going to die in a plane crash and I'm not flying to LA for an audition.' She said, 'Tim, you're not listening to me. It's not an audition. You've got the job. It starts shooting next week. Do you want it or not?'

"I said OK, hung up the phone, looked at Daphne and said, 'I just got a series.' She said, 'You go to work on your kids and I'll go to work on mine. Now give me that phone.' Then she started arranging the wedding. I had been off the plane for three hours."

The show, *Teachers Only*, was a sit-com set in a Los Angeles high school that showed promise and had a distinguished cast that included Lynn Redgrave, Norman Fell, and Jean Smart. But Reid was disappointed to see how poorly written it was—where was Hugh Wilson when he needed him?—and was not surprised when it was cancelled after a dozen episodes. Still, he was back in the television mainstream, as he discovered one day when the phone rang while he was lying in bed wondering what was next.

"We're working on a new character for *Simon and Simon*,"

said Bill Dial, who had been a writer and producer for *WKRP in Cincinnati* and was now on the staff of the popular detective series featuring two dissimilar brothers, which was going into its third year of production. "He's a detective named Downtown Brown."

"Here we go again," Reid said. "Can't I ever get a decent name?"

"Well, his real name is Marcel Proust Brown, if that helps," Dial said, and they both laughed.

For four years, Reid lived the free and easy show business life he had always dreamed of. While the stars of *Simon and Simon* worked long hours, he would show up two days a week, breeze through his lines, often opposite Daphne, who had a recurring role as a television reporter who was his love interest, and be on his way. He was living in a lovely home with his beautiful wife, spending much of his free time working out, and making more money than he ever had in his life. What could be better than this?

And then one day it hit him. The longer he stayed on *Simon and Simon*, the more in danger he was of becoming a supporting character for the rest of his career. "You see it all the time," he says. "The guy who walks in, gives a little information, tells a joke, and then leaves. He's got a career, but always as a second banana. I could see that's what was going to happen to me."

It was time, he thought, to find something he could call his own. An attempt to produce and star in a television movie about Jesse Owens had ended badly when Paramount, the studio he pitched the idea to, stole it out from under him. But once he got over the betrayal—and once his agent convinced him that filing a lawsuit would destroy his career—he felt ready to try again. Somewhere out there, Reid thought, there was a project with his name on it. All he had to do was find it.

**11**

The first time Dreesen met Frank Sinatra was in Chicago in 1975. Pat Henry, a comedian who was Sinatra's opening act, took him to the Pump Room, the famous restaurant and gathering place for celebrities, where the singer was holding court with his long-time friend Jilly Rizzo and a number of others.

"This is my friend Tom Dreesen," Henry told Sinatra. "He's working at Mr. Kelly's."

"Hi, kid," Sinatra said, reaching out his hand.

"I went home that night and wrote 'Hi, kid' on the wall," Dreesen says.

Several years later, while working in Las Vegas with Sammy Davis Jr. he quite literally bumped into Sinatra again. "I was doing the warm-up for a television roast for Dean Martin," he says, "and I was supposed to go off stage right where all the performers were waiting to come on the set. But I went off stage left and there was Frank, all alone. I didn't know what to say to him so I said I was coming to see his show."

"Thanks, kid," Sinatra said.

That's progress, Dreesen thought.

In 1982, Dreesen appeared with Smokey Robinson at Caesars Palace in Lake Tahoe while Sinatra was working a few doors away at Harrah's. "I'd seen him perform a few times and I was amazed at how the audience reacted," Dreesen says. "He created more excitement just walking up to the microphone than most people did with their entire act. I figured this was my chance to see him up close so I called over to Harrah's, where Sammy Davis and I had worked a few times, and asked if I could watch from backstage."

Since Sinatra and Robinson went on after their opening acts at about the same time, Dreesen had to move fast. "I bolted off the stage and ran down the street," he says. "I didn't even take my stage clothes off because I didn't want to miss the opening."

Arriving out of breath, Dreesen heard somebody yell, "Hey, Tommy, come over here!" He turned and saw Holmes Hendricksen, Harrah's powerful vice president for entertainment, who was standing with a heavyset man with a cigar in his mouth. Hesitating for fear of missing Sinatra's entrance, Dreesen walked over to the two men.

"Tommy, this is Mickey Rudin," Hendricksen said, a name Dreesen recognized as that of Sinatra's manager. "Mickey, this is Tom Dreesen. I think Tom would make a great opening act for Frank Sinatra."

A pained expression came across Rudin's face, one that indicated he had heard those words more times than he could count. He winked at Hendricksen and said, "Hey, kid, if I gave you a week with Frank, would you want more than $50,000?"

"Let me put it this way, Mr. Rudin," Dreesen replied. "If you gave me a week with Frank, would *you* want more than $50,000."

Rudin burst out laughing. "I like this kid," he said.

"A couple of days later, Dan Wiley got a call," Dreesen says. "Was I available to work with Frank in Atlantic City for a week in May? I figured I'd go there, do one week, get my picture taken with him, hang it in every bar in Harvey, and be happy the rest of my life."

Following his second performance in Atlantic City, Sinatra asked Dreesen to go to dinner with him and his wife, Barbara. "In the middle of the meal—I remember this like it was yesterday—Frank put his knife and fork down and looked at me," Dreesen says. "He said, 'I like your material and I like your style. I'd like you to do a few other dates with me if you're interested.' For once in my life, I didn't say something glib like 'Let me check my calendar.' What I said was, 'I'd like that.' We were together for fourteen years."

Traveling with Sinatra was like being in the center of a whirlwind. Two large men would show up at Dreesen's condominium in a limousine, carry his bags downstairs, and drive him to the Van Nuys airport where he would board Sinatra's jet for Palm Springs. "The moment Frank stepped on that plane, we were gone," Dreesen says. "He'd say, 'Let's go Spots'—his pilot's name was Johnny Spots; great name for a pilot, isn't it?—and everything had better be ready because Frank didn't want to wait. Then when we'd land, squad cars and limousines would pick us up at the airport and rush us to the arena. We'd do the show and the squad cars and limousines would rush us back to the jet. We'd be flying over the venue to the next city and look down and see people in their cars still trying to get out of the parking lot."

Dreesen soon came to see that Sinatra's performances were not simply a show but an event. His mere appearance in a town was enough to get people talking, particularly when he traveled away from the nation's largest entertainment centers. Cities like Omaha, Salt Lake City, Des Moines, and Tampa would buzz with excitement and the site of his performance—often a basketball arena or a convention center—would become *the* place to be. "I honestly think a lot of people who didn't particularly care for his music bought tickets," Dreesen says. "They just wanted to be there because how many living legends were they ever going to see?"

And far from taking this reaction for granted, Sinatra viewed it as a responsibility. "He was the star of the show, but he was also the boss," Dreesen says. "He knew his job and everybody around him had better know theirs because he wanted everything to be perfect. He used to say that every night was a command performance. And it was amazing to see how nervous he'd get before a show. He would pace around like a boxer getting ready to fight. Barbara told me she didn't like to be around him before a show because he was so edgy."

Seeing Sinatra work was a revelation. "I'd sit in the wings and watch him night after night," Dreesen says, "and I began to realize that he approached every song as a script. He understood what the writer felt the day he took pen in hand and interpreted the lyrics the way an actor would. And he was an Academy Award-winning actor, remember. But like any actor doing the same part night after night, he didn't bring the same emotion every time. Some nights, he might be in a little darker mood. It was a joy to watch."

Soon Dreesen found himself paying attention to Sinatra's effect on the audiences, which typically spanned the generations. Parents would bring their children and there was always a large number of older people, too, who had heard Sinatra's voice on their radios and record players and in their cars their entire lives. Though occasionally Sinatra would change the songs he sang, adding some and removing others, the end of his performances never varied: "My Way" followed by "New York, New York."

"I always made sure I was in the wings when he sang 'My Way,'" Dreesen says. "The lights would be turned down low and he'd be standing alone in the spotlight. He'd sing, "And now the end is near, and so I face the final curtain . . ." and I'd see people sobbing. I knew what they were thinking, that Frank wasn't young any more and neither were they. Then you'd hear *bomp ba da bomp baaaaa* . . . and he'd start singing 'New York, New York,' this big, upbeat, defiant number as if to say he's not done yet, and people would be laughing and applauding while the tears from 'My Way' were still streaming down their faces. God, it was something."

Not long after Dreesen began working with Sinatra, they were sitting at dinner after a show when a woman at the next table looked over and said, "I don't know how you can do that."

"Do what?" Sinatra asked.

"Go out there night after night in front of all those people," she said. "I can't even imagine it."

"See that guy over there," Sinatra said, pointing at Dreesen. "He's got the toughest job in show business. I'm singing a song somebody else wrote with a big band behind me. But he's all alone with just his timing and his memory. He's naked out there."

Later, when interviewers asked him about working with Sinatra, Dreesen developed these thoughts into something of a routine. "What if I told you that in five minutes you're going out there in front of 20,000 people," he would say. "I want you to hold their attention, make them laugh and pull on the strings of their emotions for forty-five minutes. You have no props, no tricks, no charts, no arrangements, no orchestra, no special lighting, nothing. Just you and the 20,000 people. Oh, and by the way, not one of those 20,000 people came to see you."

"That was my job," Dreesen says. "I'd be waiting in the wings and the lights would go down low, the orchestra would play the opening notes of 'New York, New York' and the announcer would say, 'Ladies and gentlemen, welcome to the Nassau Memorial Coliseum for our show tonight starring Frank Sinatra. Now, here's his guest star, Tom Dreesen.' I'd walk out and people would be saying, 'What the hell is this all about?' and 'I never heard of this guy,' and 'Where's Frank?' It was like opening for Sha-Na-Na all over again. Luckily, Sinatra fans were ladies and gentlemen for the most part and they were going to give you a chance. But if there was one thing I learned from working with Tim it was that I had better grab that chance fast."

Quickly, Dreesen would launch into his routine. "How many of you are seeing Frank Sinatra live for the first time tonight? Applaud. Now, how many of you thought Frank Sinatra was coming out just now? Go ahead, applaud. I know how you feel. I'm a little disappointed myself." (First laugh of the night.) "What a magnificent arena this is. How many of you are here for your very first time? Applaud if you are. All right, how many of you aren't wearing any underwear?" (Second laugh.)

The important thing, Dreesen saw, was to take charge, to have the audience respond to what he was saying and to make jokes about himself. Then, just as Tim and Tom had localized their routines for specific audiences, Dreesen would tell jokes about local politicians and personalities—the name recognition alone would usually be good for a laugh—based on information he had picked up in the limo to the arena or from someone who worked there. Who's the richest guy in town? he would ask. Given the name of a wealthy landowner in Louisville, he would say, "What a beautiful town this is. You know, on a quiet night you can hear William Bradley counting his money." Were there any recent scandals he should know about? Told about a politician who had been accused of exaggerating her academic record, he would say, "Or Sissy Williams counting her degrees." Give me the name of a small town nearby, he asked a limo driver in Dayton, Ohio, who mentioned Miamisburg, which was just down the road. "I don't know if you heard the commotion outside tonight," he would say, "but the governor said the state police were too busy to give us an escort to the arena so they sent over the entire Miamisburg police force . . . one guy on a John Deere tractor."

Audiences appreciated the fact that he had taken the time to learn something about their town and the reviews of Sinatra's performance often made mention of it. Yes, it was a tough job, he thought, but there were ways of making it easier, of getting a crowd that had not come to see him on his side.

Almost from the beginning of his relationship with Sinatra, Dreesen realized something instinctively: the last thing the man needed was one more fan. So he tried to maintain a certain distance, and never to fawn. "I'd see him do these extraordinary things on stage, but all I'd say was, 'Good crowd tonight, huh, boss?' And he'd say, 'Yeah, good crowd.' And that would be it."

But despite this deference, Dreesen found himself drawing closer to Sinatra personally and it was not hard to understand why. Both men had started out as poor Italian kids. Both had

grown up in and around saloons—Sinatra in his father's bar in
Hoboken, New Jersey, where sailors would give him a nickel
to sing along with the player piano. "A writer for the *New York
Times* once asked Frank why he kept me with him so long,"
Dreesen says, "and he said, 'If I'm a saloon singer—and I am—
then Tommy is a saloon comedian.' By that, he meant we were
just a couple of neighborhood guys."

As their friendship deepened, Dreesen began spending more
time with Sinatra when they were not working. He would often stay in a bungalow in the singer's Palm Springs compound
where Sinatra, unable to sleep, would knock on the door and
say, "Come on, Tommy, let's take a ride."

"Frank never went to bed until dawn his entire life," Dreesen
says. "He catnapped a little during the day and then he'd keep
going until the sun came up. So we'd get in the car and ride all
over the desert—hot summer nights with the windows down,
talking about being a kid in Hoboken, and about life, the good
and the bad. Or we'd go into a bar and have a few drinks and
then ride around some more. Usually, it was just two friends
talking, but there were times when he felt like a father to me,
the father I'd never really had."

As they were sitting at a table one night, a woman walked in
and asked if the bar had a jukebox.

"No," Sinatra said, "but I'll be happy to sing for you."

"No thanks," she said, and turned around and left.

"I don't think she knew who you were," Dreesen said.

"Maybe she did, Tommy," Sinatra said with a smile.

Dreesen also became close to Barbara Sinatra, who saw to
it that he was invited to Palm Springs for her elaborate parties,
often to benefit a charity. "Mingle with the guests, Tommy," she
would say. "Entertain them for us." And he would find himself
talking with the likes of Gregory Peck, Kirk Douglas, and Clint
Eastwood, and their wives. Though there was still enough of
Harvey in him to be thrilled by this, it was the final straw for
Maryellen. "This is your life, not mine!" she shouted one day
when he mentioned some of the people who would be at a party

as they drove to Palm Springs. "Turn this car around and take me home!" Dreesen pulled off the road and calmed her down and she actually enjoyed the weekend. But she was never truly comfortable in these surroundings, and never failed to let him know it.

"She felt like she didn't belong there," Dreesen says, "like she was in way over her head. She was a girl from Harvey, Illinois, and that's where she wanted to be. I was always trying to tell her to think positive, to read the books I was reading, but I just couldn't get her to do it."

The breakups became more frequent now until it became al-most inevitable that one would be final. And then, after twenty-six years of marriage, one was. "I think we both realized that sometimes there is nothing you can do," Dreesen says, "that the love is just gone."

Driving in the desert one night, Dreesen unburdened him-self to Sinatra. "I can't give you any advice on marriage, Tommy," he said, "but I can give you advice on divorce because I've been there. The important thing is to try to remain friends if you can. For her well-being and for your well-being, but most of all for the kids' well-being."

"That was good advice, wasn't it?" Dreesen says. "And Sinatra lived it, too. He stayed friends with his wives until the end."

Sinatra also gave him advice about his act. "Whenever I broke in new material, he'd listen backstage and tell me what he thought," Dreesen says. "He'd often say, 'There's no need to be dirty, Tommy. You're funny without that. There are families out there—grandmothers and grandfathers, mom and dad and the kids.' I respected that."

Occasionally, Dreesen would travel with other performers— Smokey Robinson, Natalie Cole, Frankie Avalon, Tony Orlando and Dawn—and get parts in television shows. He was cast in dramatic programs like *Columbo* and *Murder, She Wrote*, and in sit-coms like *The Facts of Life*. One day, he found himself in an episode of *WKRP in Cincinnati,* playing a white reporter for a black newspaper who is sent to interview Venus Flytrap.

"You don't know what it's like to work in a place where everybody else is one color and you're another," Dreesen said.

"Do tell," Reid replied.

"It felt a bit odd on the set at first," says Reid, who had told the show's producers of his partnership with Dreesen and suggested that he play the part. "It was like being at the finish line of a race we hadn't run."

Dreesen left the set feeling a little wistful, too. "It was good to be together with Tim again and to see him doing so well," he says, "but I couldn't help thinking about all the times we'd talked about having our own television show. All that ever came of it was that one scene."

Though these other jobs were gratifying, Dreesen's career soon began to follow a pattern. The call would come that Sinatra was going on tour again and the two large men would appear at his house to carry his bags to the limousine that would take him to the airport. He had helped create the Celebrity Golf Tour by then, and there were times when he would shake his head in wonderment. "I used to shine shoes on my hands and knees in bars where Sinatra was singing on the jukebox, and I used to carry two bags a day at Ravisloe," he says. "Now I'm flying in Frank's jet to forty-five or fifty cities a year, doing shows with him, staying in his home, and having drinks with Dean Martin and Sammy Davis Jr. And I'm playing golf on the finest courses in the land—on the celebrity tour with Michael Jordan, Johnny Bench, and John Elway, and in pro-ams with Arnold Palmer, Jack Nicklaus, and Tiger Woods. How could life get any better than this? The author Christopher Morley wrote that success is living the life you want. And I was."

And yet . . .

What was it Sammy Davis had said about moving on after two or three years, about not staying with him forever? Shouldn't he be pursuing one of those sit-com development deals the networks occasionally dangled in front of him? And look how David Letterman and Jay Leno, with whom he had struggled on the way up, had become stars of their own late-night talk shows. "You could do this, Tommy," Letterman would tell him when they went out to dinner after he had appeared on Letterman's show. He's right, Dreesen would think. I could.

"When I look back, I see there are a lot of things I could have done differently," Dreesen says. "I botched a whole bunch of great opportunities. There were a lot of talk shows in those days and maybe I should have pursued one. But I'd see how David and Jay live, how they have to come up with a show day in and day out, week in and week out, year in and year out. The ratings, the meetings, the guests, the interviews. And the more you accomplish, the more you accumulate, the more you have to be responsible for. That's a lot of stress in your life."

As for a television series, he had worked in the medium enough to learn that getting to the set at five thirty in the morning and sitting around the set all day waiting to deliver a few lines written by somebody else seemed like a wasted life. He was a stand-up comedian. That was all he had ever wanted to be, somebody who made people laugh, whether there were 15 in the room or 15,000. He didn't do it as a way to audition for roles, to be an actor, to become someone he didn't want to be. He did it because that was what he was—first, last, and always.

And so he would turn down some of the offers that came his way and not aggressively pursue others. After he passed up meetings with network producers, the Geddes Agency, frustrated in its attempts to get him regular work on television, dropped him as a client. Maybe he was making a mistake. Maybe he would have developed a bigger following and have made more money. But would he have had the same rich experiences, the same wonderful memories? "That's all we have in the end, isn't it?" Dreesen says. "The memories. I'd be lying if I said I didn't think about it, if I didn't wonder what might have been. I firmly believe that you are governed by two energies in your life, your ego and your spirit. My ego would be saying, 'Are you crazy? You've got a chance to do something on your own.' But my spirit would say, 'Wow, I'm going on tour with Frank Sinatra.' I wouldn't have missed it for the world."

So each night Dreesen would stand in the wings and listen yet again to the lyric that reduced audience after audience to tears. "Regrets? I've had a few, but then again, too few to mention," Sinatra would sing. Tell me about it, boss, he would think.

Driving to the airport in Salt Lake City one night after Sinatra's performance had received a particularly rapturous reception during which the stage had been showered with flower petals, Dreesen noticed the singer seemed strangely quiet.

"Great crowd tonight, huh, boss?" he said, just to end the silence.

"Yes," Sinatra said, a touch of sadness in his voice. "I think they thought it was the last time they were going to see me."

Sinatra was sixty-six years old when Dreesen began working with him, and eighty when he retired, and there were times when he showed every bit of his age. "I'd see him backstage when I came off and he'd be pacing and getting ready to go on and he just looked so old and tired," Dreesen says. "I'd think, 'You poor guy. You should be home playing with your grandchildren and taking life easy.' But then the orchestra would start up and he'd walk out on the stage and the lights would hit him and twenty years would fall from his face. All of a sudden, he was young again. The applause, the cheers, they were everything to him. I think he needed them to stay alive."

Seeing that Sinatra often struggled to remember lyrics, Dreesen mentioned to his road manager, Hank Cattaneo, that Sammy Davis Jr. placed a teleprompter on the floor at the front of the stage when he was breaking in new songs. Sinatra adopted the idea and soon he was inserting songs in his repertoire he hadn't sung in years, such as "Moonlight in Vermont." "Often, he didn't even look at the teleprompter," Dreesen says, "but it made him feel comfortable to know it was there. And when he did look down, it appeared that he was singing to someone in the front row. Frank learned to cheat very well that way."

Sinatra's voice had begun to falter, too, though his ability to act out the songs never did. "He'd sing, 'It's quarter to three, there's no one in the place except you and me' and everyone could just picture a man all alone in a bar whose woman has left him and he's never going to find love again," Dreesen says. "And even if he was having a bad night with some of the songs, he would always nail three or four of them."

Sinatra was beginning to forget other things, too. He would repeat stories he had told only a few minutes earlier—no one would ever dare point this out—and forget people's names. Stay close to me, he'd tell Dreesen at parties, and when someone came up to talk Dreesen would whisper the name in his ear. "Sometimes, I would be off getting a drink," he says, "and I'd see somebody talking to him and I could see the look in his eyes that said he didn't know who it was. He was starting to get dementia, I think, and it really worried him. Once, he told me he didn't even know his own phone number. I said, 'With all due respect, Mr. S., you don't have to know your phone number. All you have to do is say get Barbara on the phone or get Mickey on the phone.'"

Though Sinatra occasionally talked about retirement, few around him took him seriously. "I used to joke that one night he'd be singing, 'My Way,' and fall over and that would be it," Dreesen says. And then, on March 5, 1994, during a concert in Richmond, Virginia, it appeared to be happening right in front of him. "He was singing 'My Way,' and he passed out," Dreesen says. "He fell and hit his head on a footlight and cut it. I ran out on stage—I was the first one to get to him—and I thought, 'Oh, my God, my prophecy came true.' But he was fine. He'd been up until six in the morning and hadn't had much sleep. It was hot in the arena, too, and he hadn't drunk any water so he was just dehydrated."

Sinatra was taken to a hospital where a doctor insisted that he spend the night. Not a chance, Sinatra said. "I think he felt

the doctor just wanted to be able to say he had treated Frank Si-
natra and he didn't want anything to do with that," Dreesen says.
"A couple of hours later, we were flying home. Frank had a Jack
Daniels in one hand and an unfiltered Camel in the other."

Three weeks later, at the Mark of the Quad Cities, an arena
in Moline, Illinois, Sinatra's worst nightmare played out before
a capacity crowd of more than 10,000 people. "I did my show
and it was a great crowd, really up," Dreesen says. "Frank went
out and did three songs and was just rolling. But on his fourth
song, 'I Guess I'll Hang My Tears Out to Dry,' he blanked on the
lyrics. The teleprompter kept rolling and you could see him just
standing there all confused. He looked so forlorn and lost."

Down in the pit, the orchestra, led by Frank Sinatra Jr., continued to play until the musicians began to realize what had
happened and the sound wound down one instrument at a
time, leaving the arena in an eerie silence. "I'm sorry," Sinatra
whispered into his microphone. "I'm so sorry."

Oh, shit, Dreesen thought, as he worked his way to stage
left where Sinatra would come off. It's finally happening. What
an awful way for his career to end. Then, far up in the upper
reaches of the balcony, a man stood up and began to shout.

"THAT'S ALL RIGHT, FRANK! IT'S ALL RIGHT! WE LOVE
YOU, FRANK! IT'S ALL RIGHT!"

The man began to applaud, and then the person next to him,
and then five more, and soon the whole arena was on its feet
cheering and clapping. Sinatra acknowledged them with tears
in his eyes, then turned and began walking offstage. "He had
the microphone in his hand," Dreesen says, "and I'm thinking
he's going to lay it down and I'm going to say, 'It's been a great
run, Mr. S. Now, it's time to go home.'"

Sinatra had almost reached the wings when he looked up
and saw Dreesen waiting for him. Then, as if he had suddenly
been jolted awake, he turned and walked back to center stage
while the audience was still standing and cheering. He waited,
motioned with his hands for the people to sit and, as the noise
died down, he pointed at his son in the orchestra pit.

Frank Jr. looked up at him quizzically, as if to say "Are you sure?" and Sinatra, the look on his face saying, "Are you questioning *me*?" jabbed his finger at him. The conductor motioned to Chuck Berghofer, the bass player, who softly played several notes to create the only sound that could be heard in the arena. After a few bars, Ron Anthony's guitar joined in, and Bill Miller's piano, and Greg Fields's drums—along with perhaps the most familiar voice in the world:

*Hey, the shark has . . .*
*Pretty teeth dear . . .*

Soon, the entire orchestra was blazing its way through "Mack the Knife," led on a furious pace by the man behind the microphone. "He absolutely drilled that song," Dreesen says. "He hit every nuance, every note. I could feel the hairs standing up on the back of my neck."

When the song ended, Sinatra received another standing ovation from a crowd that knew very well what it had just witnessed and did not want to let go. Sound filled the arena until, as Sinatra looked at the orchestra in a signal he was ready to continue, it finally began to die down. And when at last he could be heard again, he pointed to a spot in the upper reaches of the balcony and shouted, "I LOVE YOU TOO, PAL!"

Sinatra finished the show, walked off the stage, patted Dreesen's cheek, gave him a wink, and disappeared into his dressing room. He toured for two more years.

In the years after Reid left *Simon and Simon,* a decision that did not make the producers of the show happy, there was little in television he didn't do. He developed "Snoops," a series for himself and Daphne in which they played a criminology professor and his wife, a U.S. State Department employee, who, in the style of Mr. and Mrs. North, continually stumble across murders to solve. The show didn't last long and his battles with network executives were maddening, but his multiple roles of co-creator, executive producer, and star paid him more than he would ever make in show business again. "Andy Griffith was making *Matlock* then and when he found out what my deal was he got really pissed," Reid says with a laugh.

For six years, he had a featured role in *Sister, Sister,* a show about twin girls who are separated at birth and discover each other by chance at a shopping mall. And he appeared in a wide variety of other TV series and movies. In 1995, Reid read Clifton Taubert's book, *Once Upon a Time When We Were Colored,* a story of black children growing up in a closely knit community in the segregated South, and was fascinated. "I know these people," he thought. "This is my story." He bought the rights, hired a cast and crew, and, for the first time, became a director as well as producer. "Thirteen weeks on the front lines taught me a les-

**12**

son I've never forgotten," he says. "How to make a high-quality, low-budget movie."

The film, which starred Al Freeman Jr., Phylicia Rashad, Richard Roundtree, and Polly Bergen, received rave reviews, and its honest portrayal of black life, along with its message of acceptance and redemption, was hailed around the world. "Black churches brought their entire congregations to see it," Reid says. "I took it to Israel where the government showed it on a day of tolerance between Palestinians and Jews. And the Hollywood premiere was very successful. Roger Ebert in particular took it to his heart. I thought it was going to change my life."

But it didn't. The calls from Hollywood he was hoping for on the strength of the movie's reception never came, and his efforts to use it as an entrée into directing television films failed as well. There was no mystery about what the problem was. He wasn't in tune with the times, he was told. His movie was too warm and fuzzy. It didn't portray the reality of black life. Hadn't he seen *Boyz n the Hood*? Now *that* was cutting edge.

"It seemed so bizarre to me," Reid says. "I'd seen people shoot up with heroin. I'd lived in a whorehouse. That wasn't cutting edge to me. But white America was enthralled by it and anybody who wanted to show real black people, people who weren't stereotypes, was pushed aside. I was in a strange situation, wasn't I? On the one hand, I was a militant black who fought the networks. On the other hand, my movie wasn't black enough."

He and Daphne were living on a farm in Charlottesville, Virginia, by then, which provided an escape from Hollywood at the price of having to commute to Los Angeles to continue their television careers. They also produced and hosted a syndicated talk show for King World, but it was only seen in Washington, Baltimore, and parts of Virginia. Reid had won some battles in his life, but when it came to going up against the phenomenon known as Oprah he quickly realized he was overmatched. "We got slaughtered," he says, "so for a while I just retired. I sold my

Mercedes and bought a tractor and for two years I just drove around on the farm. For a while, we didn't even have a television set."

Then came a call from his business manager. "Tim, do you like your farm?" he asked.

"I love it."

"Well, you better get your ass back to work if you want to keep it."

Back in Los Angeles for his role in *Sister, Sister*, Reid continued to pitch his own ideas without success. And then he had an inspiration. If the Hollywood studios weren't interested in his projects, why didn't he just build his own? "Boy, was that a crazy idea," he says with a laugh. In 1997, he used the money he had made from *Sister, Sister* to build New Millennium Studios, a state-of-the-art production facility, on a spot on the farm where soybeans once grew. Together, he and Daphne produced a number of movies, television shows, and documentaries, including a feature film, *Asunder*, a psychological thriller starring Blair Underwood, and *Linc's*, a television series for Showtime that received excellent notices and lasted for three seasons.

The show was set in a bar behind the Capitol building in Washington, that attracts everyone from prostitutes to politicians who grapple with, and laugh at, the issues of the day, and it was a crash course in television production. "We built the sets, shot it with a three-camera film crew without an audience, did it all ourselves," Reid says. "It was the first series shot outside of Hollywood and New York since *The Jackie Gleason Show*. Everybody thought we were nuts."

Somehow, though, New Millennium Studios continued to operate as one of the few independent production facilities in the country, and Reid continued to decry negative depictions of black life in America. "I'm not sure black folks fully understand the power the media has over us," he would tell audiences at various speaking engagements, often at colleges. "We are becoming who they portray us as being. We've allowed ourselves to become a collection of negative statistics. Simon says dress like a gangster, and we do. I'm amazed by what I see on television or in the movies. Either I overslept or someone stole my culture."

Reid did more than just talk about such problems, though. Working with the Entertainment Industry Council, he created an anti-drug music video called "Stop The Madness" in which a number of Hollywood stars appeared, as well as Nancy Reagan, whose Just Say No campaign made her particularly interested in its message. Before long, he and Daphne found themselves invited to a state dinner at the White House. Not bad for a country boy from Norfolk, Reid thought, as he looked around at his surroundings.

As Reid attempted to explain his ideas about the portrayal of black life in America to movie and television executives, he would occasionally hear something that indicated another reason they weren't selling. "You're the guy who did *Frank's Place*, aren't you?" someone would say. "That didn't work out so well, did it?"

It began over a tennis game at Hugh Wilson's house in Brentwood. At loose ends after leaving *Simon and Simon*—had he really been foolish enough to walk out on a steady high-paying job?—Reid had succumbed to Daphne's urging to continue trying to create something for himself and called the best television writer he knew. But Wilson wasn't working in television anymore, having parlayed his success with *WKRP in Cincinnati* into a solid movie career. He had written *Stroker Ace*, which starred Burt Reynolds and Loni Anderson, and co-written and directed *Police Academy*, the hugely successful comedy that generated six sequels. He was now moving in an entirely different direction.

"Haven't you even *thought* about doing another television series?" Reid asked him after they walked off the court.

"Only long enough to know I don't want to do it," Wilson said. "It wears you out, Tim. The actors get bored playing the same characters week after week and the writers get to the point where they can't even look at a typewriter without getting sick. You're rolling a rock uphill and every week after you shoot the show it rolls back down again."

"But it would be fun to work together again, wouldn't it?"

"You've got something in mind, don't you?" Wilson said with a sigh.

"Well, I've been thinking about a little bar or a restaurant—something like a black *Cheers*."

"But set in the South, right? The part of the country you and I know the best. That would be interesting, wouldn't it? But look, I can't get back into the grind of doing a series. I just can't. I did write the pilot for a series for Loni last year and then let other people take over. What if I did that?"

"That's fine, Hugh. I understand. Write the pilot, get it on the air. I'll take it from there."

"Let me make some calls," Wilson said, ideas already racing through his head.

By the time they met with Kim LeMasters, the vice president for programming at CBS, and Greg Maday, the network's vice president for comedy development, Wilson had come up with the broad outline of a show in which a retired professional football player buys a restaurant in Atlanta. But as soon as he said the word "restaurant," Maday interrupted him.

"I have an idea I want to talk to you about," he said, and he began describing a show about a man who inherits a restaurant from a father he never knew and is suddenly thrown into a completely unfamiliar world. "I used to hang out at a place called Dan Montgomery's when I was in college in Buffalo. The music was great and so were the people. And Cajun food is really popular now. Maybe you could set it in New Orleans."

"Gumbo, jazz, the blues, voodoo, interesting characters with the accent and attitude of the South," LeMasters said. "Something really different. What do you think?"

"Set in the black community, you mean?" Reid asked. "Nobody's ever shown black culture in the South."

"Fine," LeMasters said.

Reid and Wilson looked at each other. They could hardly believe it. They had come to pitch an idea to CBS and now CBS was pitching *them*. And pitching a wonderfully creative idea that was exactly what they had in mind. A show that would portray the reality of black life in the South, that would show a middle-class black community with love and humor and understanding.

"What do you think, Tim?" Wilson asked.

"I think we should go to New Orleans," Reid said.

The first restaurant they walked into was one of the French Quarter's finest, with linen tablecloths, a gourmet menu, and elegant service. "This is too upscale," Wilson said. "It's got to be a struggling restaurant, but one that's well known in the community."

"Let's keep looking," Reid said.

Chez Helene was not hard to find. A restaurant in a black working-class neighborhood? One that attracts people from all over town and tourists, too? You want Austin Leslie's place in the Treme, they were told. It's back behind the French Quarter, not far from the Mississippi River.

Sitting in the bar, Reid and Wilson took in the sights, sounds, and smells of a neighborhood spot with a reputation that exceeded its modest surroundings. Austin Leslie was the pioneer of a cuisine he called Creole-Soul and what a cuisine it was. Oysters Rockefeller served on bent tin pie plates. Crawfish étouffée, file gumbo, and stuffed pork chops. Mustard greens, cornbread, and fried chicken livers. Creole bread pudding with vanilla whiskey sauce. And Leslie's signature dish: fried chicken topped with a thick paste of raw garlic and parsley, served with a pepper stuffed with seafood dressing. "You couldn't fry a chicken better than Austin," New Orleans author Leah Chase wrote. "You couldn't stuff a pepper better than Austin Leslie."

Chez Helene's customers were just what they were looking for, too—a mix of people from the neighborhood, visitors from the upscale wards, local politicians, celebrities, and tourists. "Let us just sit here awhile and inhale all this good stuff," Reid said when Leslie offered them a table in the dining room. They had found what they were looking for.

After dinner, they called Leslie over and told him what they had in mind. They would like to base a television show on Chez Helene.

"We don't use that fancy French word in the neighborhood much," Leslie said. "Folks around here just call it the Chez."

Wilson smiled and took out his notebook. "We'd like to base the chef on you," he said.

"I'm not a chef," Leslie said. "I'm a cook."

Wilson wrote that down, too.

He was thinking about funeral homes, Wilson said. Funeral rituals are an important part of black culture, aren't they? Making a funeral director, or possibly an embalmer, part of the show would open up all sorts of possibilities. Perhaps his character's father could have left a funeral home as part of his estate along with the restaurant. Let's go look at some, Reid said.

The first thing they learned was that the owners of the funeral homes they visited were all women, middle-aged or older, who conveyed a powerful no-nonsense authority. But when they arrived at the Rhodes Funeral Home on Washington Avenue, they discovered that the owner, Doris Rhodes, had turned over the day-to-day operations to her pleasant young daughter, Kathleen. After chatting for a while, they asked to meet the embalmer. "We were expecting Boris Karloff," Wilson said, "but this beautiful young woman wearing a flower-print dress walks in and says, 'Hey, how y'all doing. I'm Trencia Henderson.' Tim turned to me and we both said the same thing: 'Daphne.'"

"An *embalmer!?*" Daphne said, bursting into laughter when Reid told her of their plan. "Where do I sign?"

Reid and Wilson spent several days with Henderson, driving around town as she collected dead bodies. "She was proud of the fact she could pick up a grown man," says Reid, who listened in fascination to her talk about the noises corpses made as she prepared them for viewing.

"We do full-fledged wakes," she told them. "No little cubicles. When you see your mama laid out here, it's the whole nine yards."

At one of the funerals they attended, a telephone had been painted on the inside of the casket lid along with the words, "Jesus called." Wilson reached for his notebook.

"How about the men you go out with?" Reid asked Henderson. "What do they think when they find out what you do?"

"Well, for some reason they always want to see if my hands are cold," she said. "There's a myth that embalmers have cold hands. A guy asked to feel my hands once and I had been holding a beer so when he touched them, they were ice cold. It freaked him out."

Wilson couldn't write it down fast enough.

Some weeks later, Wilson sent Reid the script for the pilot of a show called *Frank's Place*. Frank Parrish, a New England college professor, inherits a restaurant in New Orleans where he plans to stay just long enough to sell it. But he immediately becomes involved with the restaurant's employees and clientele. The latter includes Hanna Griffin, a mortician who works at a funeral home across the street that is owned by her imperious mother who, as Wilson imagines her, is confined to a wheelchair. A voodoo-tinged run of bad luck upsets Parrish's ordered life back home and against his better judgment, almost against his will, he returns to New Orleans to run Chez Louisiane, which is known to the regulars as the Chez.

As Reid read the script, he felt something he couldn't explain. And then he realized what it was. He couldn't breathe. "It was as if I had stepped into a hyperbolic chamber," he says with a laugh. "I had no sense, no thoughts. I was completely void of emotion. '*Feel* something,' I told myself, and then I did. What I was feeling was fear."

"What do you think?" Wilson asked Reid after he had put his trepidations aside long enough to pick up the phone.

"It's brilliant, Hugh," Reid said. "I've never read anything like it. But I'm worried. It's *too* good. They'll never buy it. People in television don't know this environment. They don't know these people. They won't be able to deal with it."

"Let's turn it in and see," Wilson said. "Maybe they'll surprise us."

They went back to New Orleans again and again. They took a crew with them and copied the floor plan of Chez Helene down to the smallest detail so they could recreate it on a sound stage. Later, when they shot the pilot, they brought Austin Leslie to Hollywood to prepare some of his specialties so the food would look authentic. "I had to cook every day," Leslie said. "There was never no leftovers."

On one of their trips, Daphne came along to meet Trencia Henderson and research her role. Reid dropped her off at the funeral home and when he returned an hour later he was surprised to find the relaxed friendly atmosphere he had always encountered had been replaced by a cold formality. "This way, please," he was told by someone he hadn't met before.

"I walked into a room," Reid says, "and there were Daphne, Trencia, Kathleen Rhodes, and a matriarchal-looking woman sitting at the end of a table. She dismissed the attendant standing next to her and she sat there looking at me while nobody said a word. Then I saw she was in a wheelchair and I felt a cold jolt. It was Doris Rhodes."

"Hugh, you're not going to believe this," he told Wilson, who was waiting for them in a car outside. "The woman who owns the funeral home *is* in a wheelchair."

"Step on it," said Wilson, who was beginning to wonder about this voodoo business. "Let's get out of here."

Where did Wilson find these great black actors? Reid wondered. Virginia Capers, who played Daphne's domineering mother,

Bertha Griffin-Lamour, had a long list of theatrical credits and was a Julliard-trained singer who had won a Tony for best actress in the musical *Raisin*. Francesca P. Roberts, who portrayed the sassy head waitress Anna-May, had studied in New Orleans and Paris and was ten years into a career that would make her one of the busiest actors in Hollywood. Lincoln Kilpatrick, who played one of the restaurant's regulars—a card-playing preacher named Reverend Deal, who alternates his time between searching for a pulpit and hustling real estate—had played in *Raisin in the Sun* and *Blues for Mr. Charlie* in New York and was the first black member of the Lincoln Center Repertory Company. Tony Burton, who played Big Arthur, the cook patterned after Austin Leslie, was a veteran actor who had once been a heavyweight boxer. This led to a continuing role as Sylvester Stallone's corner man in the *Rocky* movies, and to a *Frank's Place* episode, based on an only-in-New Orleans true story in which he gets into the ring with a rival chef who has stolen his recipes.

As for the two oldest members of the cast—Charles Lampkin, who was seventy-four and played the bartender Tiger Shepin, and Frances E. Williams, who was eighty-three and played the "waitress emeritus" Miss Marie—what *hadn't* they done? Lampkin was a character actor whose career went back decades while Williams had helped found the first equity theater company in Los Angeles and had been friends with Langston Hughes and Paul Robeson. In the 1930s, when she couldn't get the training as an actor she yearned for in segregated America, Robeson encouraged her to go to Moscow and study with Stanislavsky. "She'd tell us stories of harboring Robeson when he was on the lam," Reid says. "She was amazing."

Wilson also chose Robert Harper, who had a long string of acting credits, to play Bubba Weisberger, Frank's lawyer, one of the show's two white regulars. But perhaps his most inspired piece of casting came when he found the second one. Flying from Los Angeles to New Orleans, Wilson, who was trying to quit smoking, left his first-class seat to bum a cigarette in coach.

"I just found Shorty," he told Reid when he returned. "He's a gym teacher in Las Vegas."

"You're going to hire a guy who's never acted before?"

"It will be easier to teach him to act than to teach an actor to learn his accent. Wait until you hear him."

Don Yesso's portrayal of kitchen helper Shorty La Roux, whose lines Wilson occasionally rendered in subtitles, led to an acting career that continues to this day.

They broke all the rules. They didn't use a laugh track or shoot in front of an audience. They used one camera instead of the usual four so they would have the freedom to change angles, move around the set, and occasionally leave it altogether, as if they were making a movie. They insisted the actors know their lines before rehearsals started because once the show was blocked and everybody had their positions the camera was going to roll.

Four days into the filming of the pilot, Wilson announced a change of heart. "I'm going to stay" he said.

"Stay with the show?" Reid asked. "Do you mean it? What about the movies?"

"This is more fun than a movie. The only problem is I now have to sit down and do twenty-one more episodes."

"Nothing could have made me happier," Reid says.

They used Louis Armstrong singing "Do You Know What It Means to Miss New Orleans" during the opening credits, which rolled over sepia-toned images of old New Orleans. But as Wilson and the writing staff, which included the award-winning black playwright Samm-Art Williams, developed the scripts, no one could tell what might appear on the screen after the song and the opening commercial had played.

Sometimes, it would be a richly slapstick episode. In "Where's Ed?" some friends of a man who has just died steal him out of his coffin in the funeral home late one night to take him out on the town for one last celebration. He ends up in the Chez freezer just as the health inspector shows up.

Sometimes, the subject matter was as serious as it could be. In "The Bridge," a man who is dying of cancer pretends to get drunk at the Chez, then drives his truck off a bridge so his destitute wife can sue the restaurant for serving him too much liquor.

Sometimes, it would be a commentary on black culture that was almost painfully revealing. In "Frank Joins the Club," Parrish realizes that everyone in a private club is a light-skinned black and he is being recruited as its token member with a dark complexion. "All my life I've been the only black," he tells his sponsor. "I was the only black in this class. I was the only black in that organization. I was the only black on this team. Well, I'm *not* about to become the only black in a black club."

And then there were the lines Wilson and the other writers came up with.

"I can't possibly marry you," a flustered Frank tells the daughter of a minister who has suddenly thrown herself into his arms. "I'm a Darwinian evolutionist."

"I'd drown myself, I'd stick my head in the oven before I'd come to work for you," Big Arthur tells a gangster who is threatening him with violence if he does not leave the Chez. Then, without changing expressions, he says, "I'd sit through 900 half-time shows."

Before long, it became impossible to know just when the writers' sense of humor might show up, or how. In one episode, Dizzy Gillespie arrives at the Chez accompanied by a group of African musicians. Shorty La Roux's Cajun dialect is given subtitles while the Africans speak in their native tongues with no translation.

Though Reid was delighted with the scripts, there were times when he grew concerned about how the show would be received. So much of it was so sly, so subtle. Were they asking too much of the audience? Would the range of subject matter, the fact that some episodes were comic while others were far more serious, be off-putting? How would viewers react to an old lady in a wheelchair and the other elderly cast members?

But there were other times when he felt differently. "We'd finish a scene and I'd think, 'This is it. These are my people,'" he says. "And I would literally weep."

Reid went to New York to promote *Frank's Place* at CBS. The buzz had already begun—he and Wilson had been interviewed by a few curious journalists who wrote positive articles—and he wanted to build on the enthusiasm by showing a few of the early episodes to the network's publicists, ad salesmen, and anyone else who wanted to see them. As he was screening the show in the employees' lunchroom, he received a phone call from CBS president Tom Leahy.

"William Paley wants to see you," Leahy said.

"What?!"

"He heard you're here and he wants to see you. This never happens, Tim. I don't think he's talked to a performer since Jackie Gleason."

"Tom, I'm wearing a flowered shirt and yellow pants. I look like a peacock threw up on me. I can't see William Paley dressed like this."

"You'd better come up here."

For an hour, Reid was briefed on how to behave in the presence of the legendary head of CBS, the man who virtually invented network television. He speaks very low so you have to listen carefully, Reid was told. And be sure to notice his art collection. He's very proud of it. Taking the only elevator in the building that went to Paley's office on the top floor, Reid and Leahy entered a lobby the size of a basketball court decorated with some of the most magnificent art work he had ever seen. Where am I? he wondered. The Uffizi? Ushered into Paley's private office, they nearly bumped into an exquisite Greco-Roman marble statue and saw more beautiful paintings on the walls. Sitting with his back to a window, sunshine streaming in from behind as if he were in a perfectly lit movie scene, Paley motioned them to sit.

"Young man," he said without preamble, "I saw your show. I

have to tell you I would have been proud to have it on the schedule when I was running the network."

Reid's mouth fell open. Wow. What do I say to that?

"It's certainly unique," Paley continued. "Now let me ask you. What are your intentions?"

My *intentions*? Boy, I'd better answer this one right.

"Well, I want to . . ." he could feel himself fumbling for words and then he stopped. He wants to know if I have an agenda, he thought. He's saying art is propaganda and he wants to know what mine is.

"Mr. Paley," Reid said, beginning again, "the community I grew up in was segregated, but culturally it was one of the richest in America and I seldom see the richness of that culture on television. My goal is to introduce you and the world to some wonderful folks I've known in the hope that it will inspire people to want to know more about our community and help us try to improve it."

He was babbling, he knew it, but he was getting his point across, too. And the way Paley was nodding indicated that he seemed to be in agreement.

"Are your writers going to stay with you?"

"Yes, sir. I believe so."

"That's very important. Thank you, young man. I wish you a lot of luck with this."

*Frank's Place* made its debut on September 14, 1987, and the reviews were beyond anything they had dared hope for.

"The new CBS series 'Frank's Place' is such a terrific hoot, such pure, smoky, filmy joy that it's hard to know where to begin," wrote Howard Rosenberg in the *Los Angeles Times*. "Often hilarious, 'Frank's Place' is also deep-dish television, soulful, thoughtful and unconventional, a show of many faces, moods, rhythms and textures, a comedy that's not always a comedy. Whatever propels 'Frank's Place' should be bottled by CBS and spread around."

"'Frank's Place' takes its people seriously, capturing the

special warmth of New Orleans without tumbling into pa-
tronizing caricatures," wrote John J. O'Connor in the *New York
Times*.

"Eleven characters haunt the 'Chez Louisiane' restaurant-
lounge in 'Frank's Place,' and every one of them is deliciously
appealing—as tasty as gumbo creole and bouillabaisse," wrote
Mark Schwed of UPI.

"The marvelous mix of ingredients and ensemble casting
make the Cajun-and-Creole-tinged 'Frank's Place' surely one of
network television's brightest new shows," wrote Bob Niedt in
the *Syracuse Post-Standard*.

"A work of art compared to usual series television," wrote a
reviewer in Portland's *Oregonian*. "The scripts treat the characters with respect and dignity, and credit the audience with
enough intelligence that the punchlines, when they finally
come, don't have to be slammed out like handballs into a wall."

"'Frank's Place' can stand proudly beside such notable fictional emporiums as Duffy's Tavern and the 'Cheers' bar," wrote
Tom Shales in the *Washington Post*. "How easy it is to pull up a
chair and make oneself at home."

The morning after the show's premiere one more review arrived in a telegram. It was from Bill Cosby and it contained one
word: Bravo.


Things went wrong almost from the start. Though the ratings for the pilot beat the other networks in its time slot, they
quickly began to fall off. CBS, which was in an uncharacteristic
ratings slump that was exacerbated by the turmoil surrounding
financier Laurence Tisch's recent controversial purchase of the
network, began shuffling the show around the schedule with
little notice, and occasionally pre-empted it altogether. In all,
*Frank's Place* occupied six different time slots on four different
nights. "We were moved around so much my mother couldn't
find it," Reid says. "One day, *I* couldn't find it. TV Guide said it
was on, but they had changed the time two days earlier without
telling anybody."

Inevitably, Reid and Wilson started second-guessing themselves. Should they use a laugh track? Should more of the episodes have a voodoo theme? Should they give Bubba Weisberger more to do? They would have to think about it. But the critical reaction continued to be positive and LeMasters remained resolute. The history of television was filled with hit shows that took a season or two to succeed, he said, particularly shows that broke new ground. *All in the Family* was a prime example. *Frank's Place* would find its audience, he insisted, and he ordered enough scripts to fill out a twenty-two-episode season. "I've never been prouder to be associated with anything in my life," LeMasters told reporters. "If America doesn't get it, it's America's problem."

The show got a big boost from the Emmy Awards, where it earned nine nominations, including two for Reid as the show's lead actor and producer. He remains one of the few African Americans ever nominated in both categories. And it won three Emmys—one for Wilson's script of "The Bridge"—while the Television Critics Association voted it the outstanding comedy of the year. And Reid, who had once attended the NAACP Image Awards as Della Reese's escort, returned in triumph to win an award of his own.

But his jubilation turned to sadness when, shortly after the Emmy nominations were announced, his mother died. "We had just gotten to the point when for the first time in our lives we were at peace with each other," he says. "At least, she got to see her son at the top of the world."

Reid was hurt when *Variety* and the *Los Angeles Times* refused his request to run Tina Wilkins's obituary, but that same day a car drove up to his house and delivered a telegram of condolence. It was from Ronald and Nancy Reagan in the White House. "I don't know how they found out she had died," he says, "but when I read that telegram in front of her old girlfriends at her funeral back in Norfolk, you would have thought the Queen of England had died. Here was a woman who never had a break in her life, who worked in white folks' homes until I could finally take care of her, and now she was being honored by the president of the United States. I will always have a soft spot in my heart for Ronald Reagan, politics be damned."

Wilson went to work on the scripts for the second season of *Frank's Place*. He sent a writer to New Orleans to research new episodes, one about the blacks who dress up as Indians during Mardi Gras that would feature Sammy Davis Jr. He made plans to shoot more exteriors in New Orleans to show more of the city's flavor. And he vowed to make more of the romance between Frank and Hanna, which had occasionally been sidetracked during the first season as *Frank's Place* explored weightier themes. LeMasters ordered thirteen scripts and shooting dates were scheduled. "I feel the next thirteen episodes are going to be some of the finest television anyone will ever see," he told the press. "I know it will be."

And then the show was cancelled.

"But we've been picked up!" Reid shouted when LeMasters called to tell him the news. "We've built the sets. We've hired the crews. We start shooting in three days. Everybody's under contract. It's going to cost CBS a fortune. Nobody cancels a show when the season is just beginning. They cancel it at the end, or in the middle."

"I know, Tim," LeMasters said. "I don't understand it, either."

"But now it's too late for anybody to get another job. All the other shows have already started production. Kim, it's crazy."

"Tim, I can't explain it. I'm not sure I'll ever be able to explain it."

Defeated, devastated, Reid sat down and cried.

It sounded like the voice of God as it boomed across Sixth Avenue. "TIM REID!" it called. "Wait there a minute. I want to talk to you."

That's Walter Cronkite! Reid thought, recognizing the voice

even before he turned and saw the celebrated newscaster getting out of a cab and walking toward him. Walter Cronkite knows who I am?

"Come with me, young man. I think you're owed an explanation," Cronkite said, and he steered Reid into a bar near the CBS building.

"I'm on the board of CBS," Cronkite said after they had ordered drinks, "and I want to tell you that we talked about *Frank's Place* at all of our meetings. Everybody just loved it. I think it's one of the finest shows of recent times. And I want to tell you why it was cancelled. It was because of one episode."

One episode? thought Reid, who was in New York hoping to find a place for *Snoops* on the CBS schedule. It was a year since *Frank's Place* had been cancelled and the wounds were still raw. Nor had his battles with the network for the money he'd been owed, money he'd used to finance *Snoops*, improved his mood. "At one point, I called the NAACP, which sent over some pickets to help convince them," Reid says. "It wasn't exactly the March on Selma, but it got the point across."

The episode that killed *Frank's Place*, Cronkite said, was the last one of the season, "The King of Wall Street." It was one of Wilson's most heartfelt scripts in which he poured out his feelings about the wave of junk bonds and leveraged buyouts that was sweeping across corporate America. A businessman stops in the Chez where he gets a phone call telling him he has been the victim of a corporate raider. Stunned, he pours his heart out to Frank. My great-grandfather made chairs, he says, wonderful sturdy chairs that I sit in today. My grandfather took over the business and he, too, made beautiful chairs. Then my father took over the business, but nobody wanted quality chairs any more so the business died. Today, I sell junk. I add no value to anything I sell. Yet in one transaction I make more money than all the generations of my family made put together. Something's wrong with that."

"That episode really got Laurence Tisch upset," Cronkite told Reid. "He viewed it as a direct slap in the face."

"I guess if I owned a network I'd bought with junk bonds, I'd be upset too," Reid said. "But to cancel the show over one episode?"

"We tried to convince him," Cronkite said. "We all did. But he wouldn't relent. He said, 'Not on a network I own,' and that was that. I'm sorry, Tim. We tried."

Over the years, *Frank's Place* would acquire an almost mythic status. The show was not released on video tape or DVD, and, except for a brief reprise on the BET network, it was never seen again on television. So unlike *WKRP in Cincinnati*, which developed a new generation of viewers when it became a hit in syndication, *Frank's Place* existed only in the memories of those who treasured its six-month run. Some university professors showed whatever clips they could find in their media-studies and television writing classes, and the significance of the show was occasionally discussed in books and articles by scholars of popular culture. Typical was an article in the *New York Times* in which Harvard professor Henry Louis Gates detected a key difference between *Frank's Place* and the wildly popular *Cosby* show. While *Cosby* was "remarkably successful at introducing most Americans to traditional black cultural values, customs and norms," Gates wrote, "it has not succeeded at introducing America to a truly different world. The show that came closest—that presented the fullest range of black character types—was *Frank's Place*."

The coming of the Internet gave rise to chat rooms where fans could discuss their favorite moments from the show and lament their inability to obtain tapes or DVDs. In 1994, the New Orleans press reported that Austin Leslie, always a better cook than businessman, closed Chez Helene and went to work in other restaurants. In 2005, Hurricane Katrina forced Leslie and his wife into the attic of their home where they spent two days before they were rescued by neighbors and evacuated to the squalor of the New Orleans Convention Center. They made their way to Atlanta where Leslie died of a heart attack less than a month later. He received the first jazz funeral following the hurricane in the still largely deserted city, and the procession stopped along the way at the site of Chez Helene.

The Rhodes Funeral Home on Washington Avenue was also destroyed, and Trencia Henderson lost all her possessions and was driven from her home. She moved across the river to Algiers and returned to work as a funeral director and embalmer. "It's a mess," she said in 2007 of trying to deal with what remained of the city's bureaucracy. "It takes months to get a death certificate now. It's just so depressing."

Some of the critics who had championed the show also kept its memory alive, placing it high on lists they would occasionally compile of shows too good for television.

"*Frank's Place* wasn't just the best dramatic series with a predominantly black cast ever to grace prime time," Noel Holston wrote in the *Fort Lauderdale Sun-Sentinel* in 2002. "It was also a shining example, seldom if ever followed, of how a real, knowledgeable sense of place can enrich a show and lift it from the ordinary."

"Personally," wrote James Endrst in *Newsday* seven years after the show was cancelled, "I still miss *Frank's Place* more than I can say."

# 13

The call came in the afternoon of May 15, 1998.

"He's gone, Tommy," a voice whispered.

"Oh, Barbara, no," Dreesen said, and he felt his knees buckle. "I can't believe it."

"He was at peace, Tommy. He's not suffering any more."

"What can I do, Barbara? How can I help you?"

"I'll need you at the funeral, Tommy. To be a pallbearer and say a few words. I know how much he meant to you."

"Anything, Barbara. Anything at all."

He sat and thought about Sinatra's final months, which had not been kind to him. Following a heart attack, he was confined to his home in Los Angeles where only his family and his closest friends visited. There had been no farewell concert, no official goodbye. He had simply stopped singing. His final performance had come shortly before he was stricken, at a dinner preceding a golf tournament he sponsored to benefit the Barbara Sinatra Children's Center near Palm Springs. He was supposed to sing three songs, but he sang six and received a standing ovation after every one. The last song he ever sang in public was "The Best Is Yet to Come," words that would be engraved on his tombstone.

"Don't put away that suitcase," Sinatra told Dreesen when he came off the stage, the applause ringing in his ears.

Great, Dreesen thought. We're going on the road again. But they never did.

Dreesen would visit occasionally, sometimes alone to watch boxing on television, which Sinatra enjoyed, and sometimes with groups of people Barbara invited over. There was a large party on Sinatra's eighty-second birthday, December 12, 1997, where the discussion turned to the best place in the world to live. Gregory Peck talked about his villa in the south of France, Robert Wagner and Jill St. John said how much they liked Aspen, and Jack Lemmon, Kirk Douglas, and Sidney Poitier mentioned their favorite places. Then Sinatra, who hadn't spoken for some time, said, "The best place in the world to live is where your friends are." The room grew silent in assent.

Dreesen went back a week later and saw that Sinatra had taken a turn for the worse. He was all but immobile and sat wrapped in a shawl as he was fed from a spoon by Vine, the elderly black woman who had been with him for decades. They chatted for a while and then Dreesen realized it was time to leave.

"I've got to go, Mr. S.," he said. "My ex is in town and the kids are getting us all together for Christmas."

"Oh, good, Tommy," Sinatra said. "Tell them I said hello."

"I will. They'll be thrilled."

"You know I love you, Tommy."

Dreesen was stunned. He didn't say, "I love ya, pal," the way he sometimes did with a wink and a kiss on the cheek. He said, "I love you," with a grave solemnity.

"I love you, too, boss," he stammered. And then, out of sheer nervousness, he said, "Let's go back on the road again."

Stupid! Exactly the wrong thing to say. He could have bitten his tongue out.

"Tommy, you're going to have to go on the road by yourself from now on," Sinatra said, and he reached up to put his hand on his cheek.

"I'll talk to you later," Dreesen said and he turned and walked away. The last thing he was going to do was let Frank Sinatra see him cry.

Barbara followed him outside. "Are you OK?" she asked.

"It's tough, Barbara," he said.

"I know, Tommy, but you should come visit him again. He likes it when you're here."

"I will, Barbara," he said, and he did.

In the days following Sinatra's death, something happened that Dreesen was not prepared for. The phone never stopped ringing. He was expecting calls from the media, of course, and from his family and friends. But people he hardly knew called, too, and people he didn't know at all. There were so many calls that his daughters, Amy and Jennifer, and Dan Wiley had to handle some of them. These people needed to tell someone how they felt, Dreesen realized, and they chose him because he was as close to Sinatra as they could get.

Driving back from Sinatra's house after discussing funeral arrangements with Barbara, he listened to a woman on a radio call-in show whose host had asked for his listeners' responses to Sinatra's death. Something was the matter with her husband, she said. He was a tough guy who had fought in Korea and Vietnam, and who hadn't cried at his own father's funeral. But now he was in the bedroom with the door shut, crying like a baby. She didn't know what was wrong, she said. She didn't know why it mattered so much.

Dreesen thought he knew. Just as he had listened to Sinatra on the tavern jukebox while he was shining shoes in Harvey, much of America had grown up to his music, too. They had gone steady to it, gone to war to it, gotten engaged to it, gotten married to it, gotten divorced to it, gotten remarried to it, to him singing "The Second Time Around." And as long as they could read in the paper that Sinatra was still singing somewhere, they were as young as they were the first time they heard his voice. But now they had to face it, not just as an abstraction but as reality. If Frank Sinatra could die, they were going to die, too.

He worked his way up to the front of the Good Shepherd Roman Catholic Church in Beverly Hills so he could be near the lectern when it was time to speak. He stood off to the side and looked out at the crowd. Amazing, he thought. Actors like Gregory Peck, Kirk Douglas, Sidney Poitier, Anthony Quinn, Jack Lemmon, Tony Curtis. Singers like Tony Bennett, Liza Minnelli, Bob Dylan, Bruce Springsteen, Steve Lawrence, Eydie Gorme, Diahann Carroll, Vic Damone. Comedians like Milton Berle, Don Rickles, Jerry Lewis, Joey Bishop. Quincy Jones, who had arranged some of his finest albums. Barbara, of course, and his ex-wives, Nancy Sinatra and Mia Farrow. His leading ladies, Betty Garrett from *On the Town*, Debbie Reynolds from *The Tender Trap*, Sophia Loren from *The Pride and the Passion*, Angie Dickinson from *Ocean's 11*. So many more, including Nancy Reagan, who arrived late and whose Secret Service contingent kicked Ed McMahon out of his seat.

He stood listening to the prayers and the music, waiting to go to the lectern, and he could hear Sinatra in his brain giving him instructions: be brief and be funny. He thought again about what he would say, about the time they arrived in Fort Lauderdale late at night and all he wanted to do was go to bed so he could play golf in the morning. But five minutes after he got to his room, there was a knock at the door and a bellhop the size of a linebacker standing outside.

"Mr. Sinatra wants you downstairs in the lounge," he said.

"I'll give you twenty dollars if you tell him you couldn't find me," Dreesen said.

"Mr. Sinatra gave me a hundred dollars to tell you he wants you in the lounge," the bellhop said.

"Can't you please tell him you couldn't find me?"

"He said if you resist, he'll give me an extra hundred to drag you down there."

Dreesen thought about what he wouldn't say, too. He wouldn't say that he knew a lot of people in the audience had wanted Sinatra to stop performing long before he did. But they hadn't been with him every night and they didn't know how good it made him feel if he could sing just one song the way he used to.

There was a lull and he looked over at Cardinal Roger Mahony, the archbishop of Los Angeles, who shook his head and motioned him to stay where he was. The choir began to sing "Ave Maria" and he could feel tears forming. Don't cry, he could hear Sinatra say. Sicilians cry alone. He stared at the wall and busied himself thinking it needed a coat of paint, maybe another window. Anything to keep from crying.

The choir finished and the church grew so quiet he could hear pews creaking as people stirred in their seats. A few moments passed and he looked at Mahony again but got the same signal—not yet. And then Sinatra's voice came over the loudspeaker.

*Put your dreams away for another day*
*And I will take their place in your heart*

He began to cry and he looked around and saw that everybody else in the church was crying, too, crying without shame. The song ended and he looked up and saw Mahony motioning him forward. He smiled through his tears as he walked to the lectern. "You did it to me again, boss," he thought. He took a deep breath and began telling jokes once more to an audience that had not come to see him.

**14**

Every once in a while over the years, someone would approach Reid or Dreesen and say they ought to work together again. Host a television show, perhaps, or make a movie. Show business had changed so much since the days of Tim and Tom. Black and white performers working together had become so common that nobody gave it a second thought. It would be so much easier now and their humor, their approach, would still be fresh and relevant.

But they had long been on their separate paths by then—Reid acting, directing, and producing at his studio in Virginia and in Hollywood; Dreesen appearing on television and doing stand-up comedy at clubs, corporate dinners, and benefits around the country. They were so involved with their own projects and travels that they simply didn't have time. To come up with new routines, to rehearse and look for places to perform, would require a commitment neither one could make.

They did appear together casually a few times, once on a television show called *All-Star Secrets* where Bob Eubanks brought Reid onto the set as a surprise to Dreesen, and once at the LA Improv where they took turns introducing young comedians. But when Dick Clark called to ask if they would be interested in hosting a half-hour comedy show, Reid was not available. After a brief discussion of being paired with Arsenio Hall, Dreesen passed, too. It was clear by then there would be no going back.

There was no ambivalence about how they felt about each other, though. Whenever they were together, there were hugs and smiles and retelling some of the old stories of all they had shared. Whatever animosity and bitterness they had once felt belonged to another time, a time that was long gone. Look at us, they would think. We got what we wanted. We made it in show business. They had not gotten there as Tim and Tom, but they would not have gotten there without Tim and Tom, either.

"Remember Sidney Poitier and Tony Curtis in *The Defiant Ones*?" Dreesen says. "Remember how even when they broke the chain that was holding them together, it was still there? That's us. Everything I am, everything I have, is because I met Tim."

"Same here," Reid says.

# Acknowledgments

The authors wish to thank Rita Reid, Daphne Maxwell Reid, Dick Owings, Steve Sperry, and Trencia Henderson for sharing their memories of some of the events related in this book. Thanks also to Mike Downey for his help in getting the project underway, to Rick Kogan, whose article about Tom Dreesen in the *Chicago Tribune* magazine was particularly helpful, and to John Schulian and Bill Zehme for their valuable suggestions. The reporting of Dave Walker in the *New Orleans Times-Picayune* and other writers noted in the text was useful in helping to reconstruct the story of *Frank's Place*.

Thanks to John Tryneski, Rodney Powell, Mara Naselli, Levi Stahl, Ryan Li, and others at the University of Chicago Press for their enthusiasm and support. Thanks as well to Dale Hoffer for overseeing the tape transcriptions and to Joan Rapoport for her careful initial reading of the manuscript.

# About the Authors

**TIM REID** is an actor, producer, and director who has created and performed in many television shows and movies. Perhaps best remembered by television viewers as the overnight disc jockey Venus Flytrap in *WKRP in Cincinnati*, Reid now operates his own production studio in Petersburg, Virginia.

**TOM DREESEN** is a stand-up comedian who has appeared scores of times on *The Tonight Show* and *Late Show with David Letterman*, and was Frank Sinatra's opening act for fourteen years. Dreesen performs at clubs and special events around the country and in his one-man show, "Shining Shoes and Sinatra."

**RON RAPOPORT** has been a sports columnist for the *Chicago Sun-Times* and the *Los Angeles Daily News* and a sports commentator for National Public Radio's *Weekend Edition Saturday*. His books include *Betty Garrett and Other Songs: A Life on Stage and Screen* and *The Immortal Bobby: Bobby Jones and the Golden Age of Golf*.